TABLE OF CONTENTS

DOWNLOAD YOUR FILES

Downloading your files is simple. To access your digital files, please go to the last page of this book and follow the instructions.

For technical assistance, please email: info@vaulteditions.com

Copyright

Bibliographical Note

This book is a new work created by Vault Editions Ltd.

ISBN: 978-1-922966-66-7

SKULL – FRONTAL VIEW

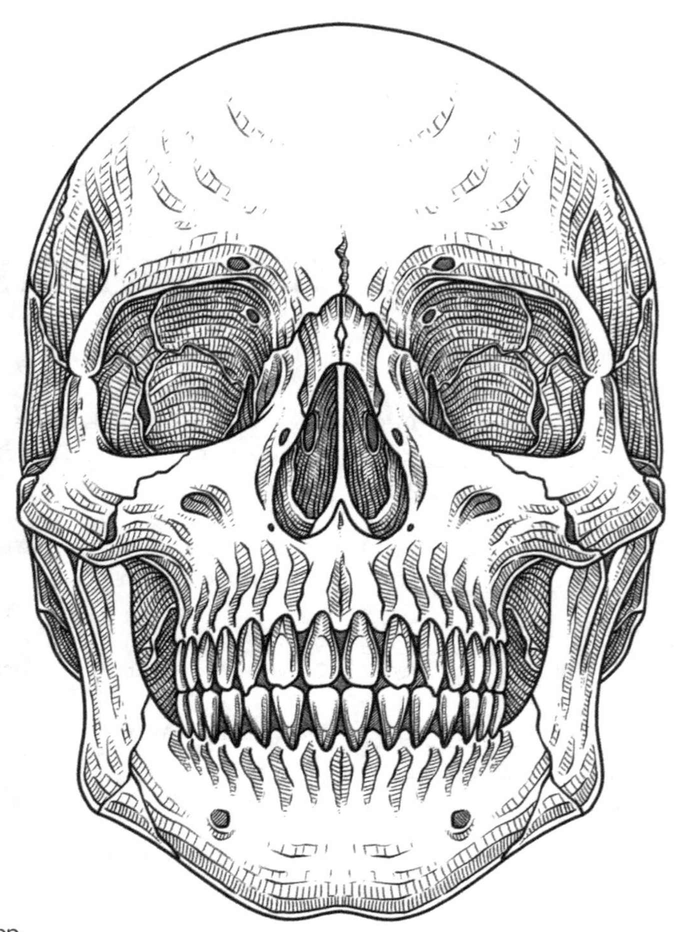

Pro Tip: Use a centre line to keep symmetry. Pay close attention to the angled eye sockets and jaw shape to build accurate proportions.

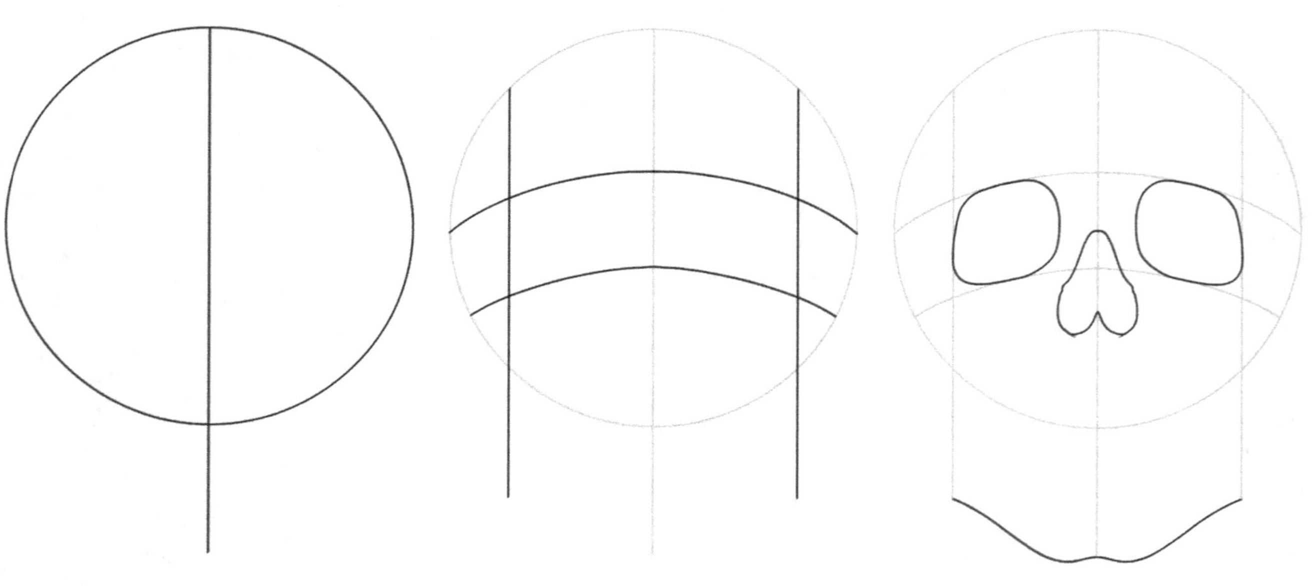

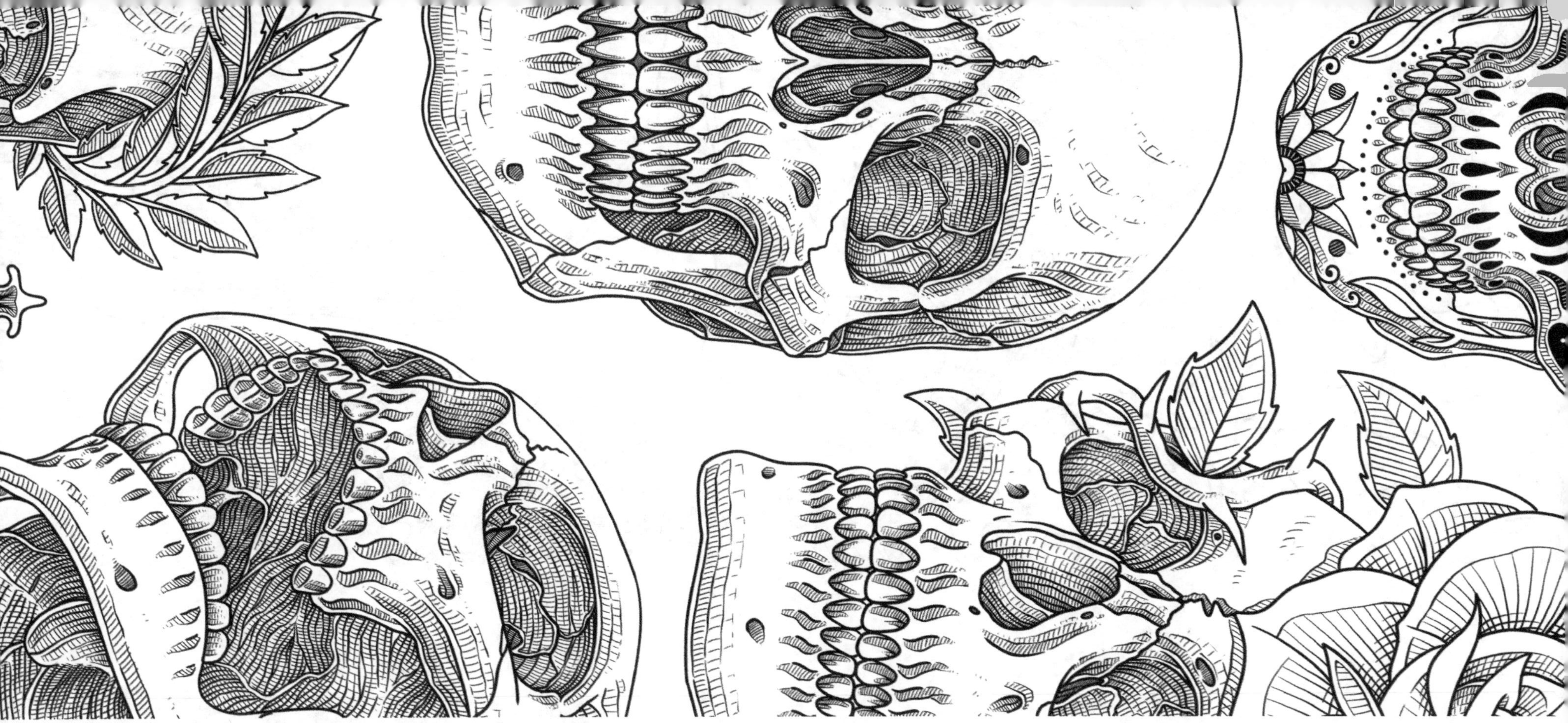
EDITIONS Vault

HAND DRAWN
UNIQUE 40 DESIGNS
BEST QUALITY

STEP BY STEP

A HELPFUL MANUAL FOR ARTISTS AND DESIGNERS

HOW TO DRAW
SKULLS

THE VAULT EDITIONS GUIDE TO
MASTERING
THE ART OF
DRAWING

INTRODUCTION

The skull has been a powerful symbol in art, tattooing, and design for centuries. It represents everything from mortality, impermanence, and transformation to strength, defiance, and protection. Its universal presence transcends cultures and styles, whether it's found in classical anatomical studies, traditional tattoo flash, or modern graphic art.

This book is designed as a practical guide to mastering the art of drawing skulls. Whether you're a tattooer, illustrator, designer, or hobbyist, the goal is simple: give you the tools to confidently draw skulls from multiple angles and in a variety of compositions.

Inside, you'll find step-by-step guides that break down complex forms into clear, manageable stages, from accurate anatomical skull studies to stylised designs featuring roses, snakes, wings, flames, and more. Every design has been crafted to help you understand structure, flow, and proportion.

This book isn't about rigid rules. It's about learning the foundational shapes and techniques so you can adapt them to your own style, whether that's bold, traditional tattooing, delicate fine-line work, or anything in between.

As with every Vault Editions title, each drawing was developed with a focus on clarity, accuracy, and practical application. You'll learn not only how to construct skulls, but also how to build compositions, balancing elements like horns, wings, or crowns so they flow naturally with the form of the skull.

Use this book as a study guide, as a reference tool, or as a jumping-off point for creating your own designs. Whatever your intention, it's designed to help sharpen your craft and push your drawing skills further.

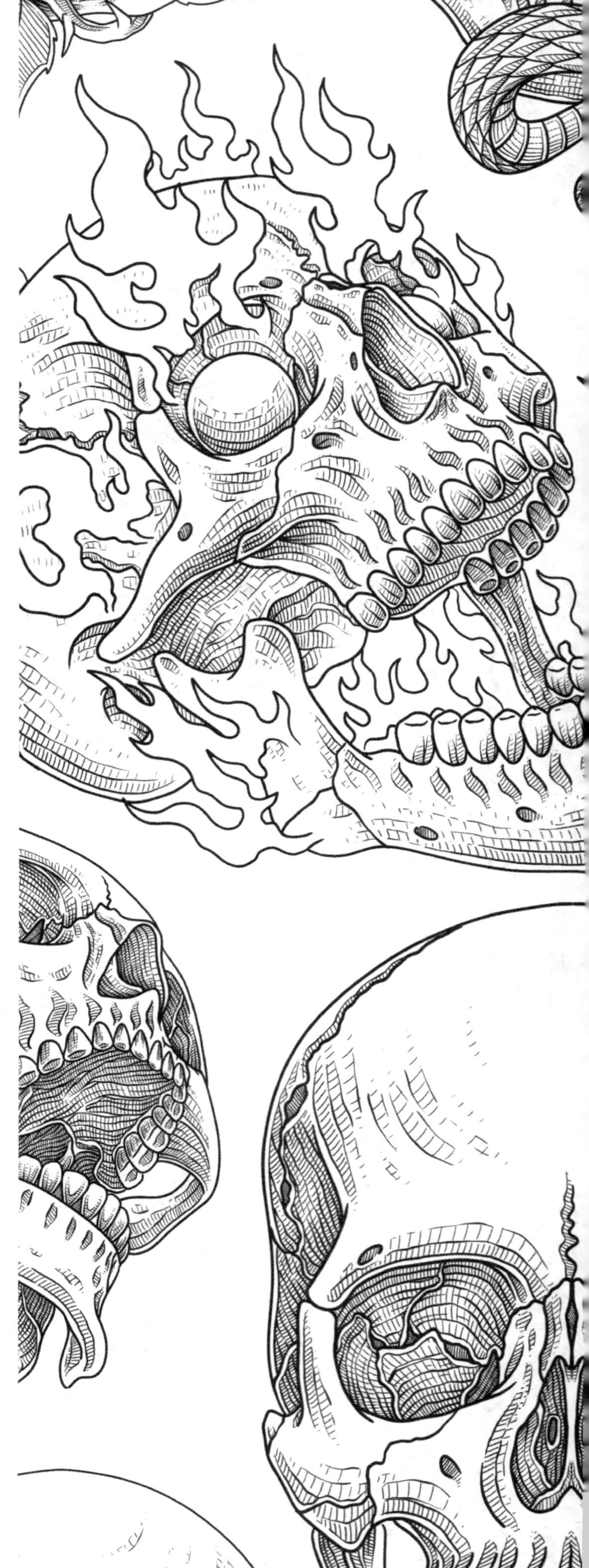

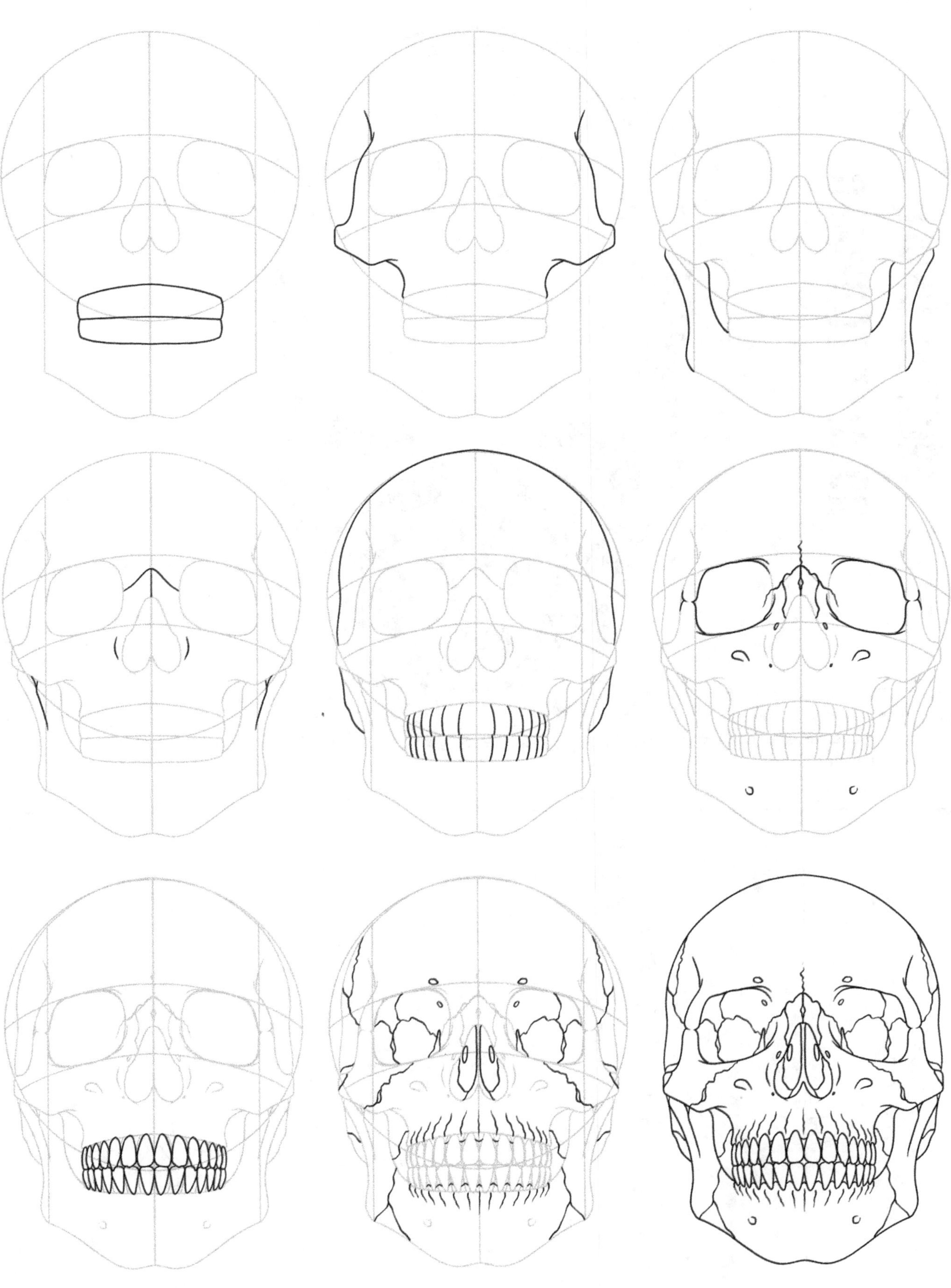

HOW TO DRAW SKULLS

FRONTAL SKULL ROTATED FORWARD

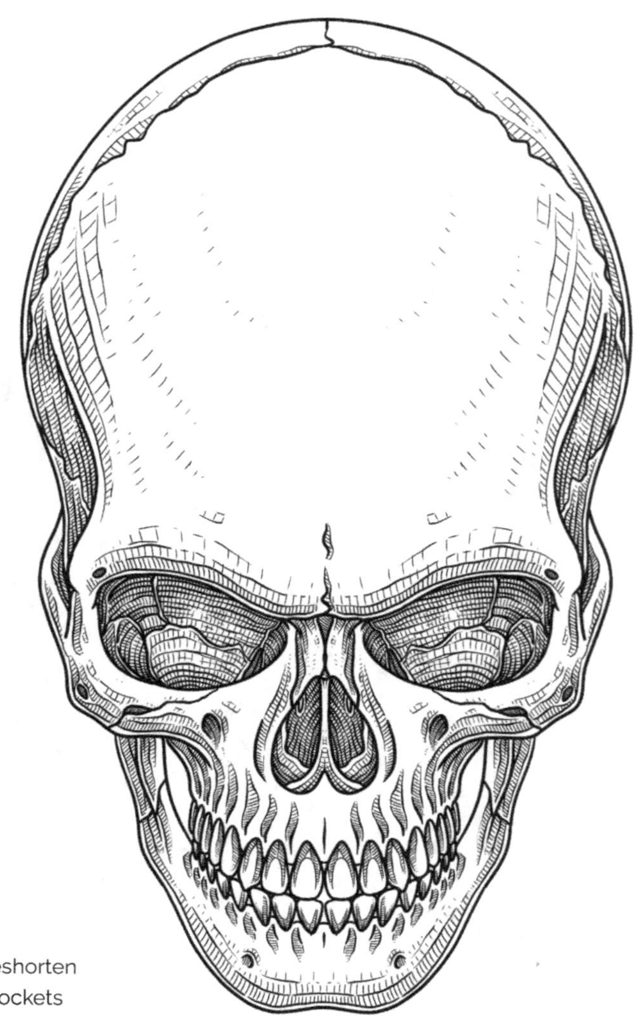

Pro Tip: Tilting the skull distorts proportions. Shorten the jaw, foreshorten the cranium, and curve the eye sockets to show the angle.

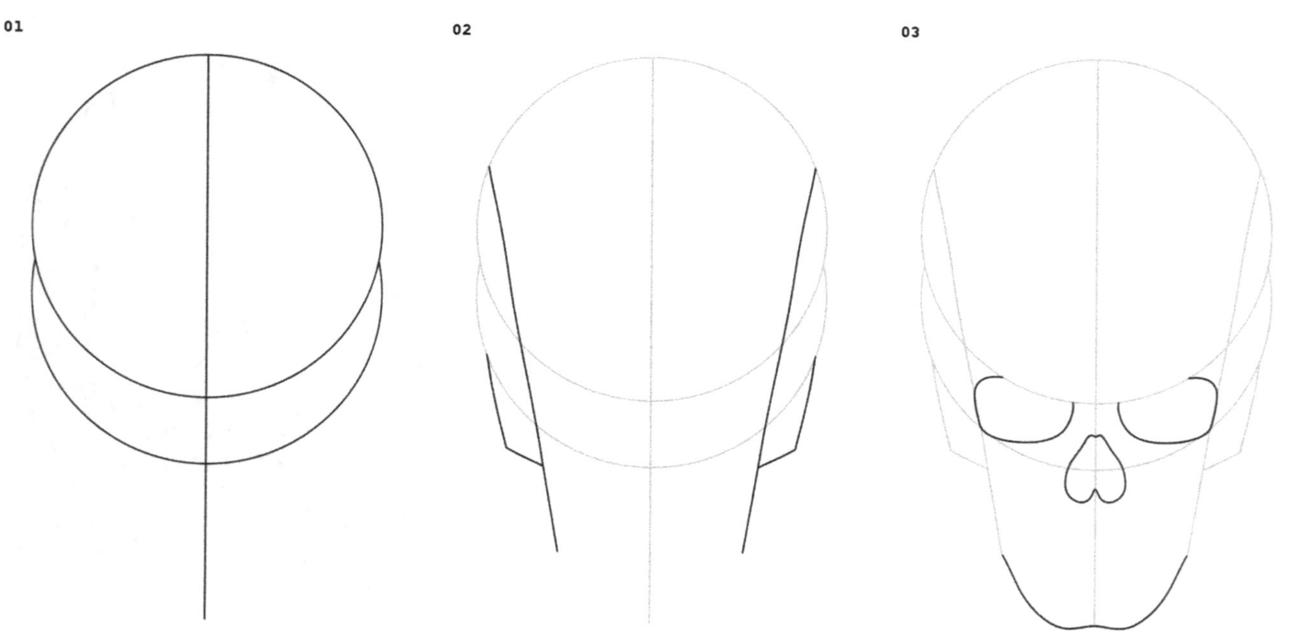

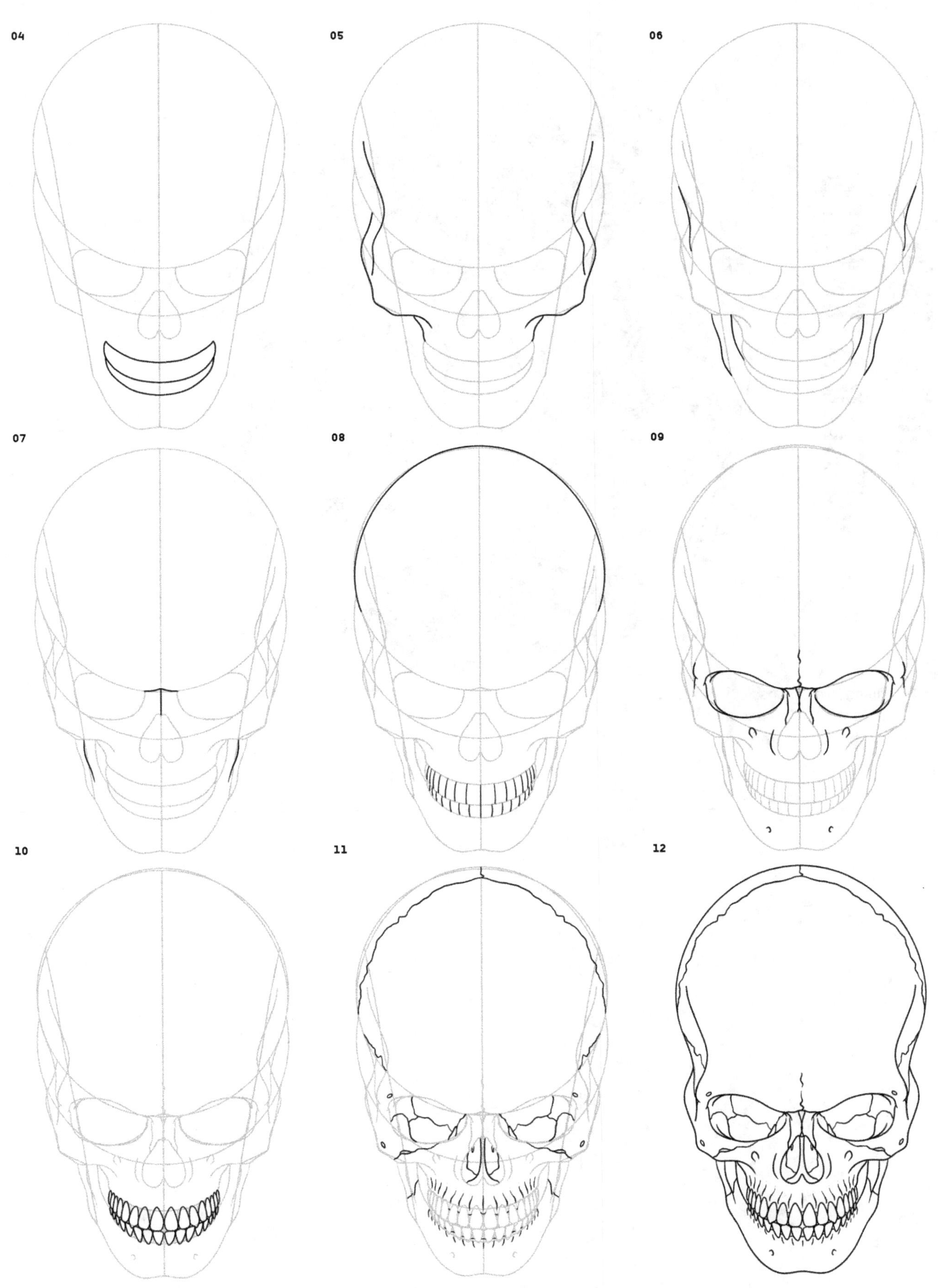

04
05
06
07
08
09
10
11
12
HOW TO DRAW SKULLS

FRONTAL SKULL ROTATED BACKWARD

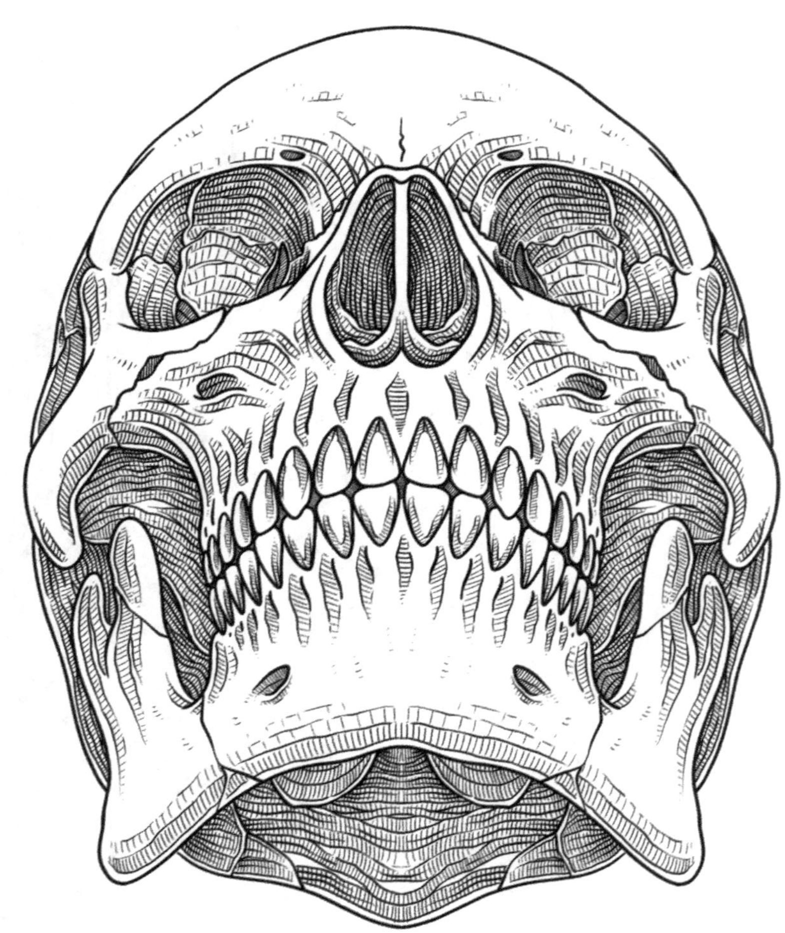

Pro Tip: Tilting back exposes the jaw and underside. Foreshorten the teeth and exaggerate the curve of the eye sockets and cheekbones.

01

02

03

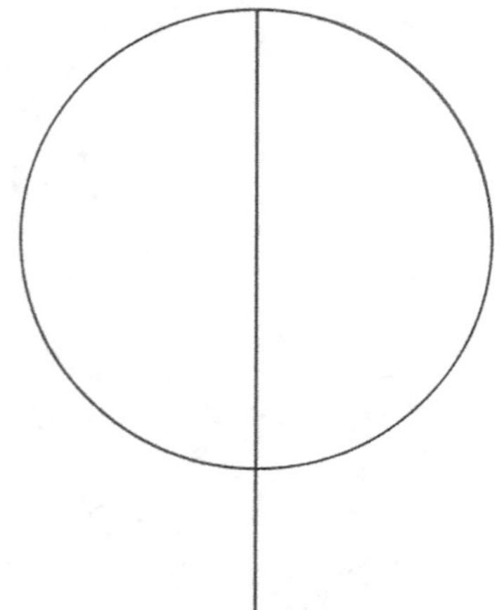

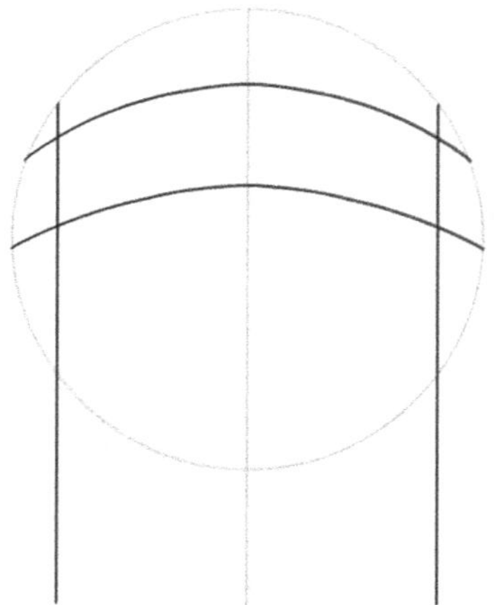

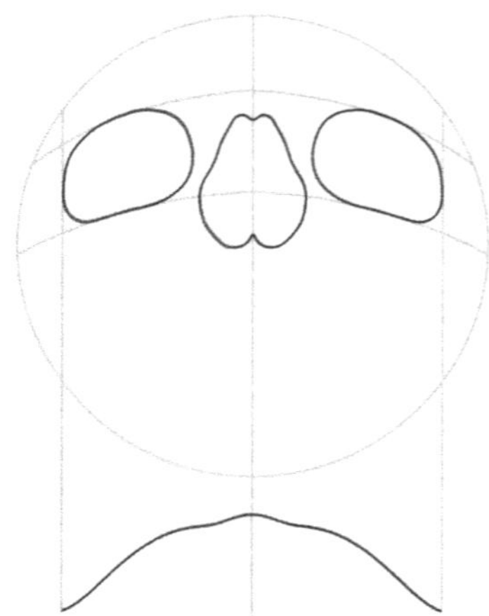

04

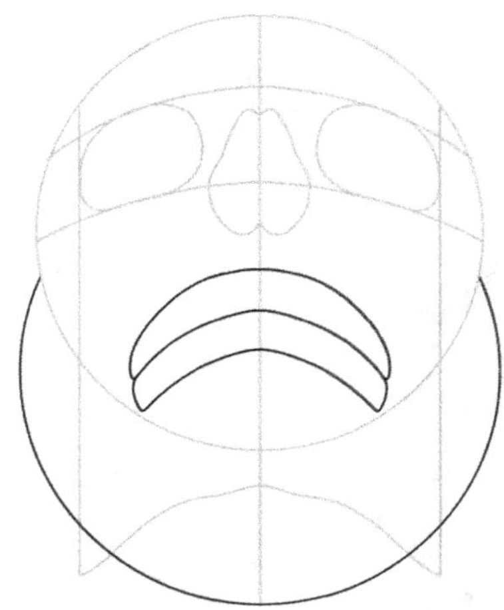

05

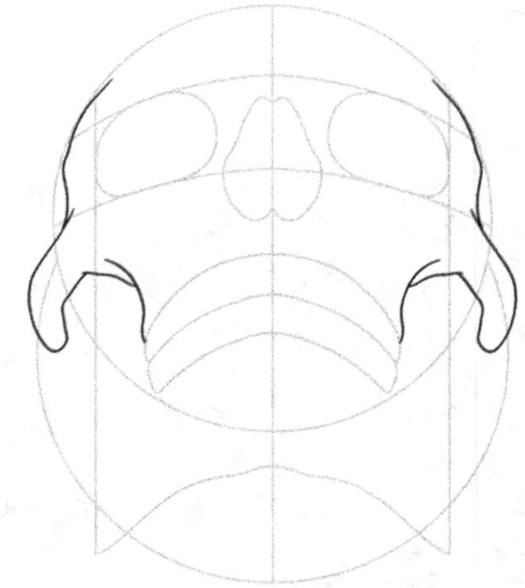

06

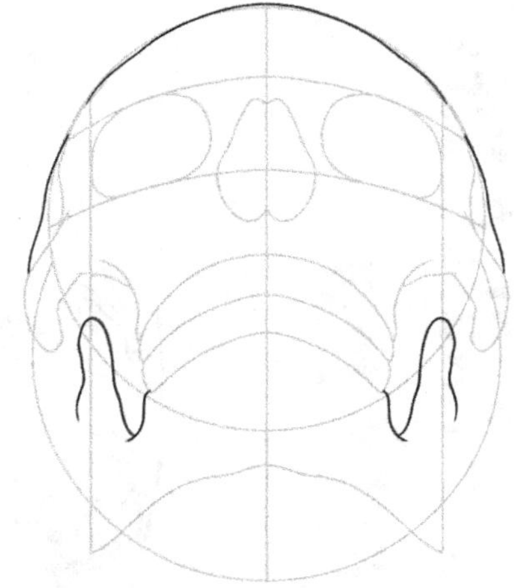

07

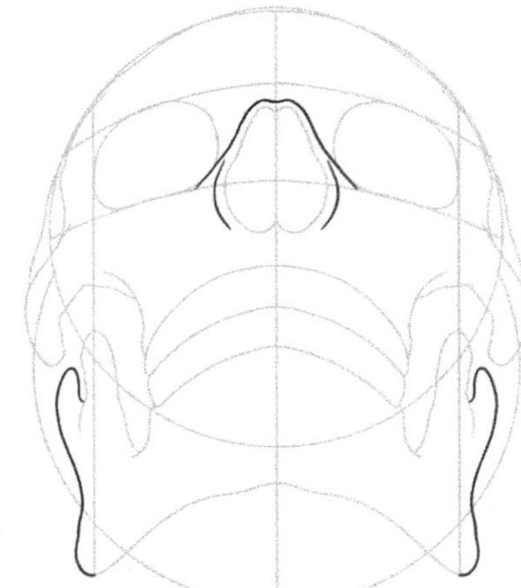

08

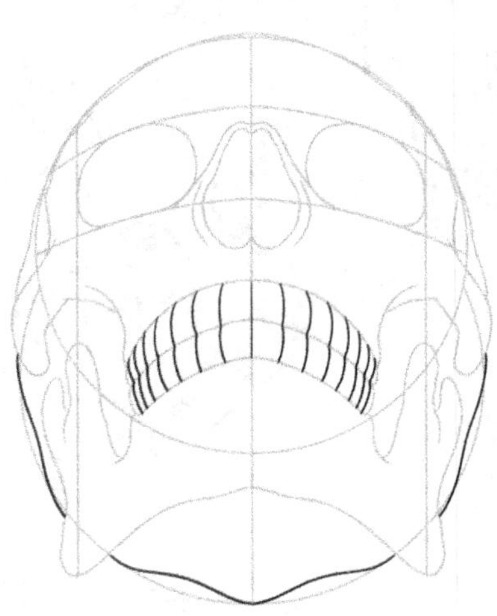

09

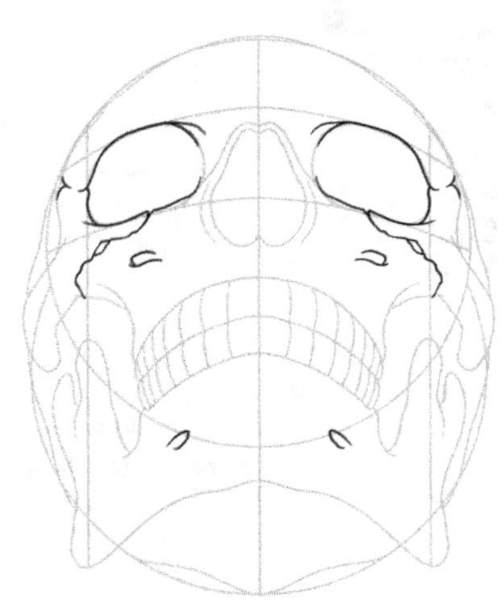

10

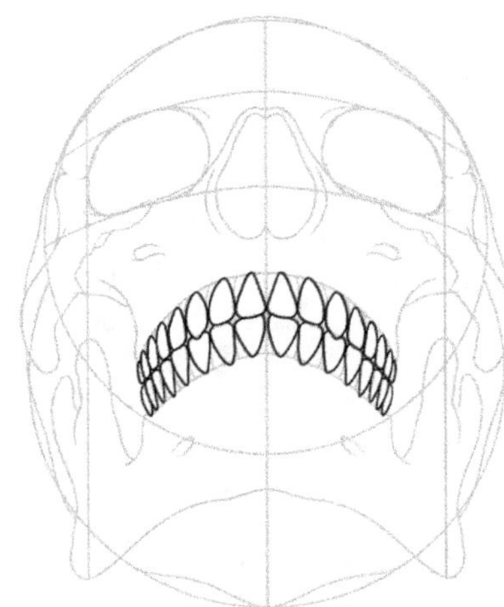

11

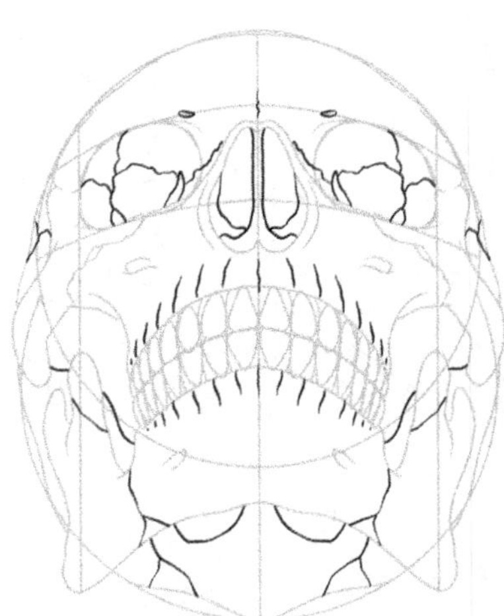

12

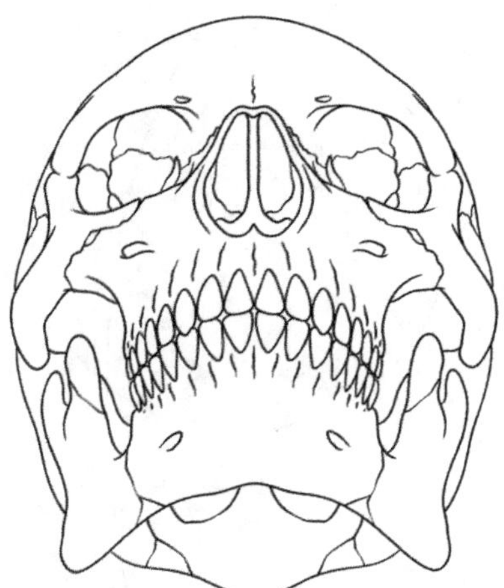

FRONTAL SKULL – ANGLED VIEW WITH OPEN JAW

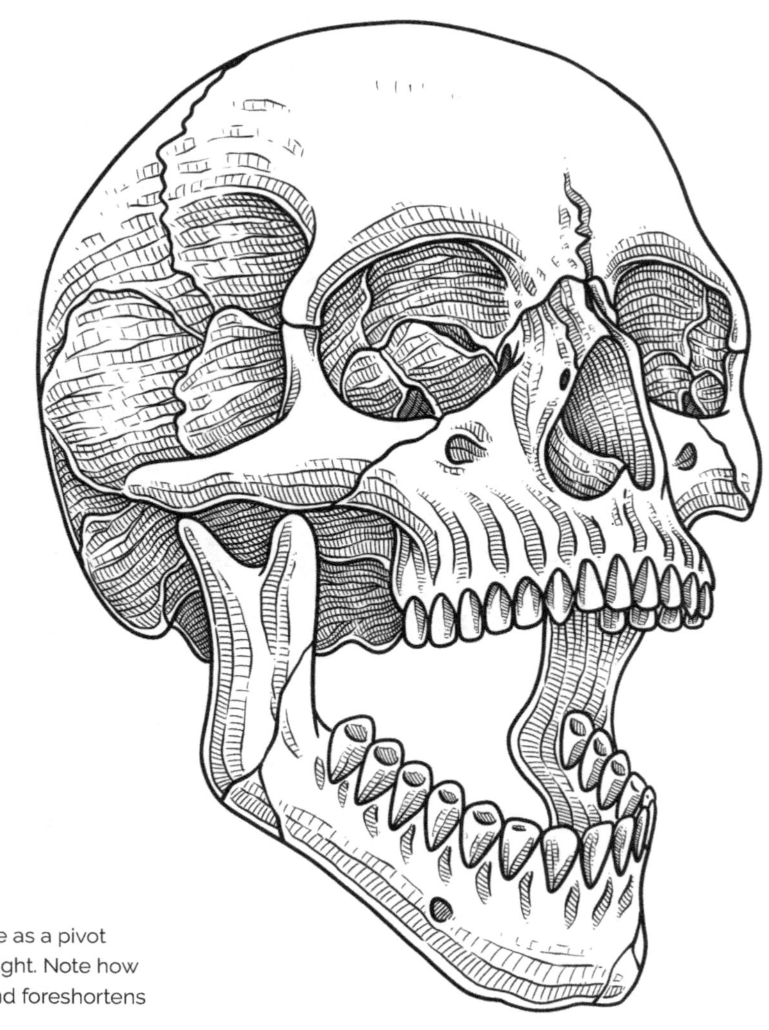

Pro Tip: Use the jaw hinge as a pivot point. Keep perspective tight. Note how the jaw curves forward and foreshortens when open.

01

02

03

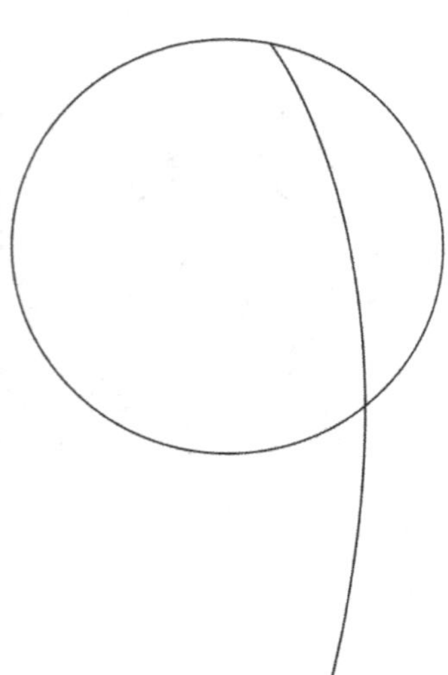

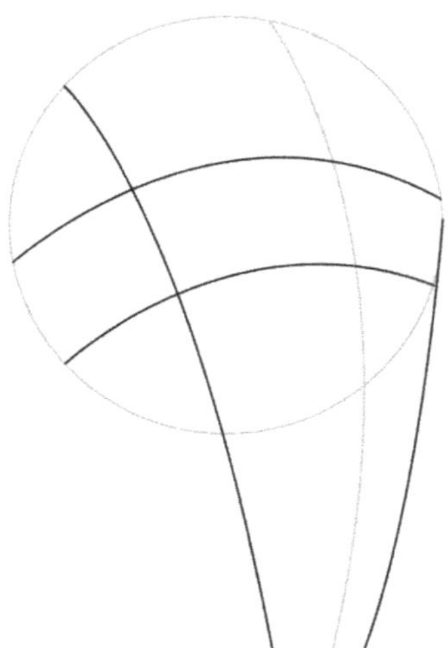

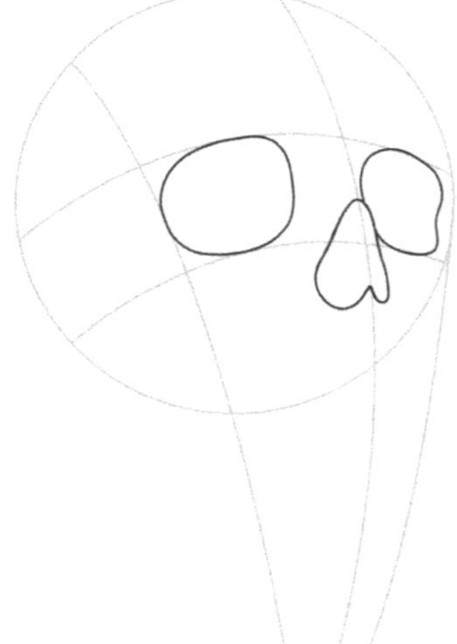

04

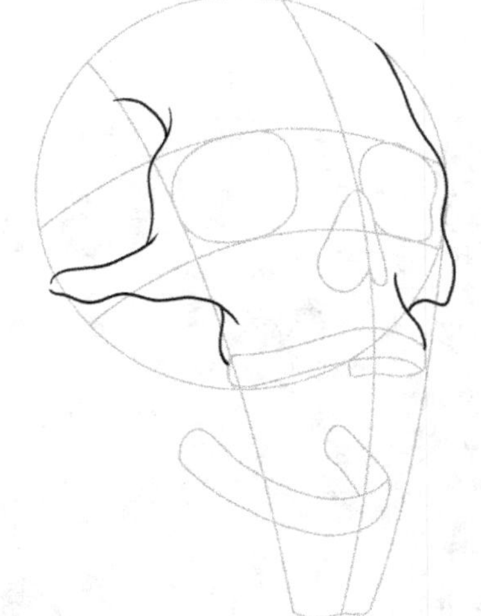

05

06

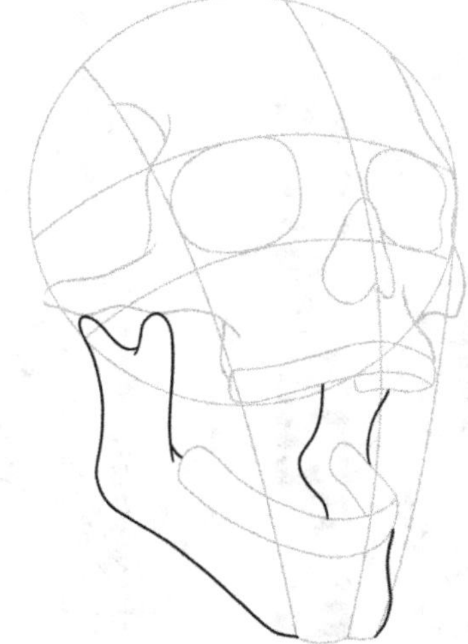

07

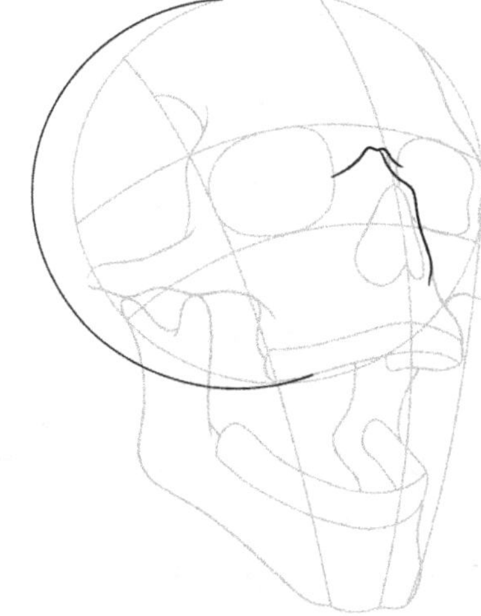

08

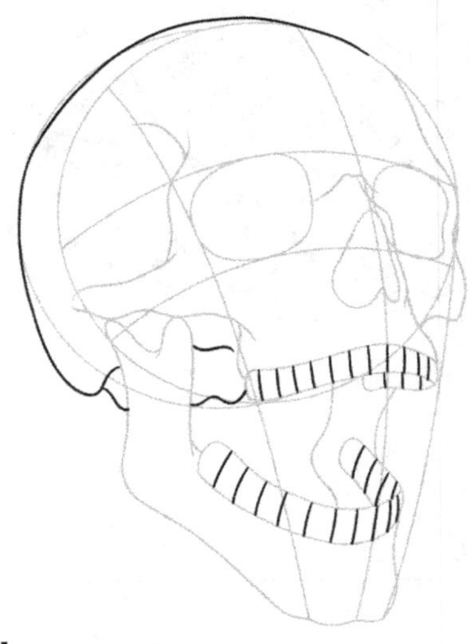

09

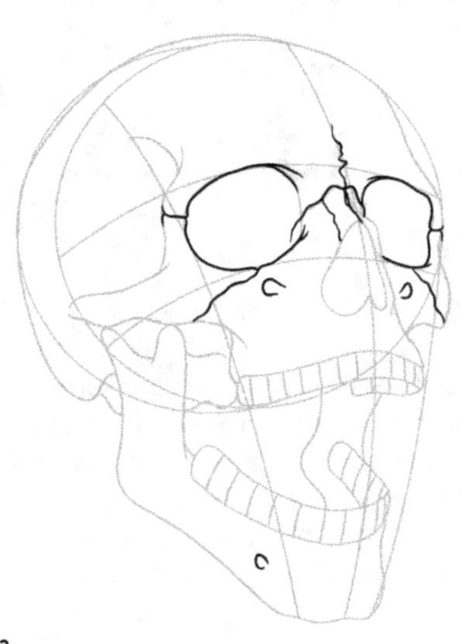

10

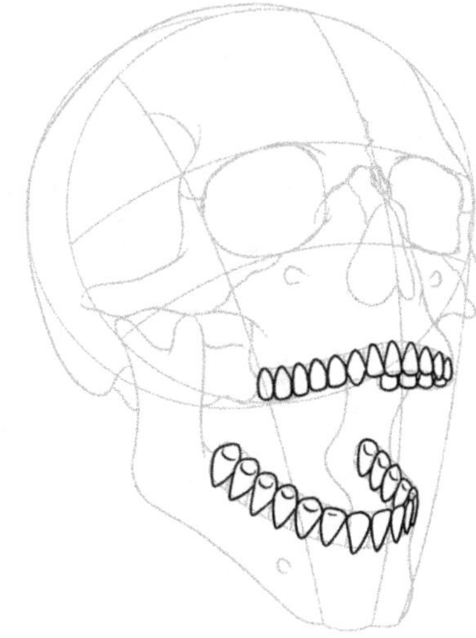

11

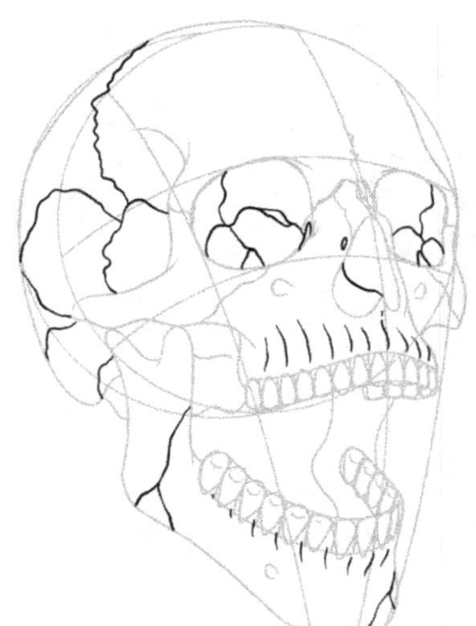

12

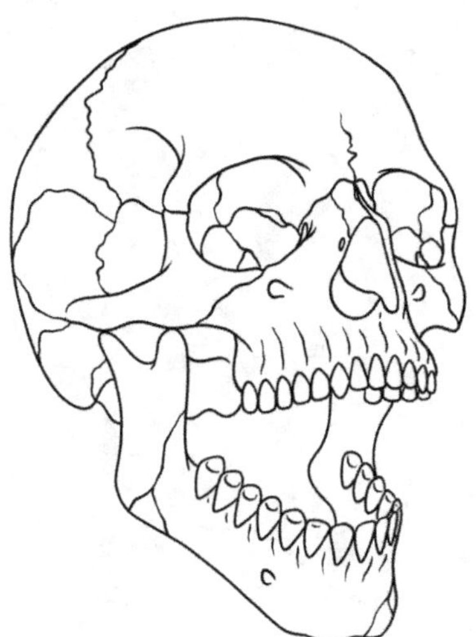

FRONTAL SKULL UNDERSIDE PERSPECTIVE

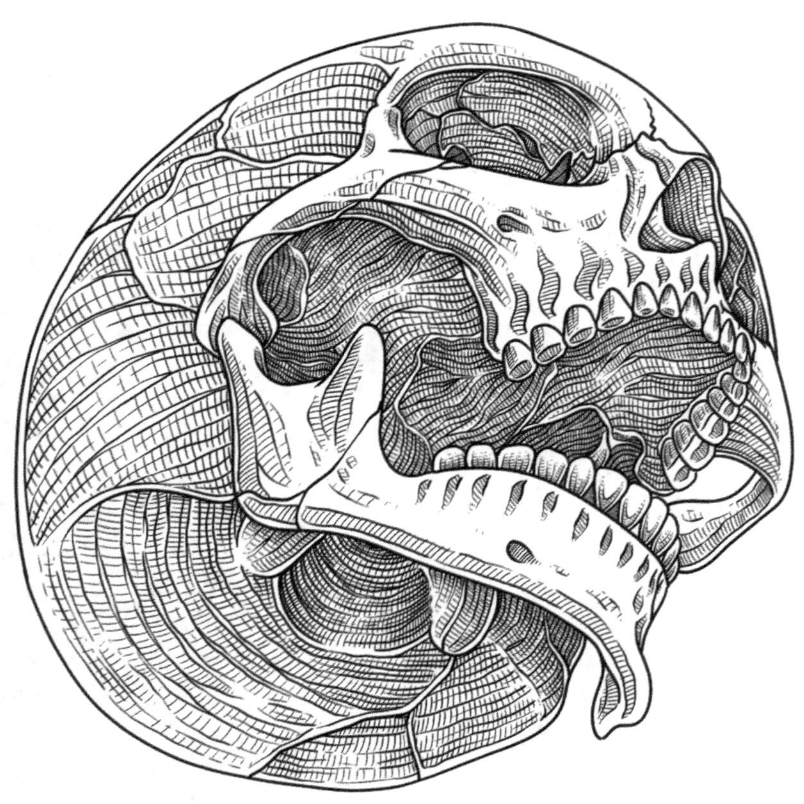

Pro Tip: Extreme angles distort forms. Focus on foreshortening the teeth and jaw, and exaggerate curves to show the skull's underside.

01   02   03

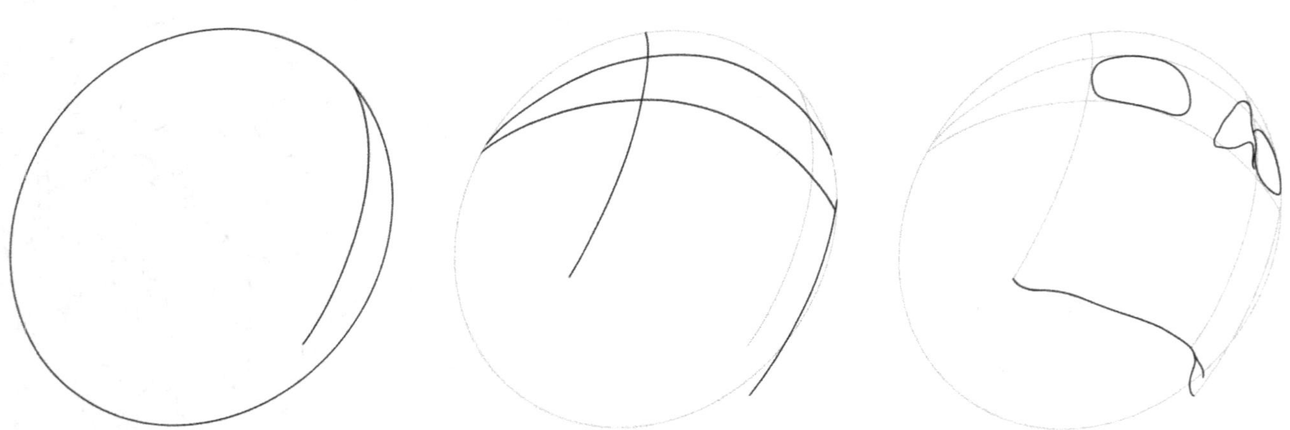

04

05

06

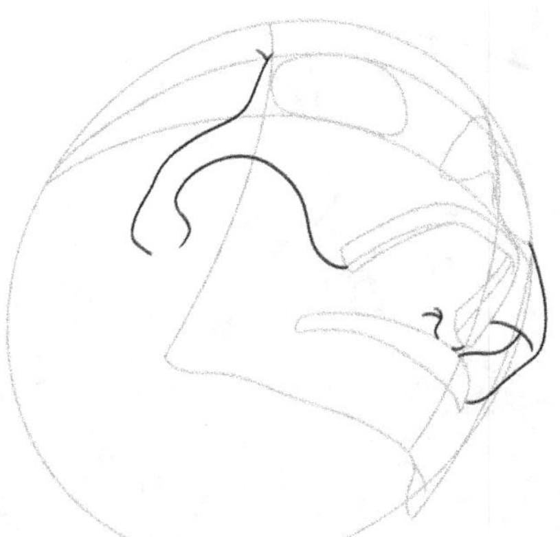

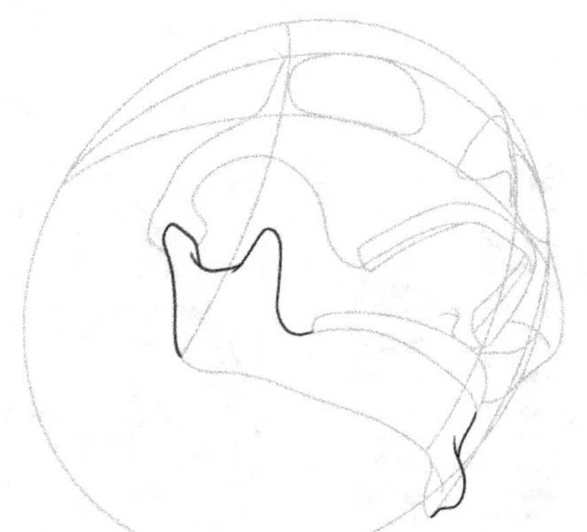

07

08

09

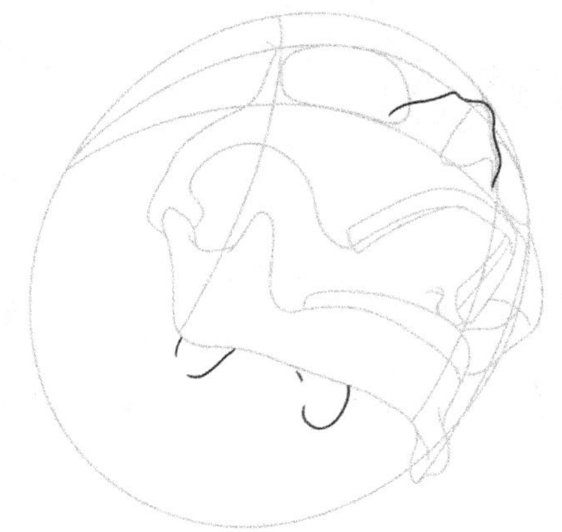

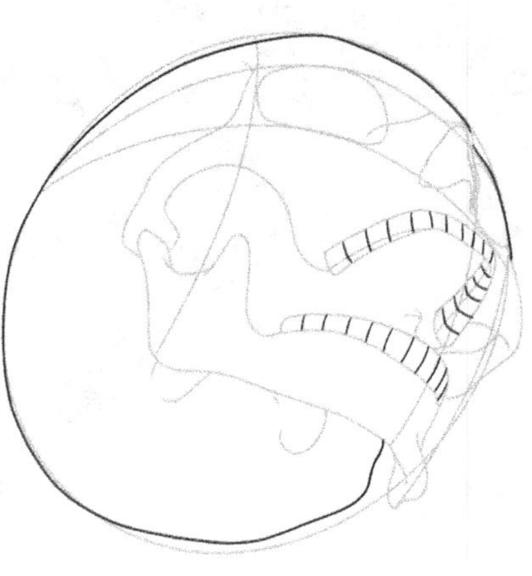

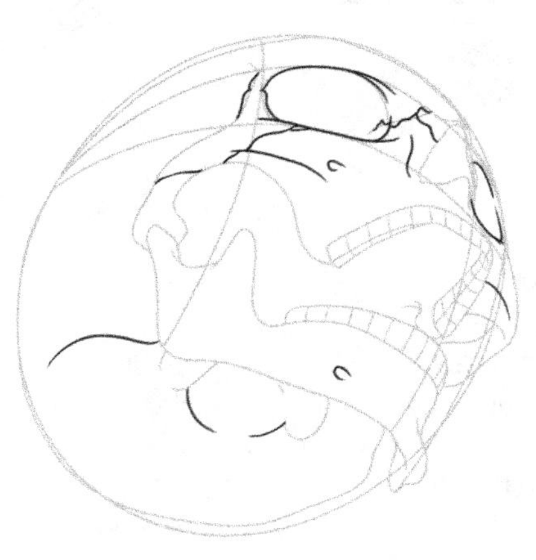

10

11

12

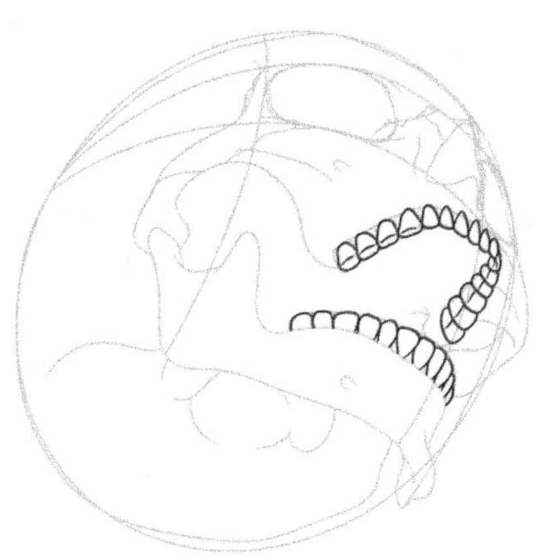

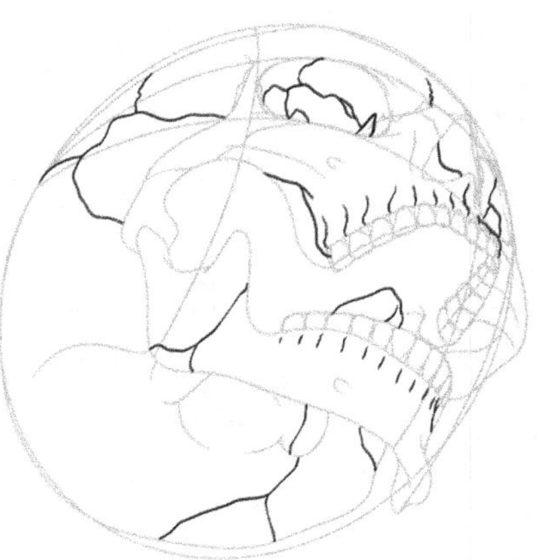

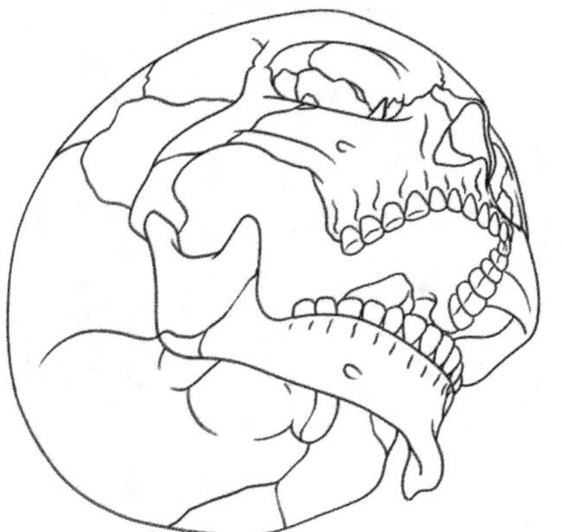

SKULL – PROFILE VIEW WITH OPEN JAW

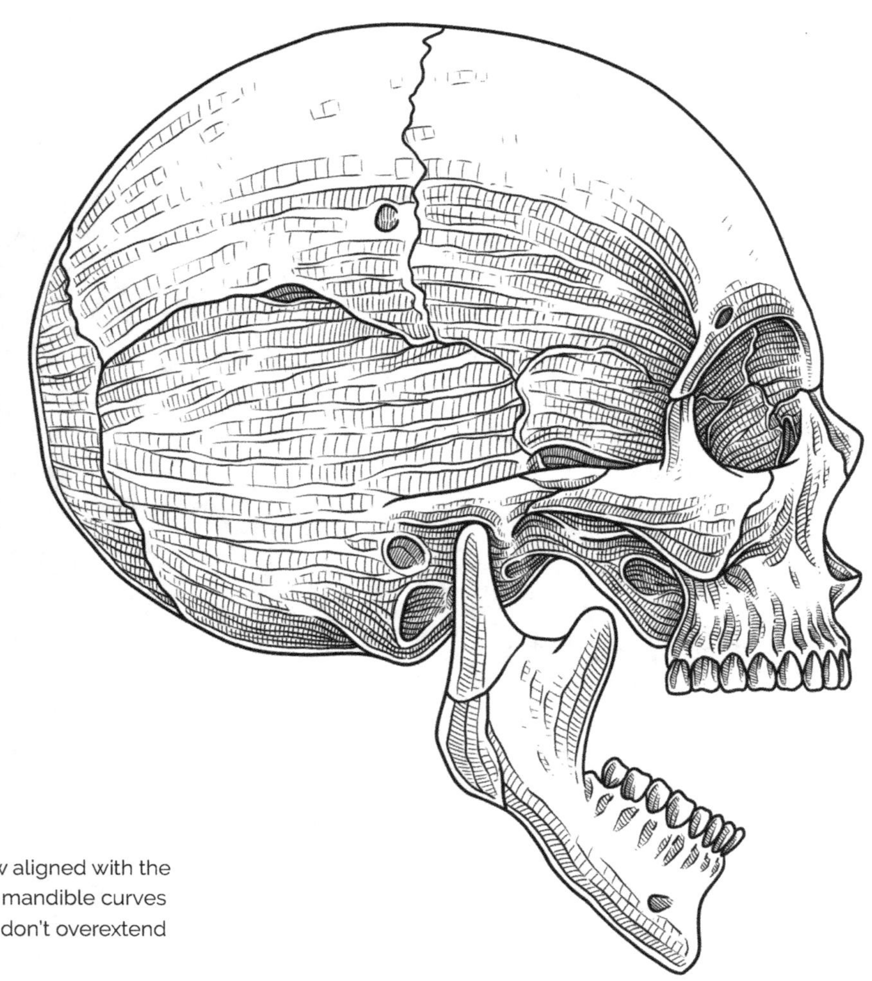

Pro Tip: Keep the jaw aligned with the hinge. Note how the mandible curves forward when open, don't overextend past the joint.

01

02

03

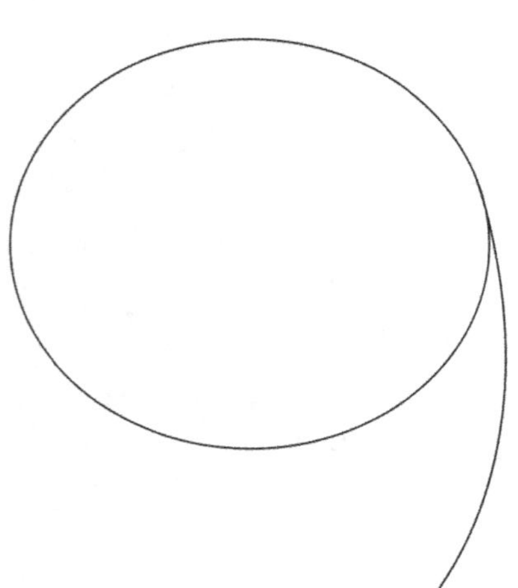

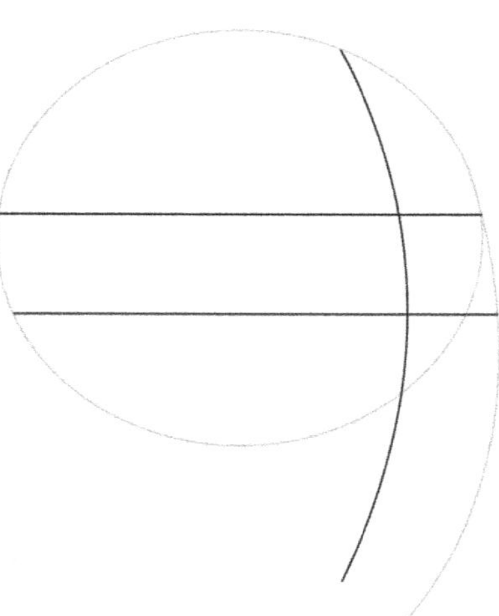

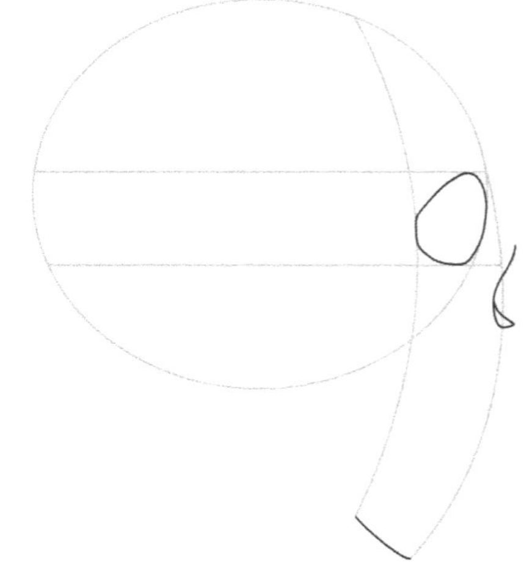

04

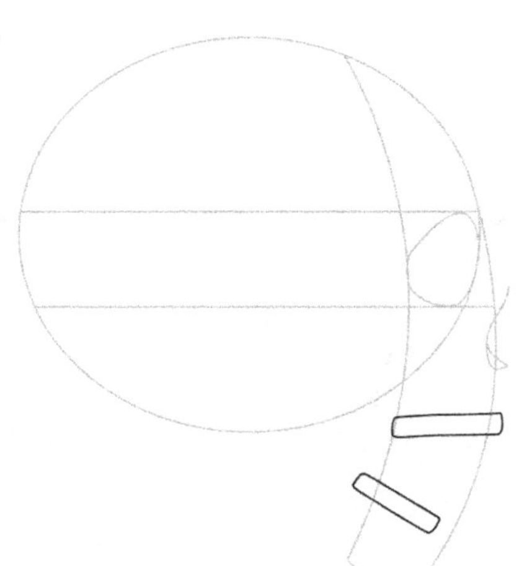

05

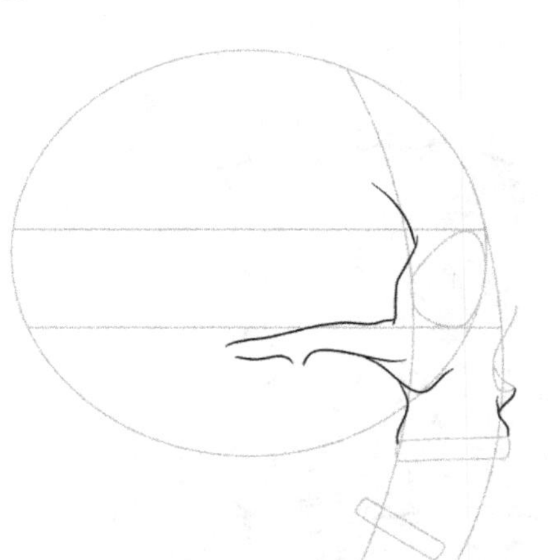

06

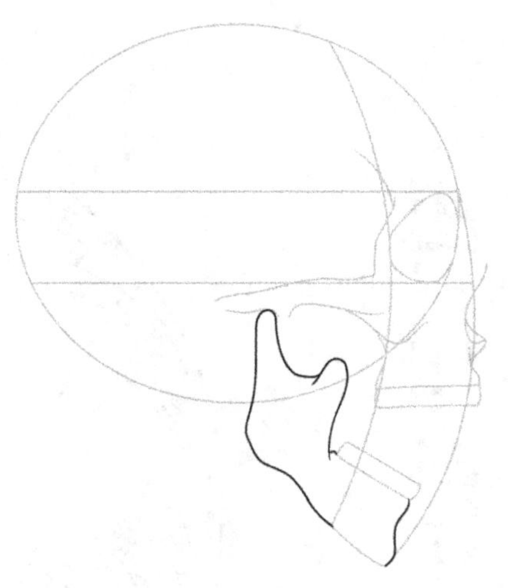

07

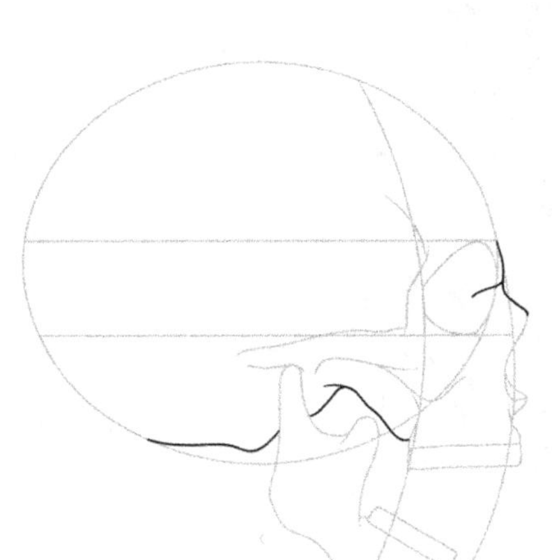

08

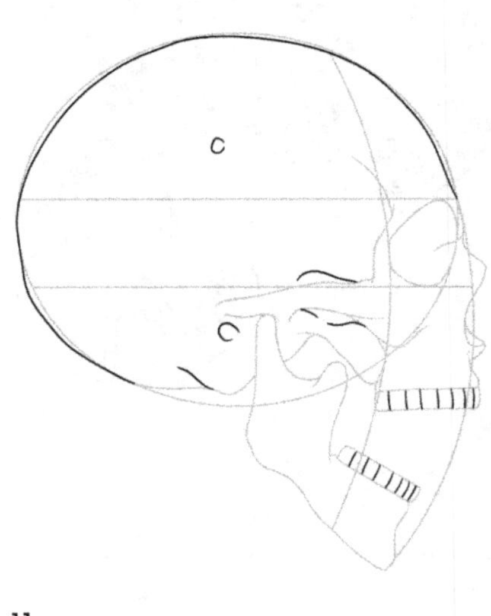

09

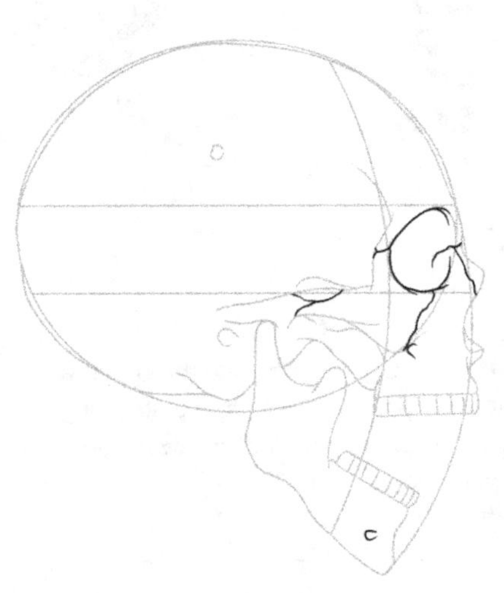

10

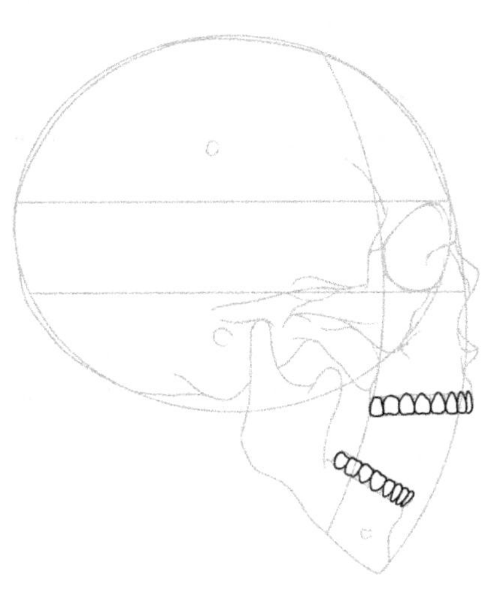

11

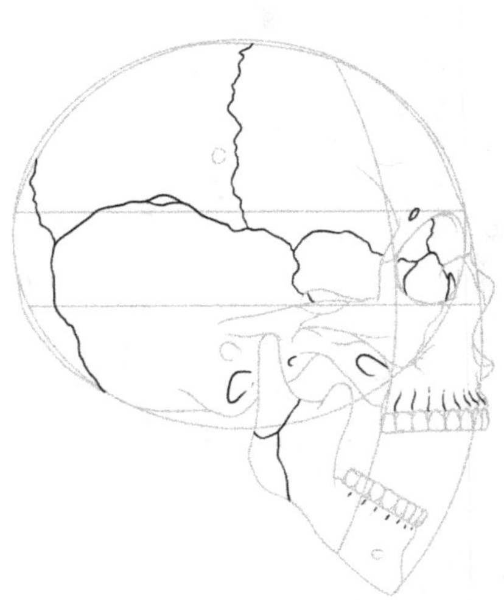

12

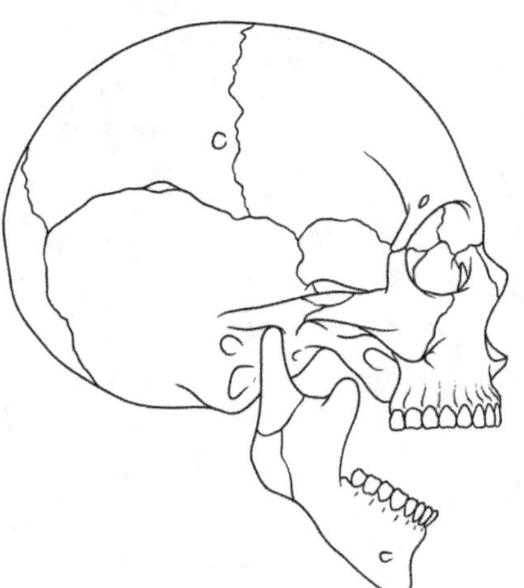

SKULL – PROFILE VIEW

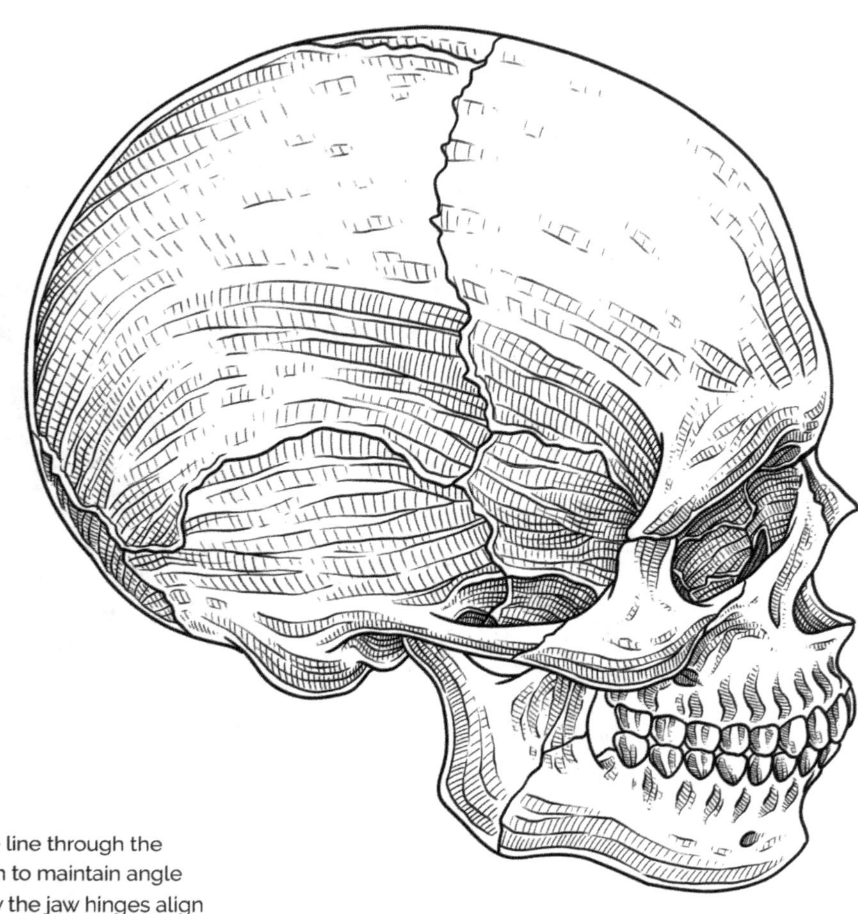

Pro Tip: Use a centre line through the brow, nose, and teeth to maintain angle accuracy. Watch how the jaw hinges align with the ear canal.

01

02

03

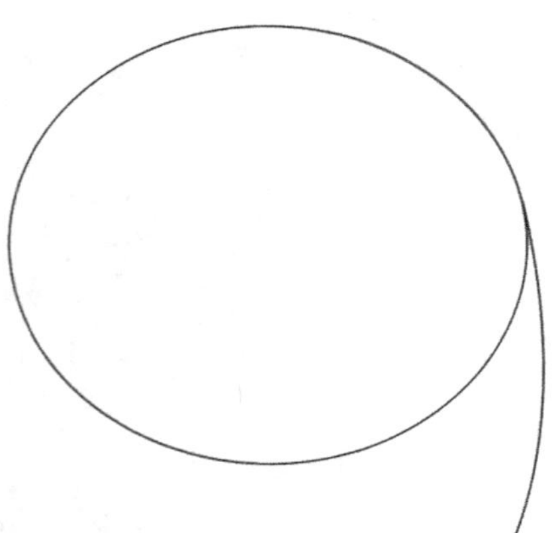

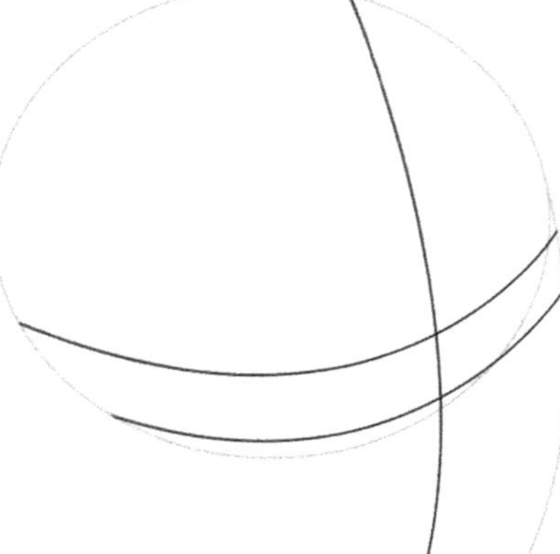

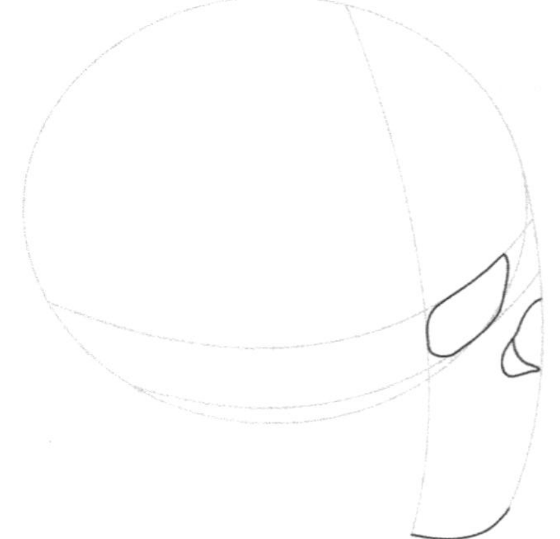

04

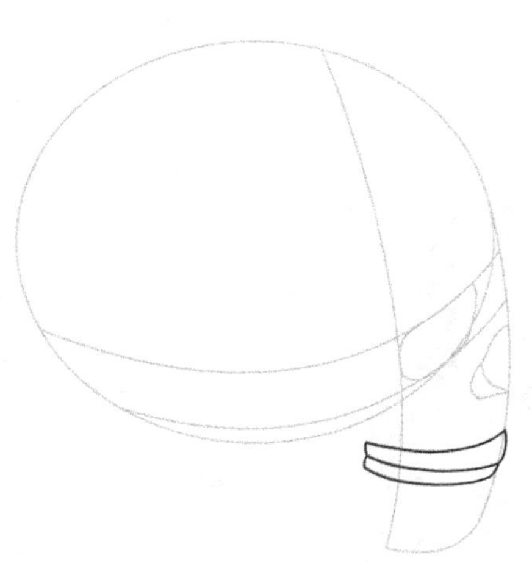

05

06

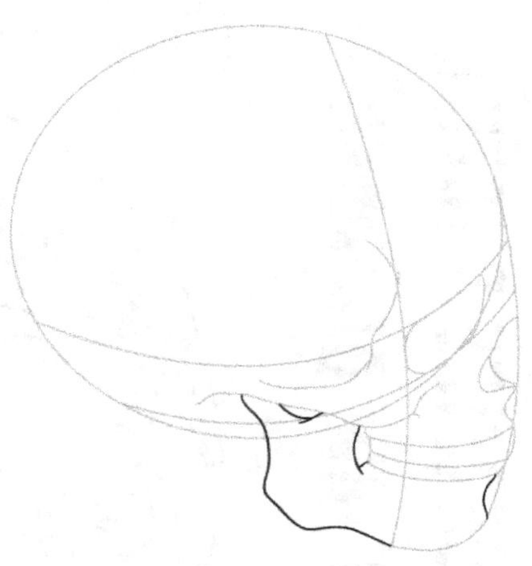

07

08

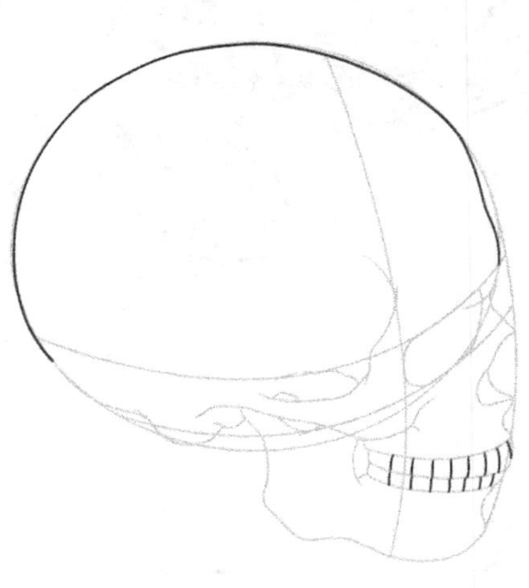

09

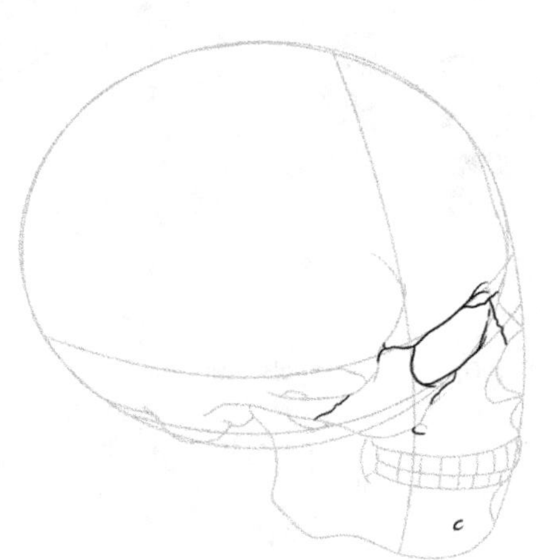

10

11

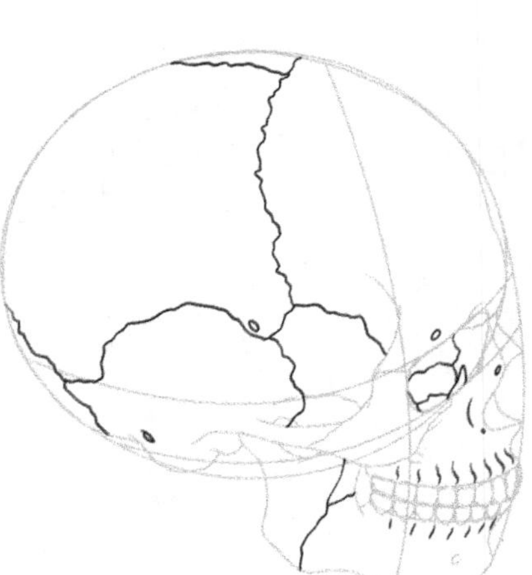

12

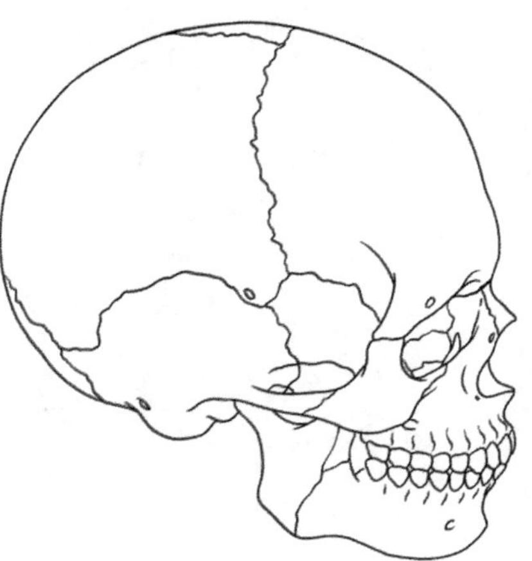

SKULL — UNDERSIDE PROFILE VIEW WITH JAW DROPPED

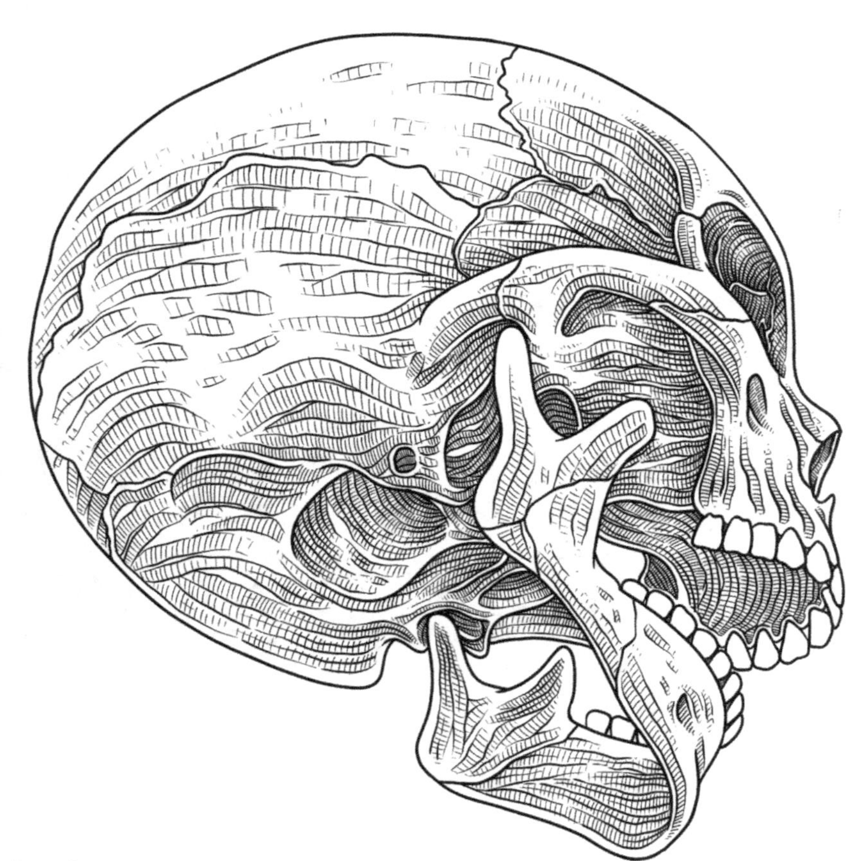

Pro Tip: The jaw pivots from the hinge, moving downward and slightly back. Keep the curve of the mandible consistent as it opens.

01   02   03

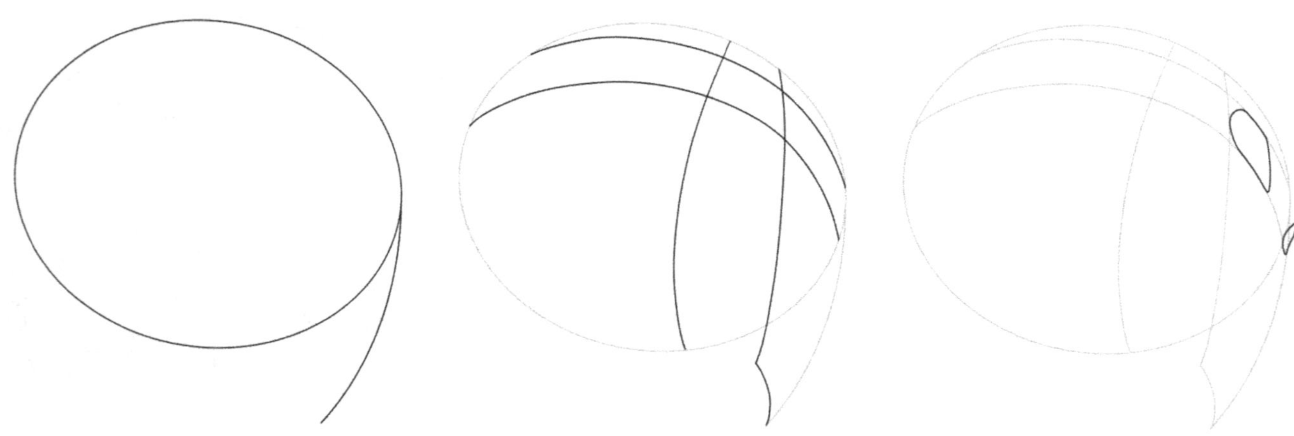

04
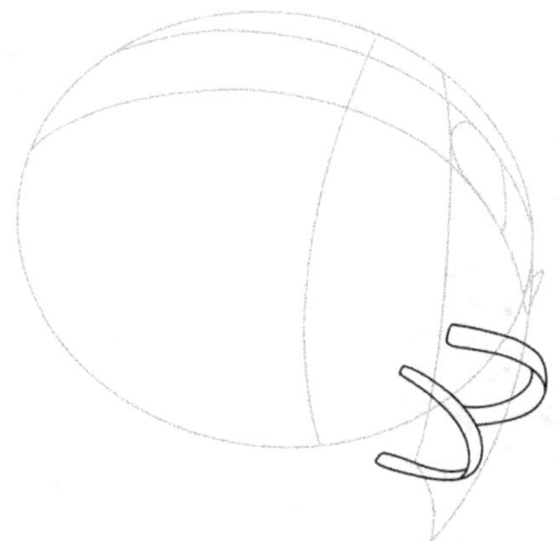

05
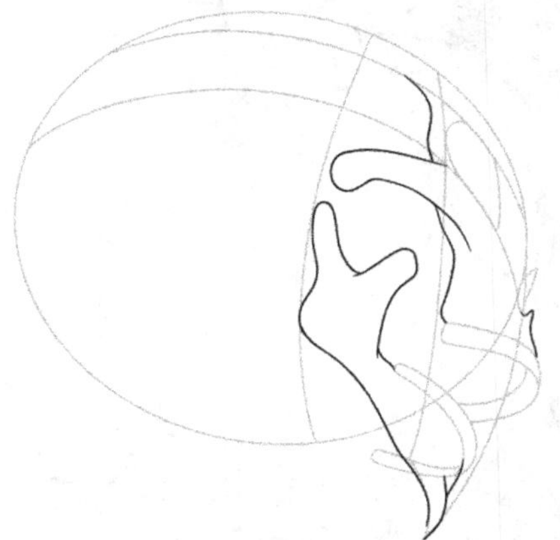

06
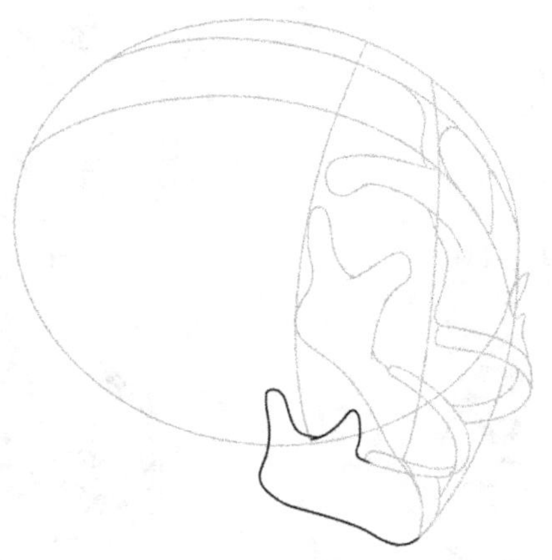

07
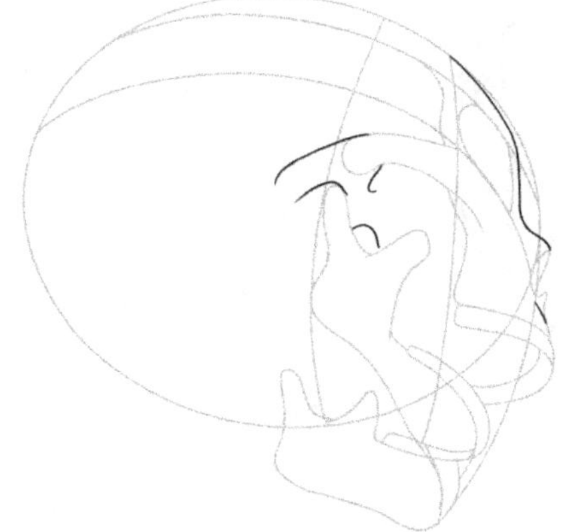

08
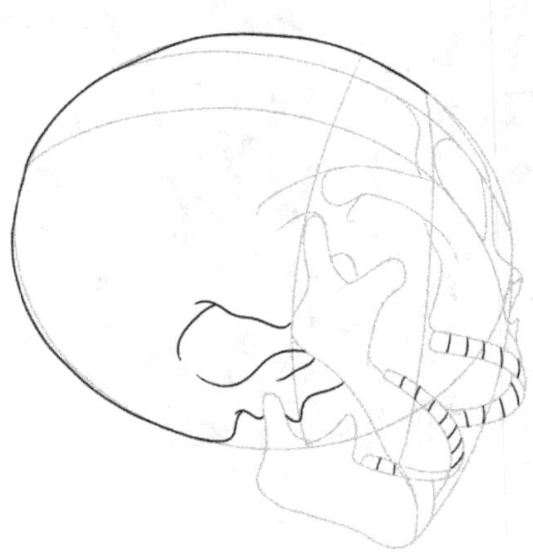

09
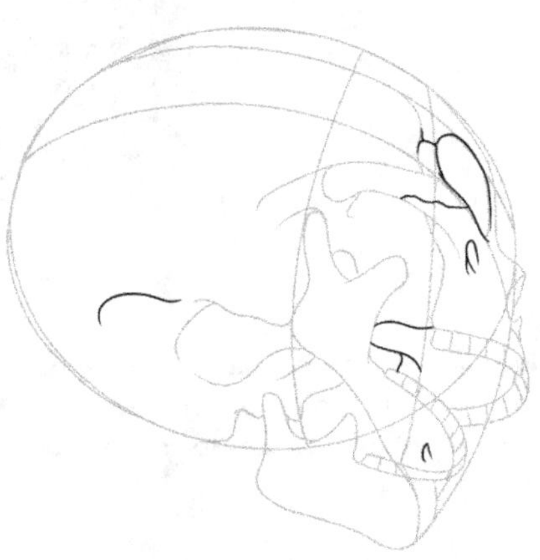

10
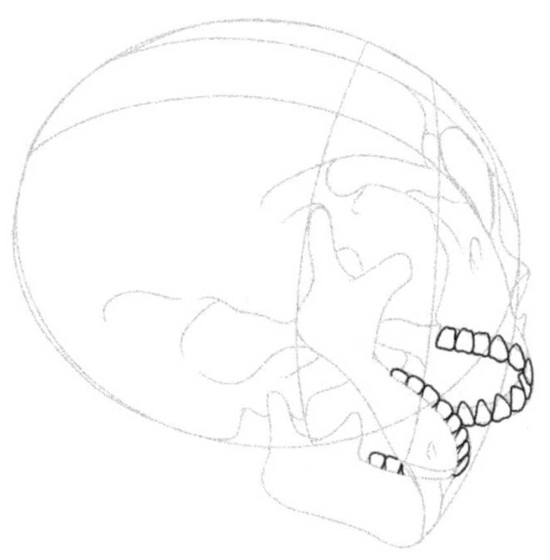

11
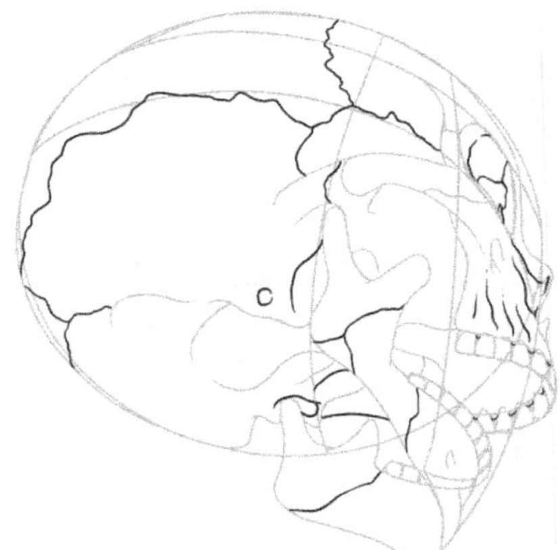

12
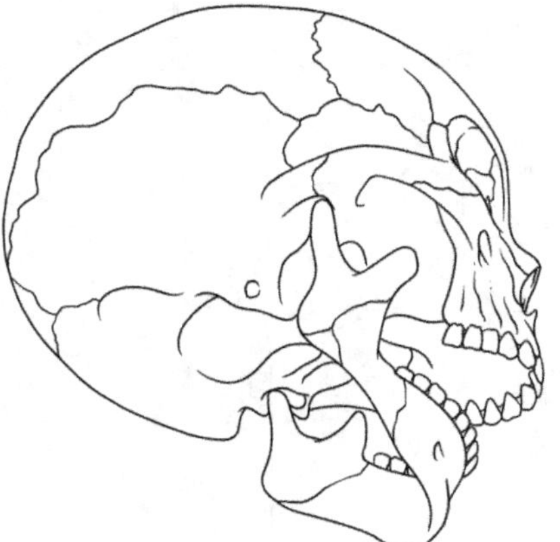

SKULL & SNAKE

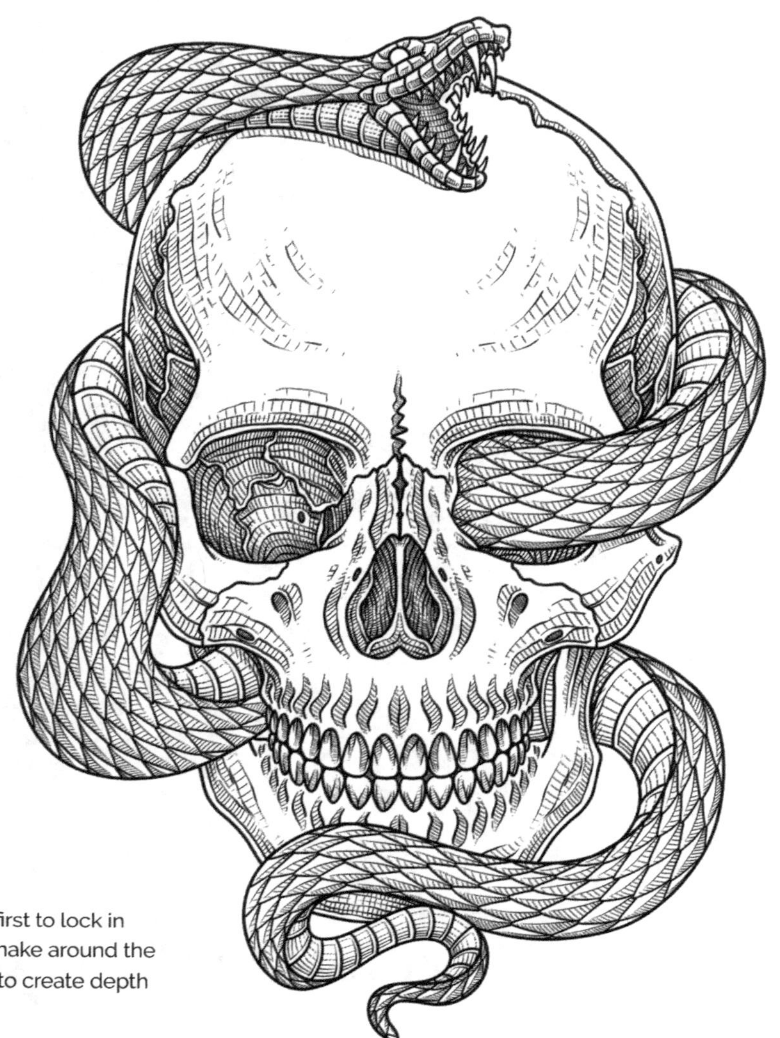

Pro Tip: Sketch the skull first to lock in the form. Then flow the snake around the contours, using overlaps to create depth and movement.

01

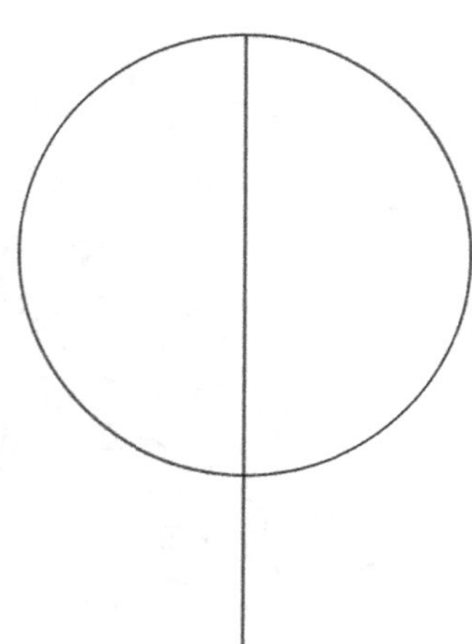

02

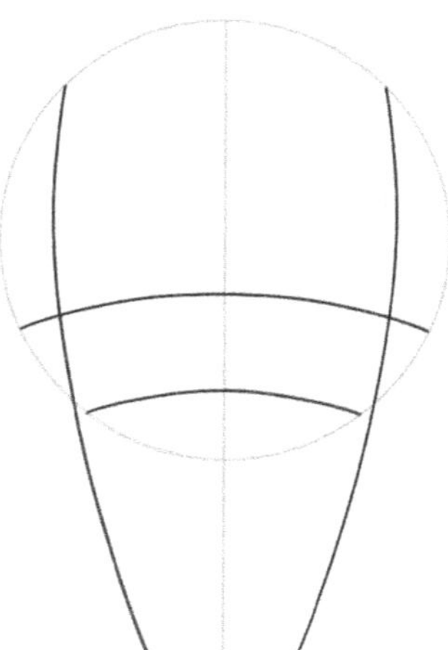

03

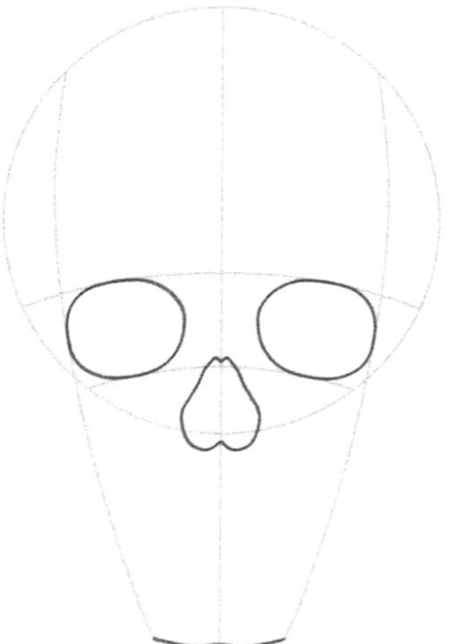

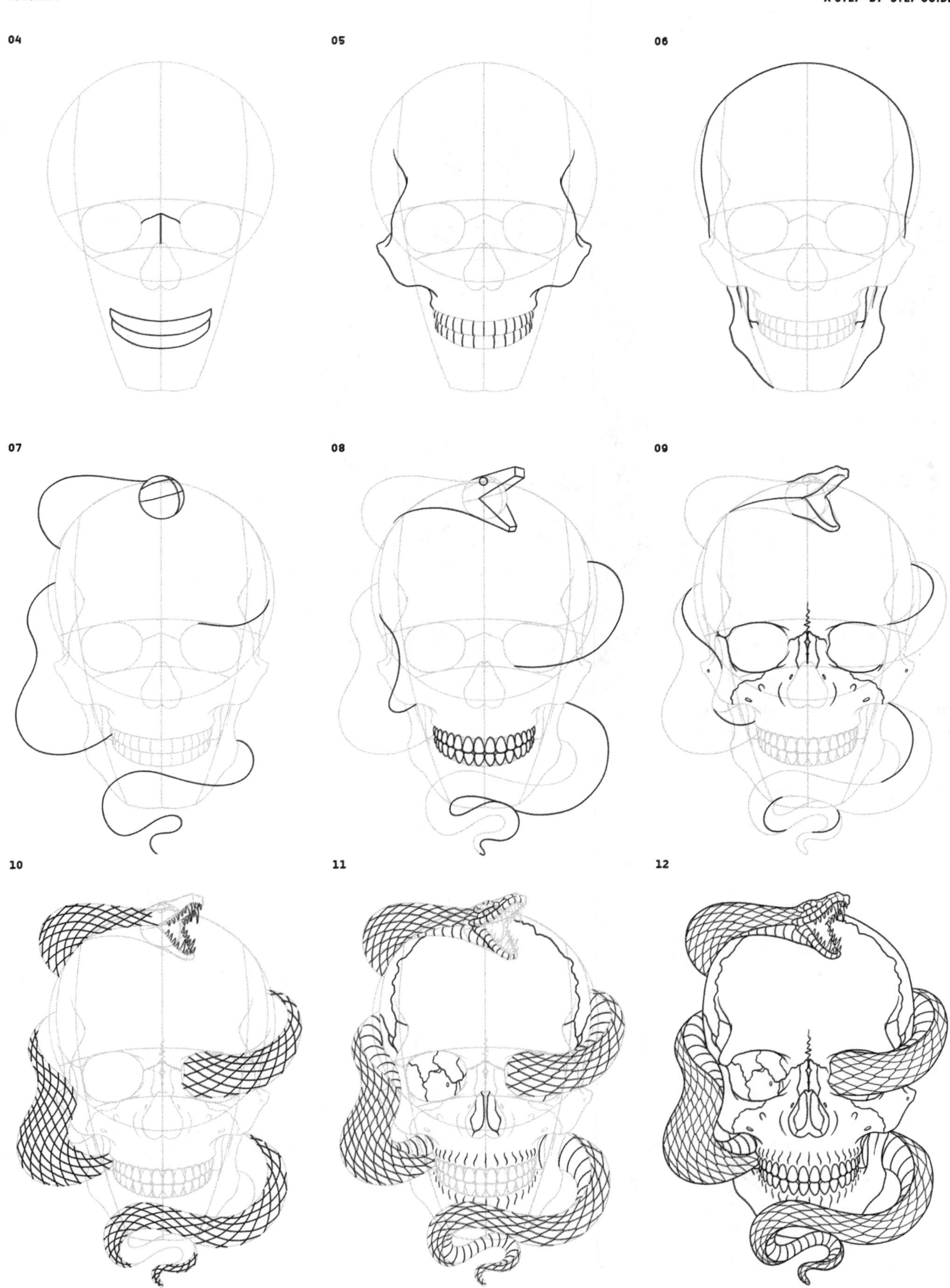
04
05
06
07
08
09
10
11
12
HOW TO DRAW SKULLS

SKULL & ANCHOR

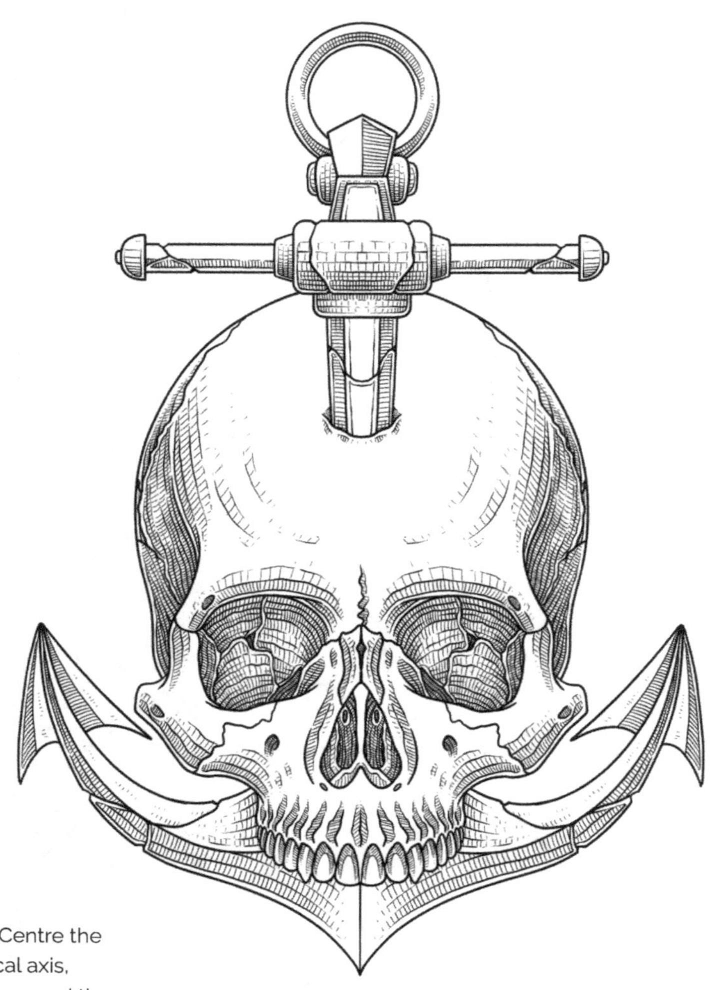

Pro Tip: Focus on symmetry. Centre the anchor along the skull's vertical axis, aligning the shank with the nose and the flukes with the jawline.

01

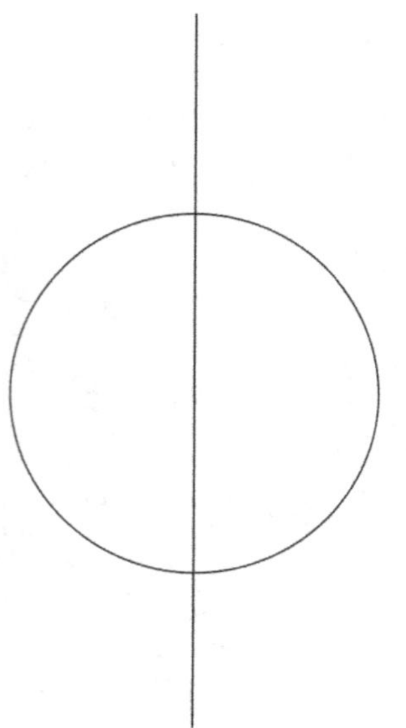

02

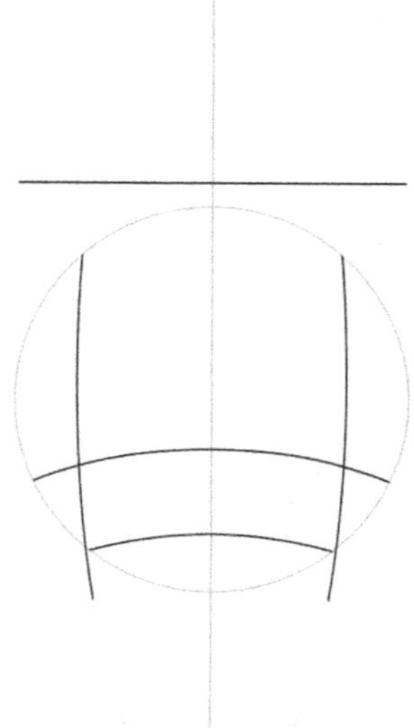

03

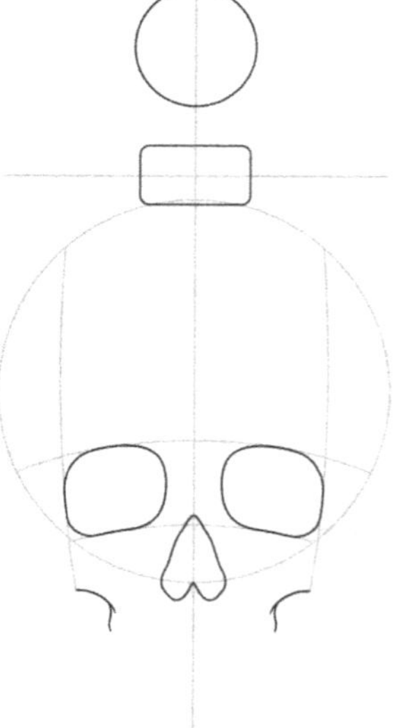

04

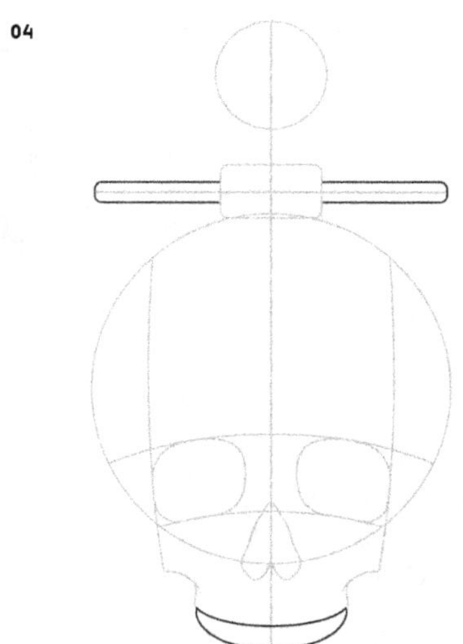

05

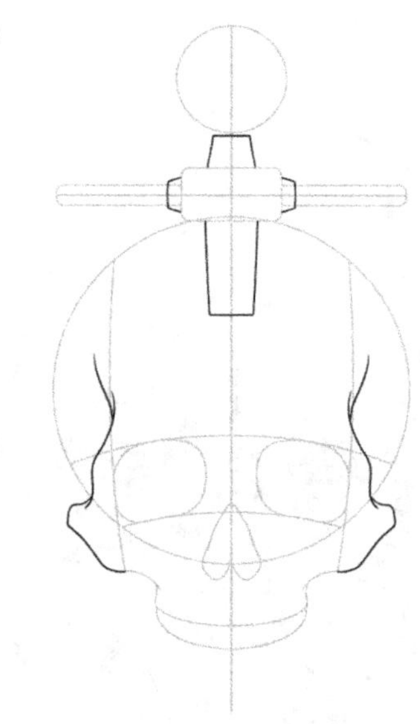

06

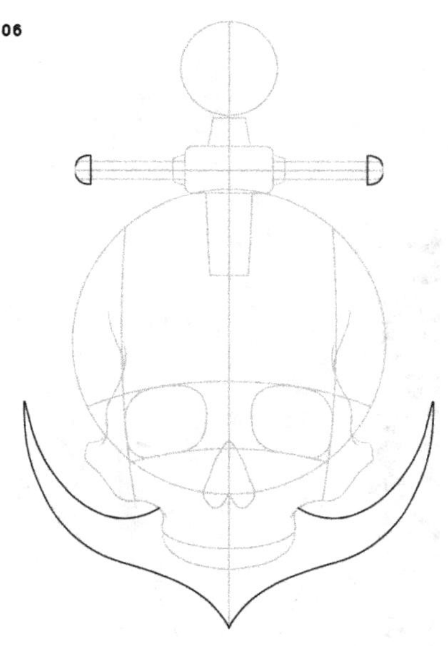

07

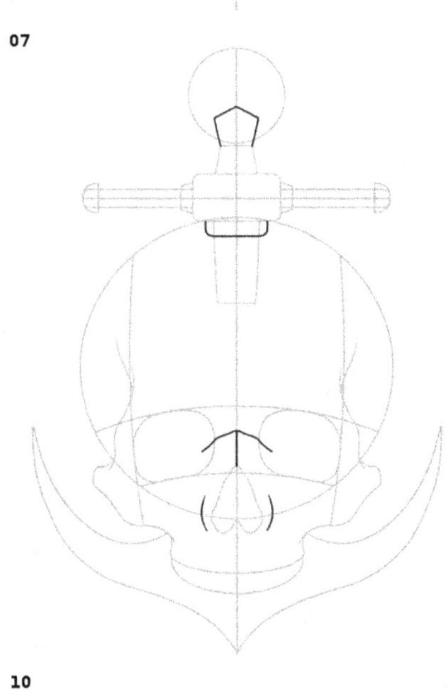

08

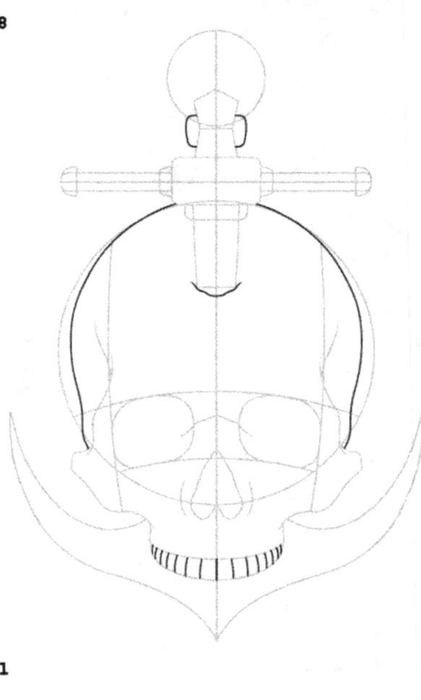

09

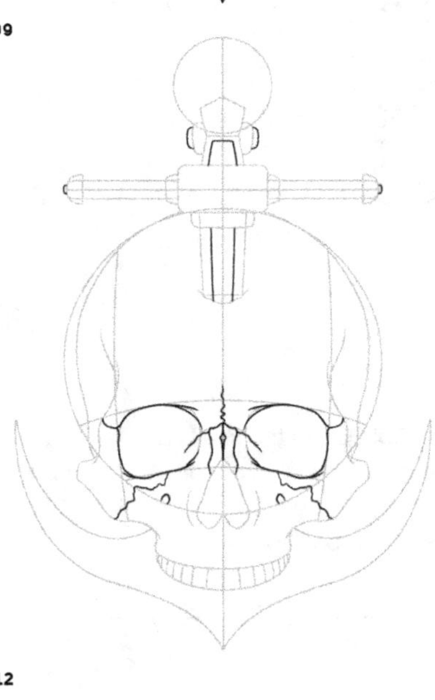

10

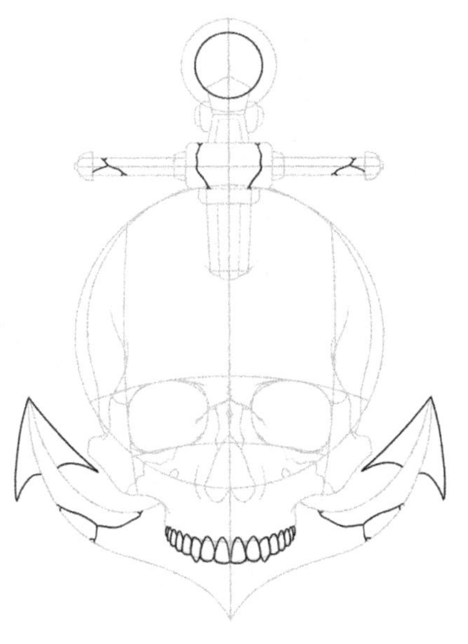

11

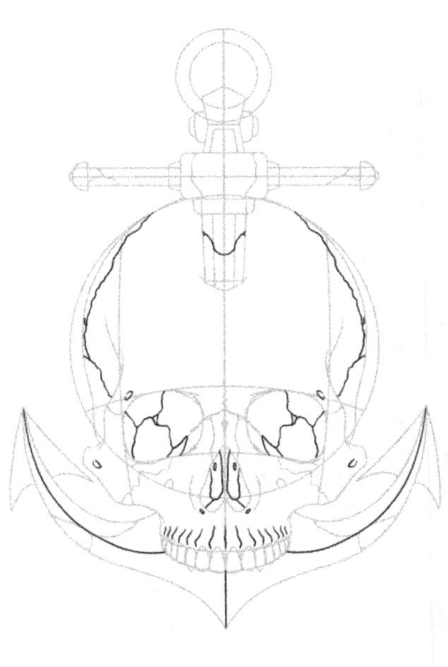

12

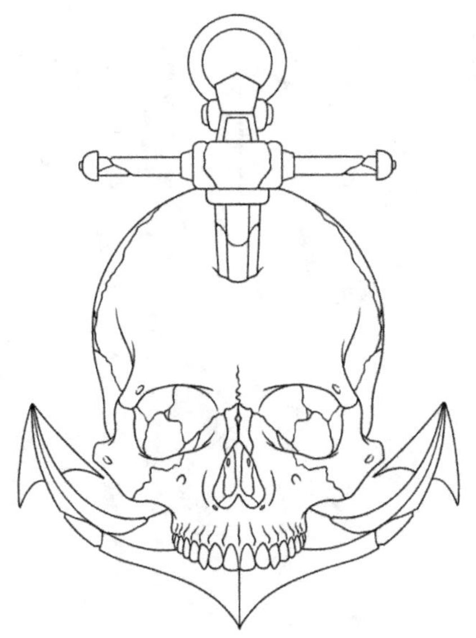

HOW TO DRAW SKULLS

SKULL & CROSSBONES

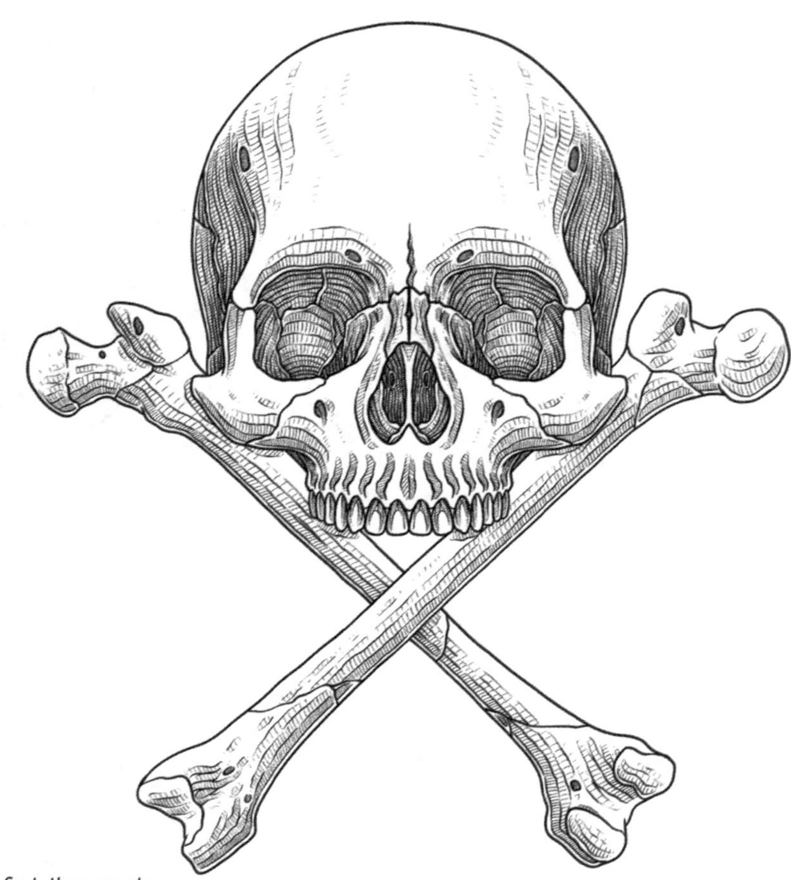

Pro Tip: Centre the skull first, then angle the bones evenly beneath it. Keep both bones balanced and symmetrical for a clean composition.

01

02

03

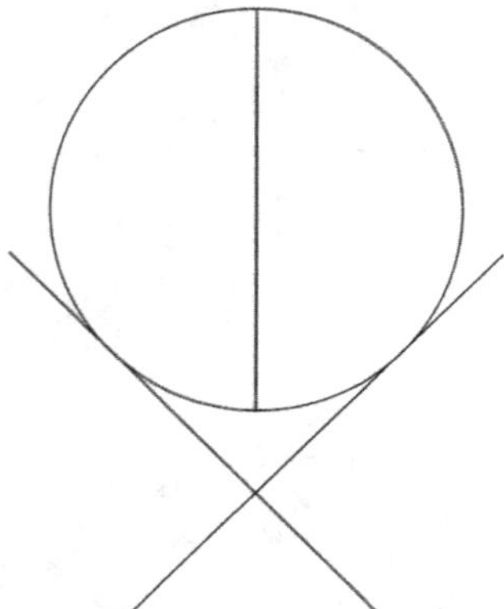

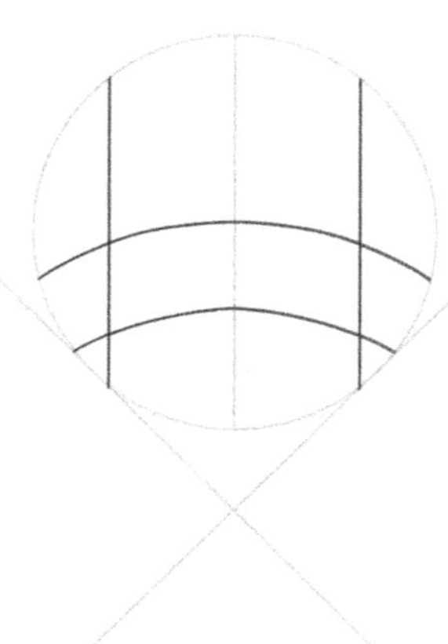

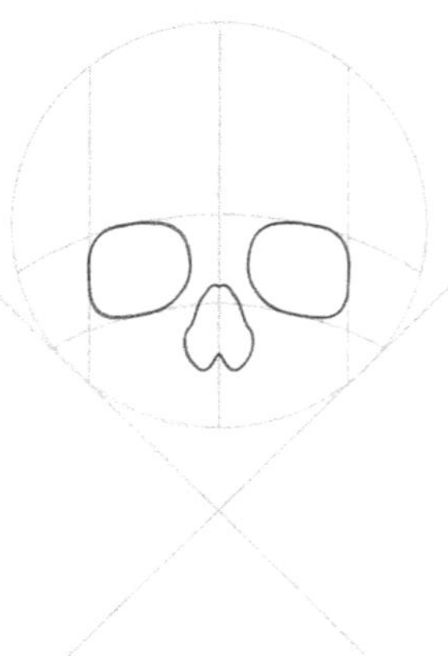

04

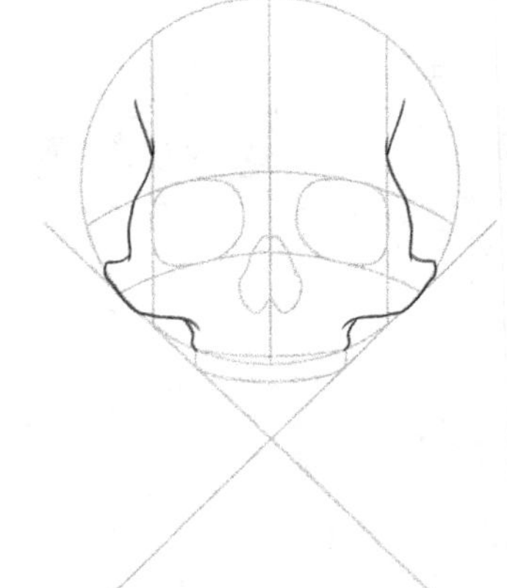

05

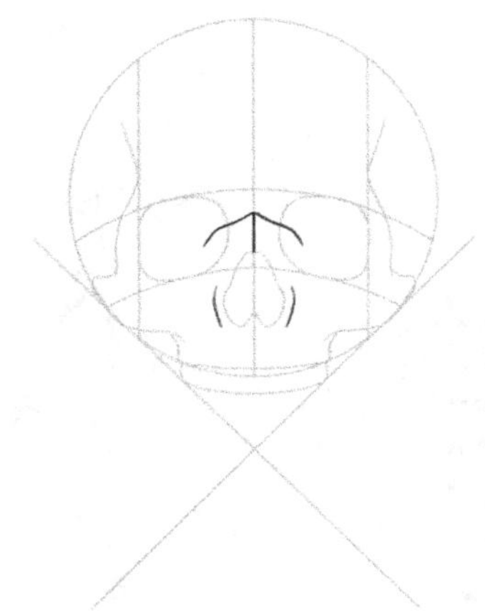

06

07

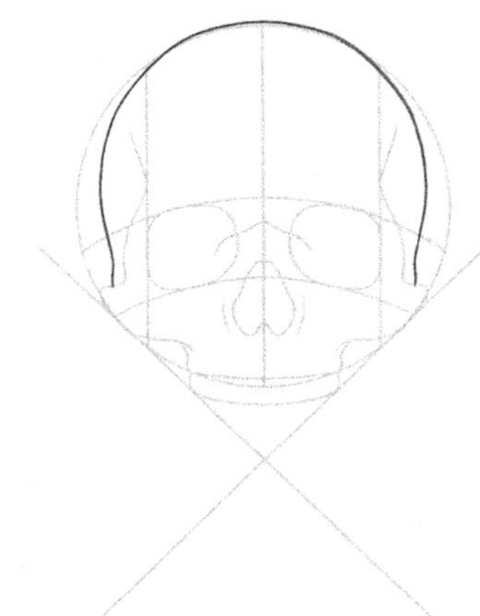

08

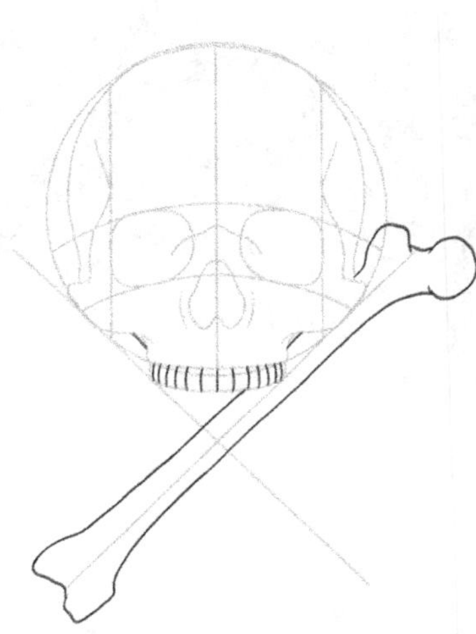

09

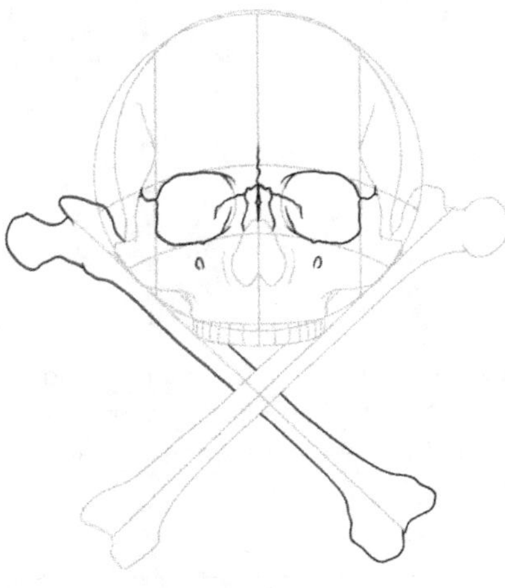

10

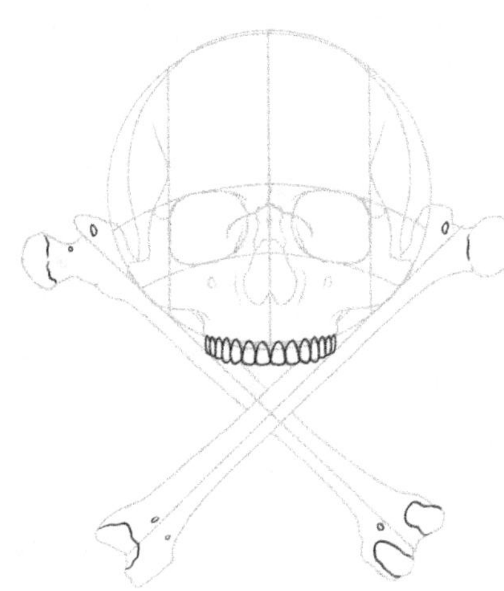

11

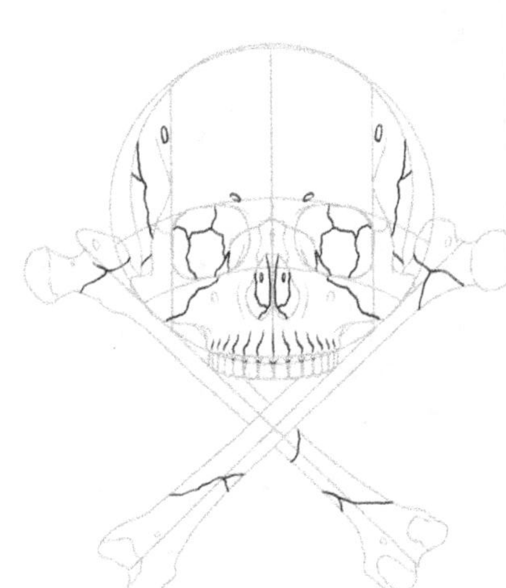

12

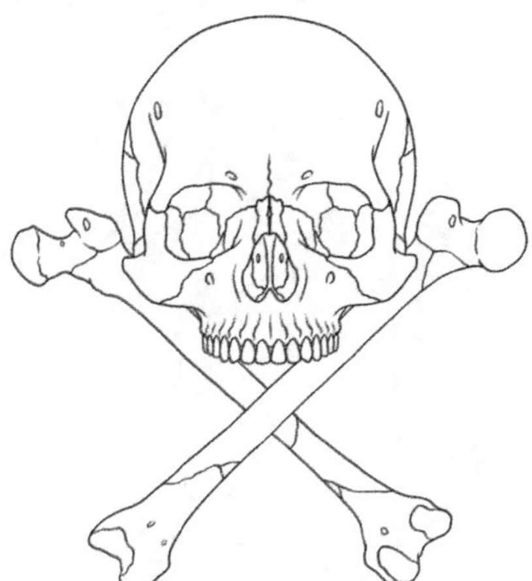

HOW TO DRAW SKULLS

SKULL & SCYTHE

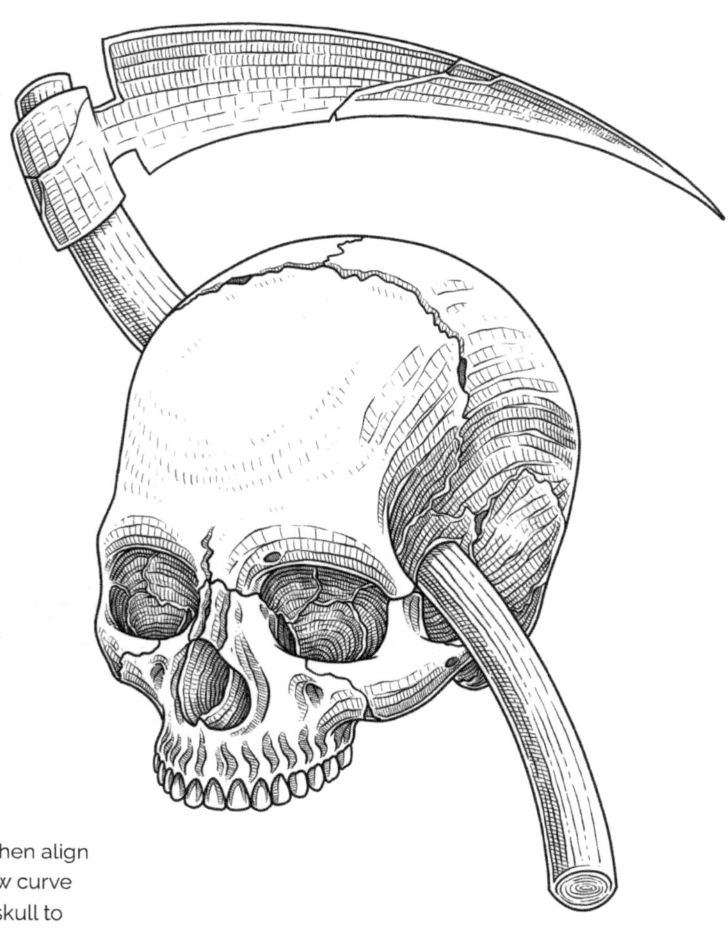

Pro Tip: Sketch the skull first. Then align the scythe's handle with the jaw curve and let the blade arc over the skull to balance the composition.

01

02

03

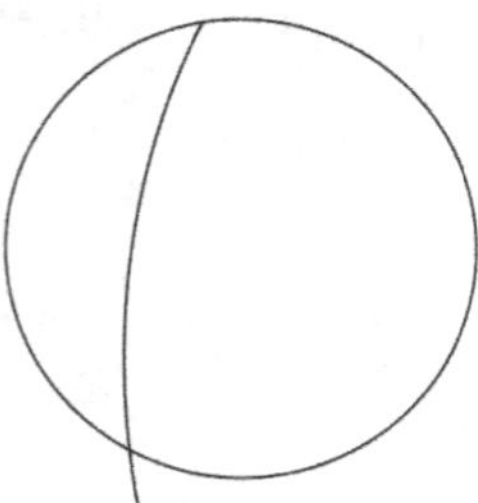

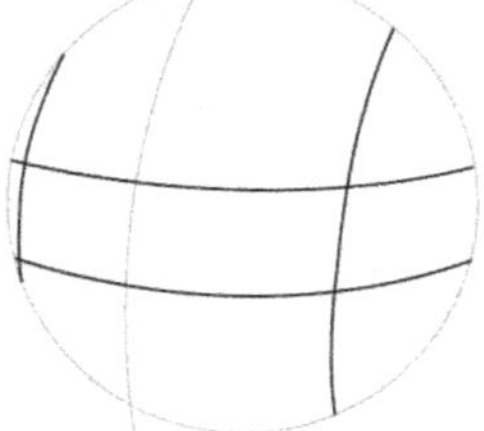

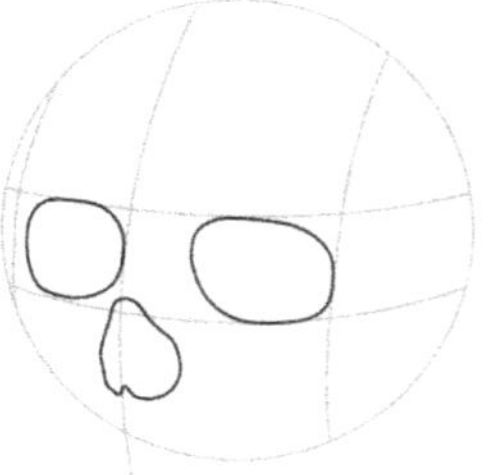

04

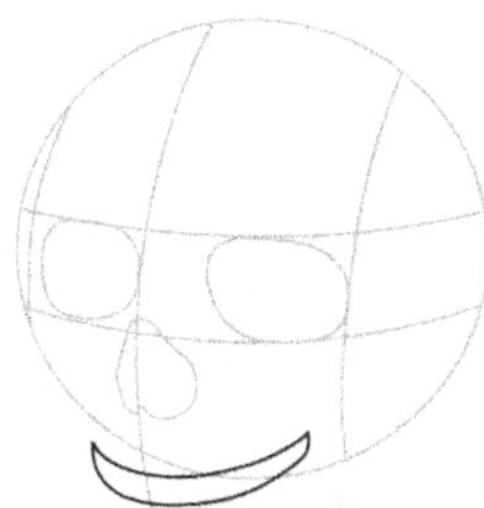

05

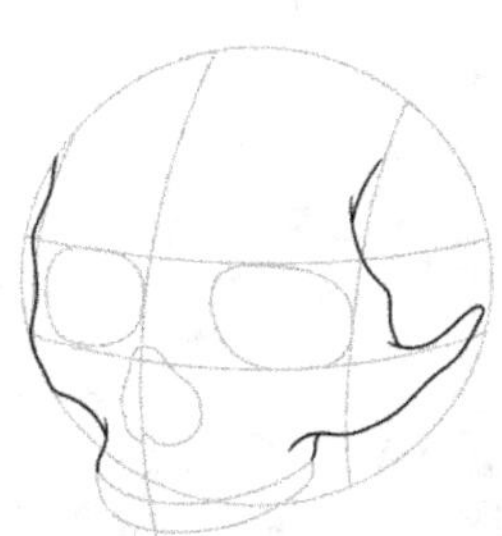

06

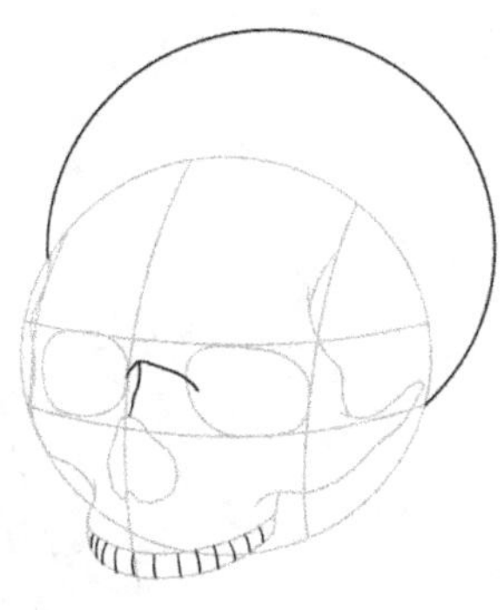

07

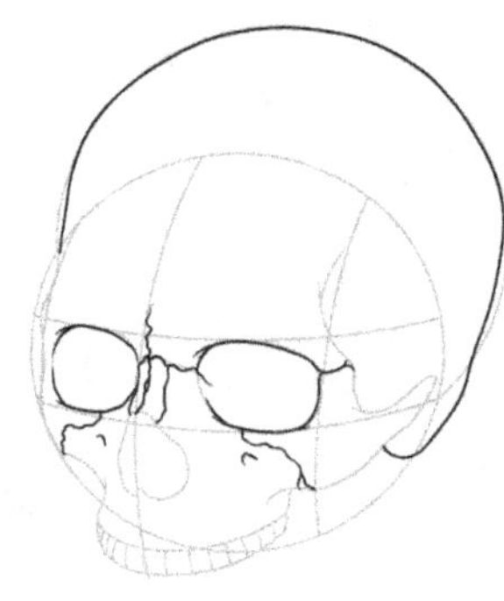

08

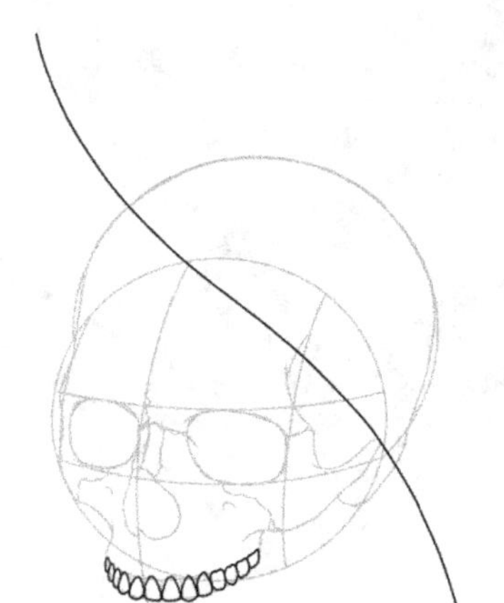

09

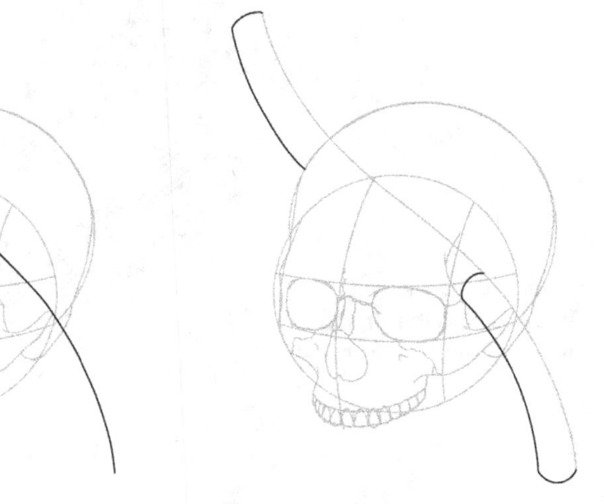

10

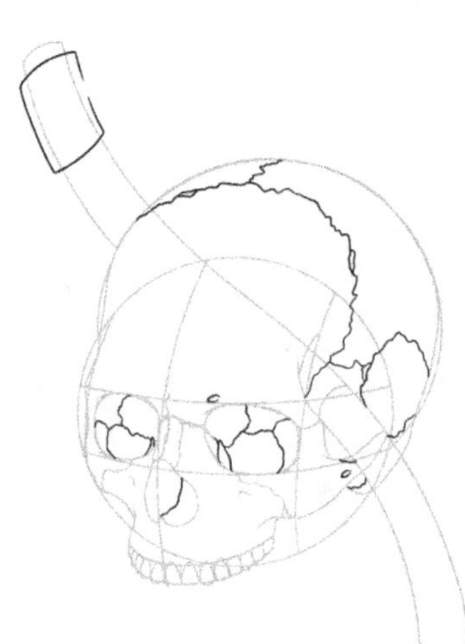

11

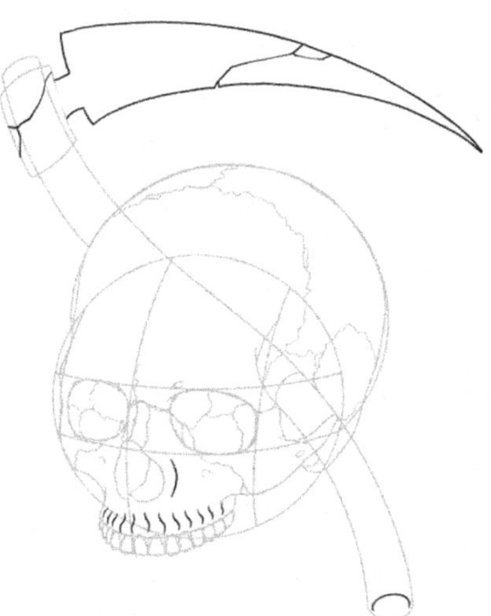

12

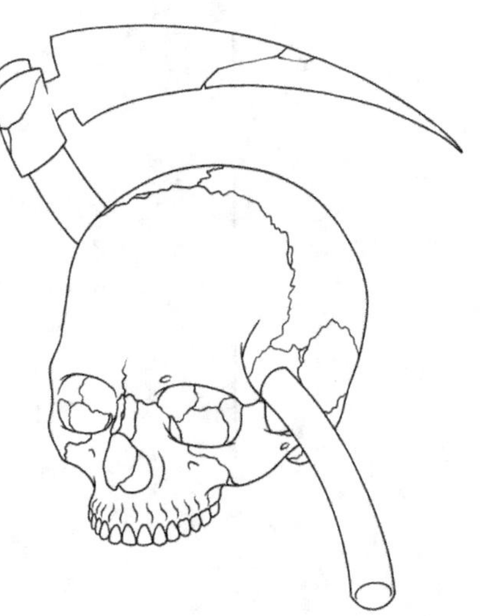

CLOAKED SKULL

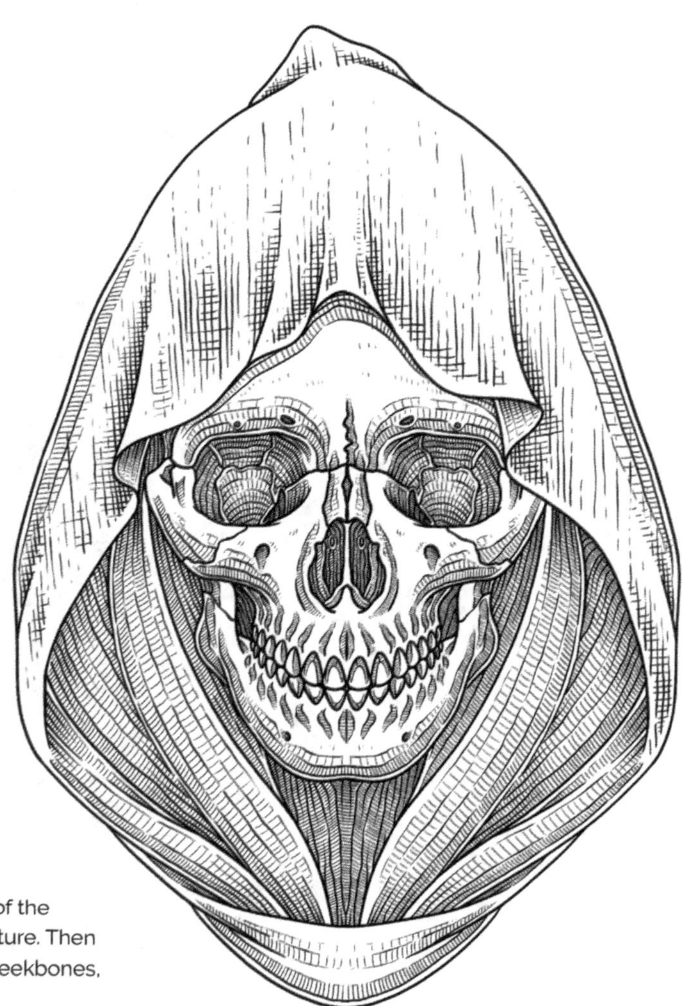

Pro Tip: Sketch the lower half of the skull first to establish the structure. Then shape the cloak around the cheekbones, jaw, and chin for natural flow.

01

02

03

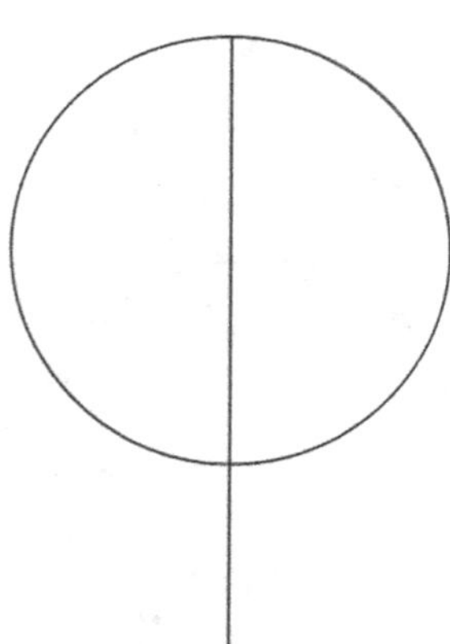

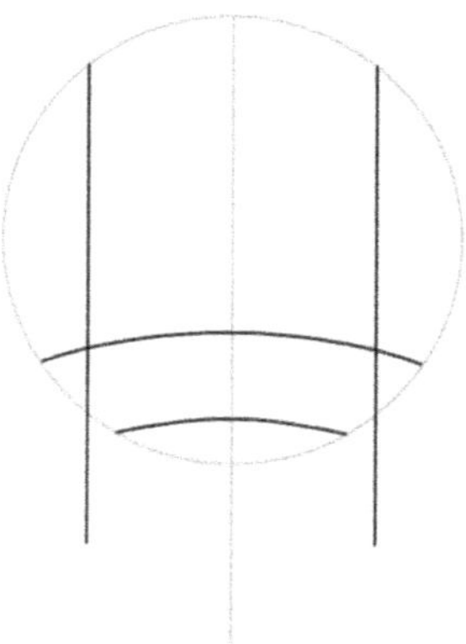

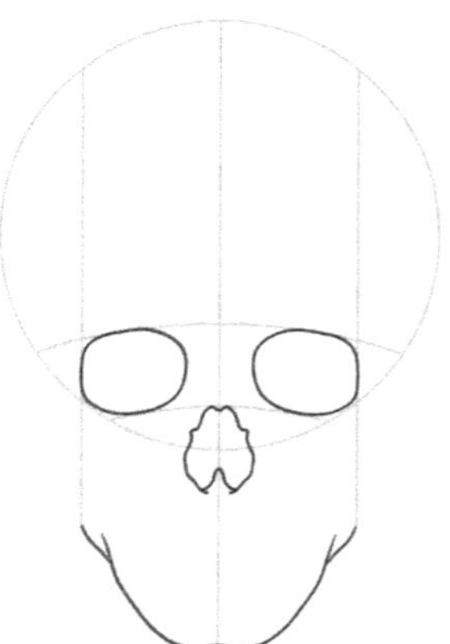

04

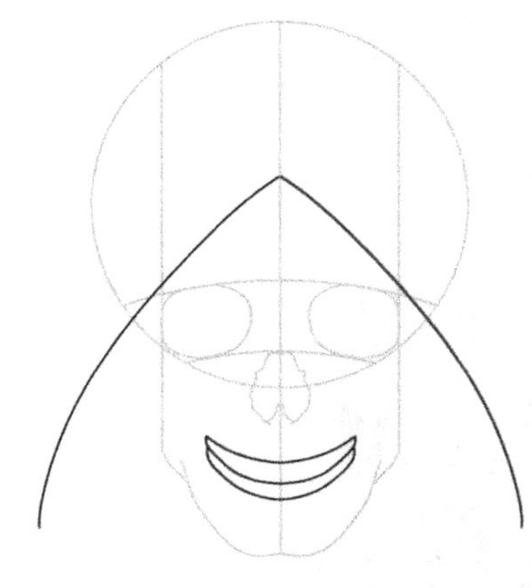

05

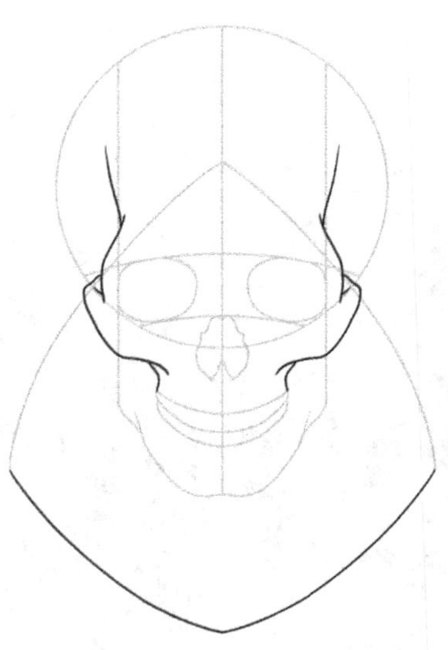

06

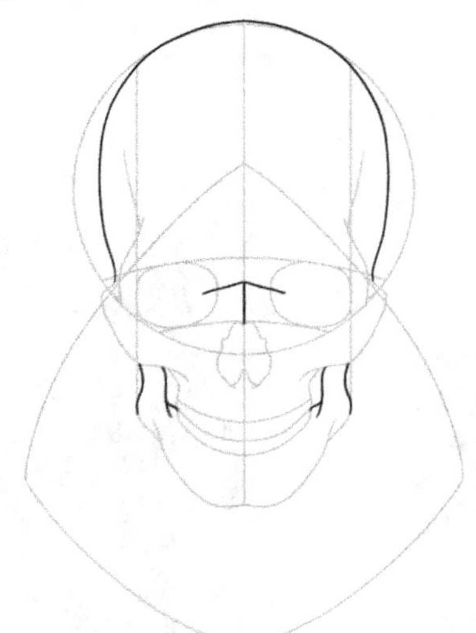

07

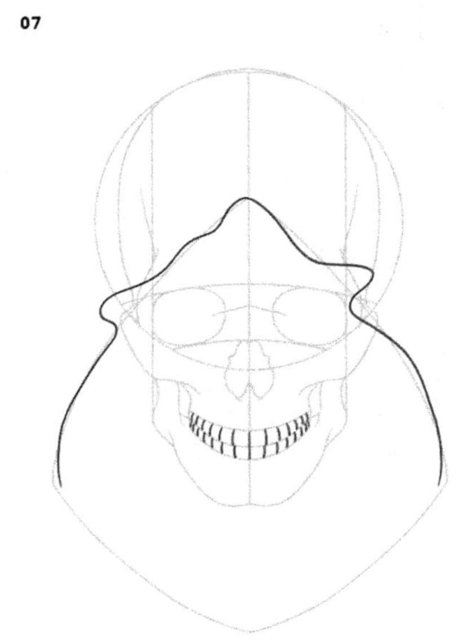

08

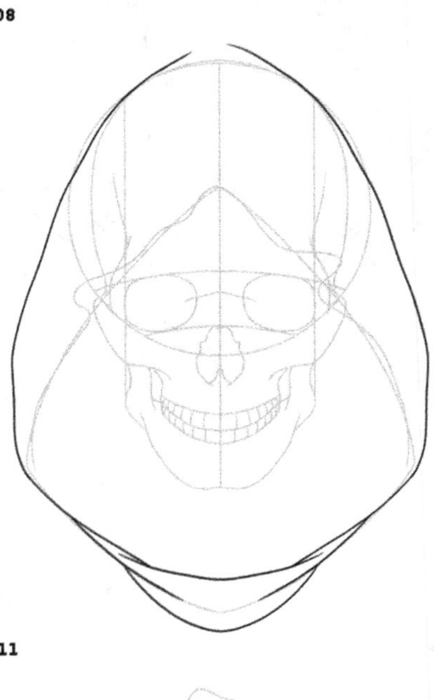

09

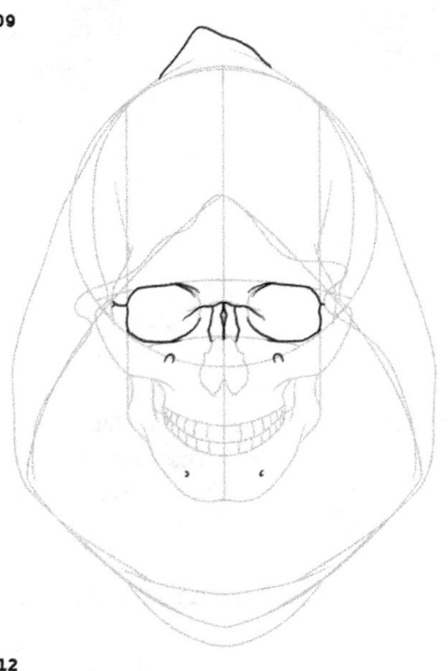

10

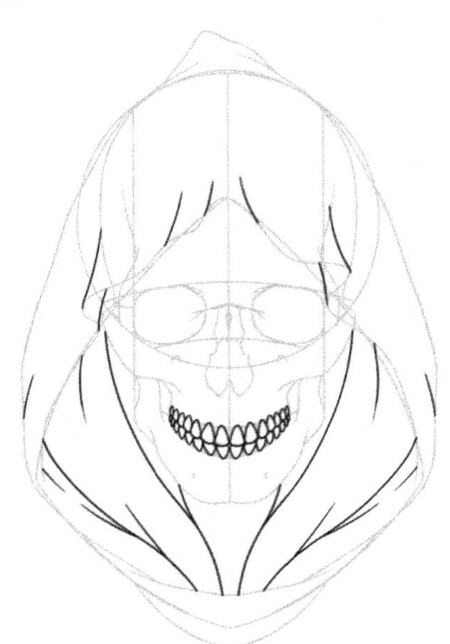

11

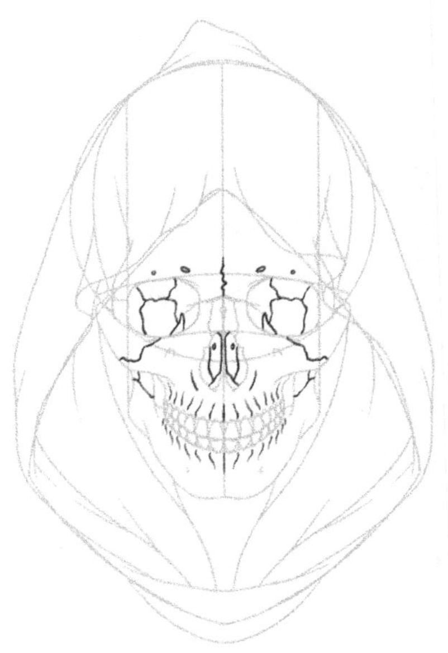

12

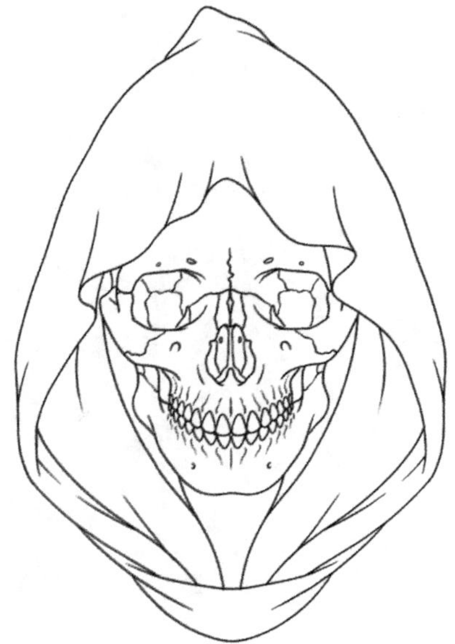

SKULL HEART

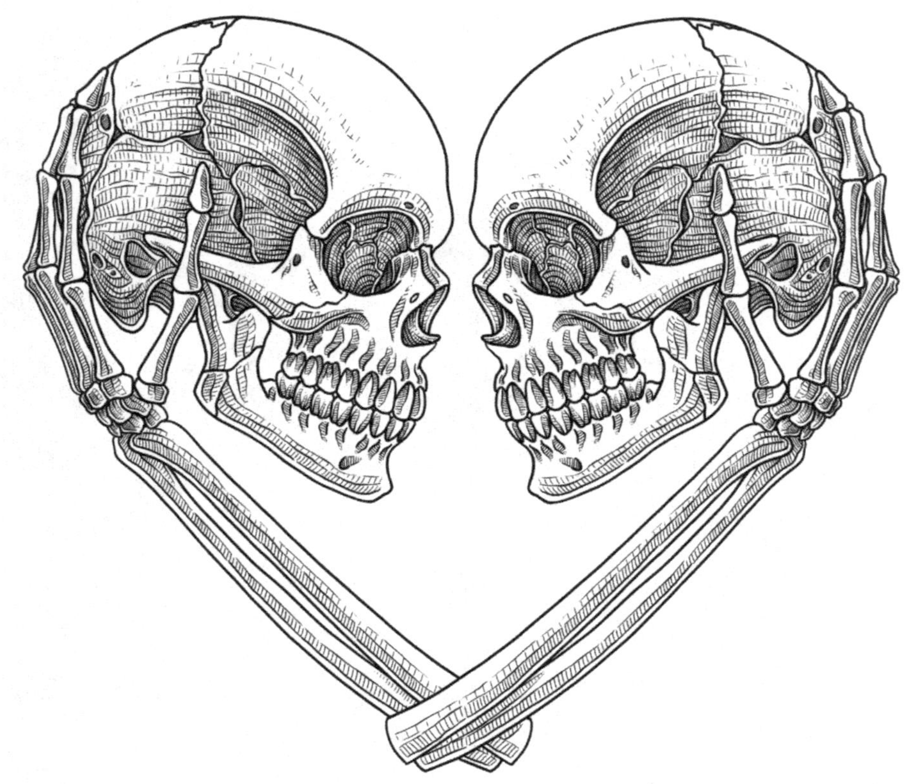

Pro Tip: Sketch the shape and tilt of both skulls first to lock in the heart form. Then connect the arms and bones to complete the flow.

01

02

03

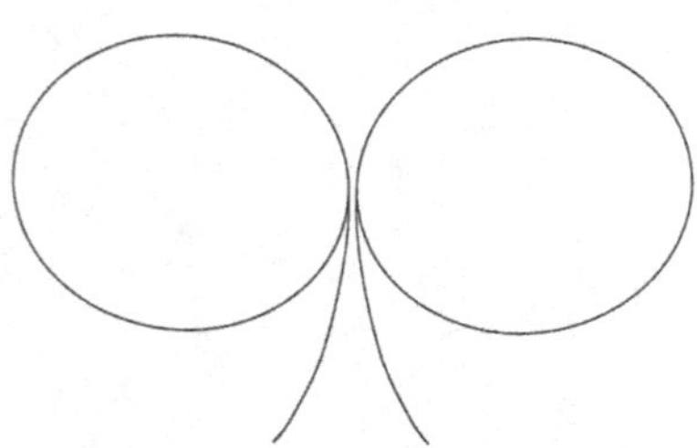

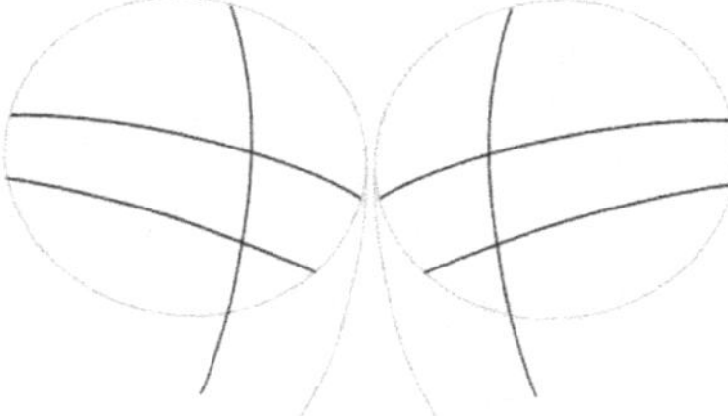

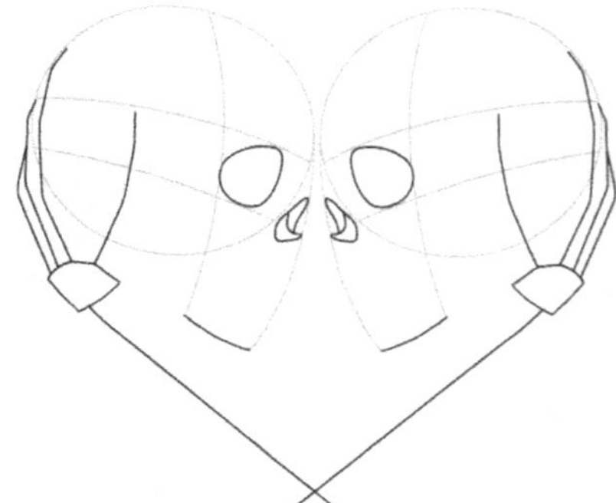

04

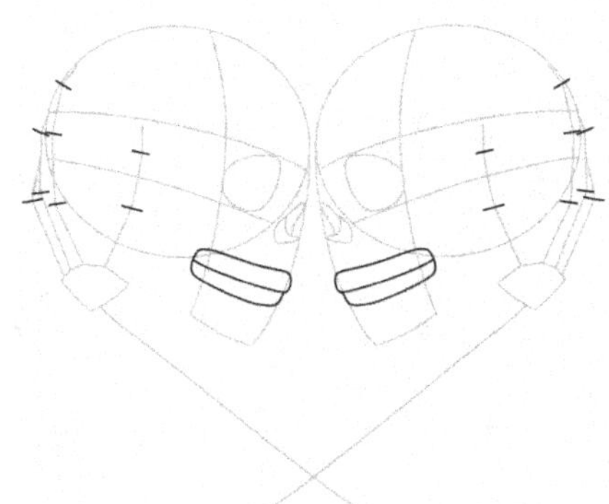

05

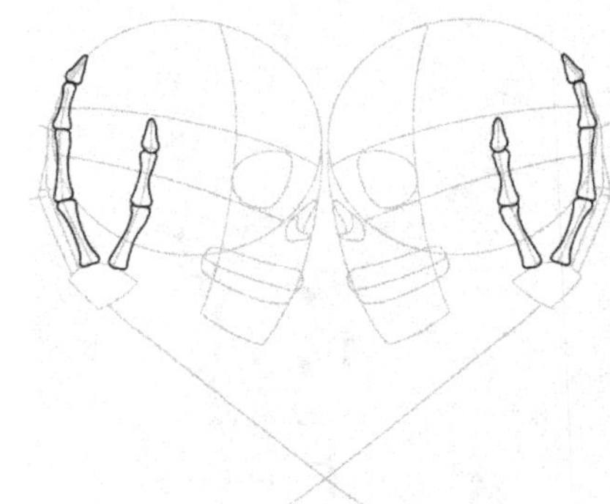

06

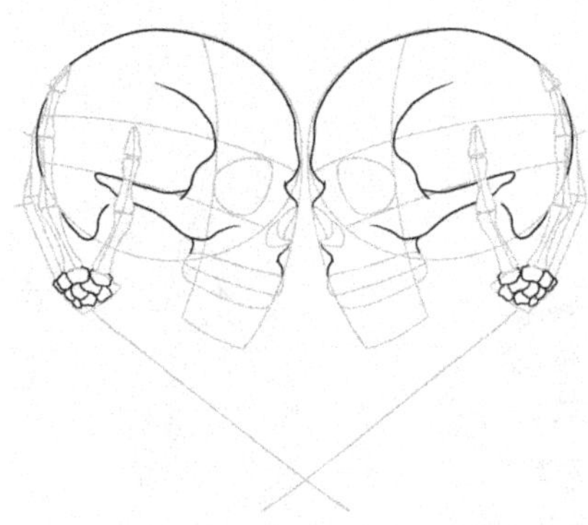

07

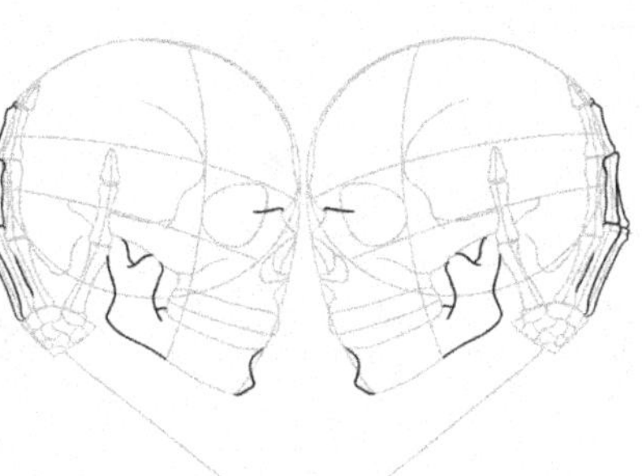

08

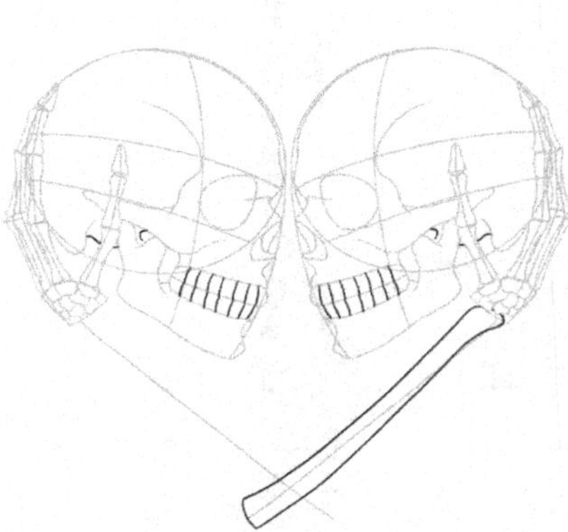

09

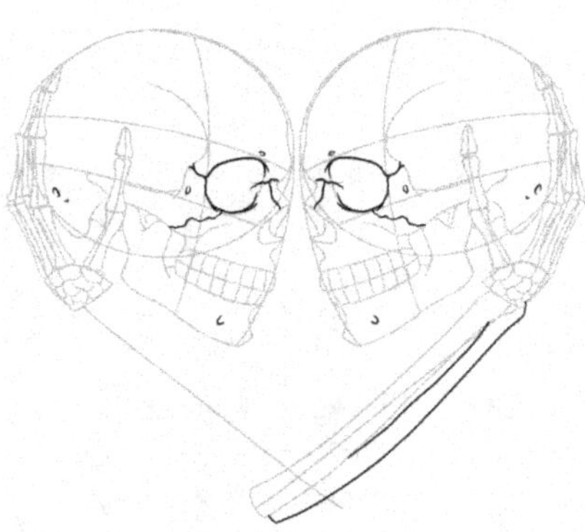

10

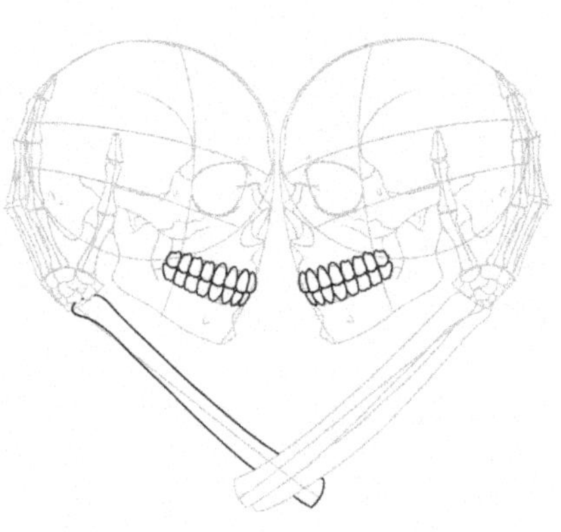

11

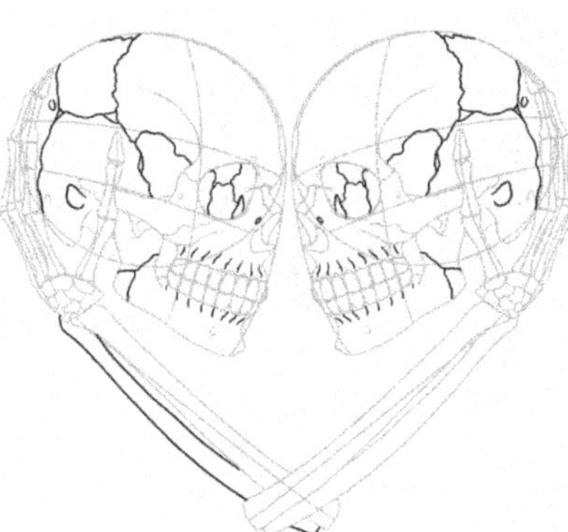

12

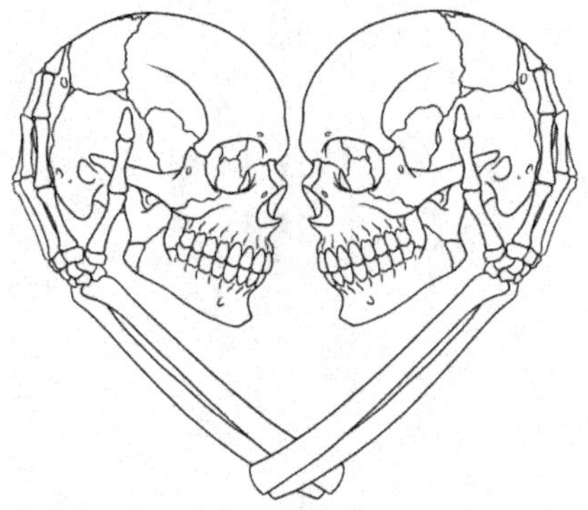

HOW TO DRAW SKULLS

SKELETON KEY

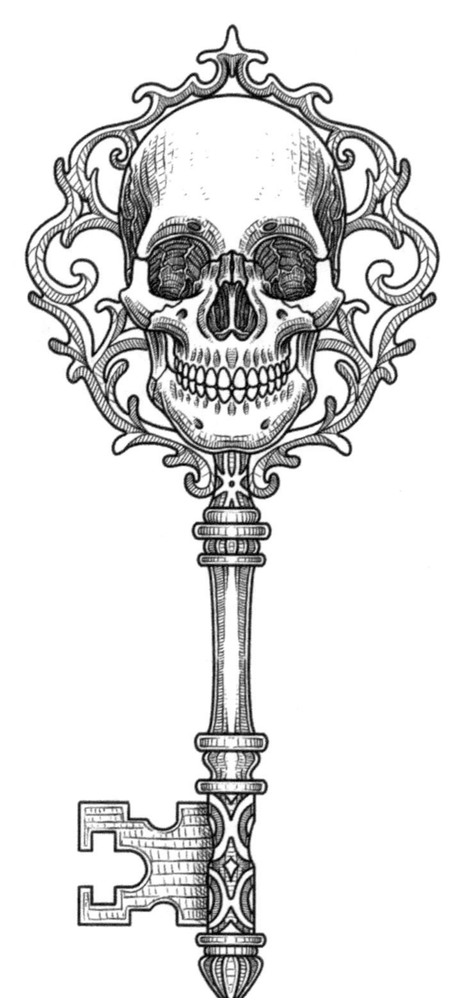

Pro Tip: Keep the key's shaft around twice the length of the skull for clean proportions and balanced composition.

01

02

03

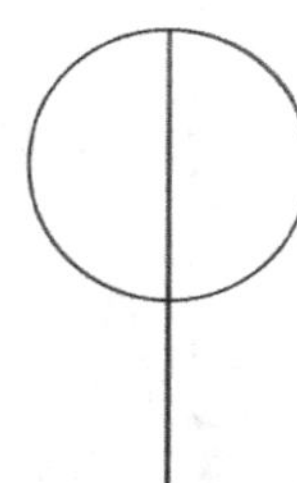

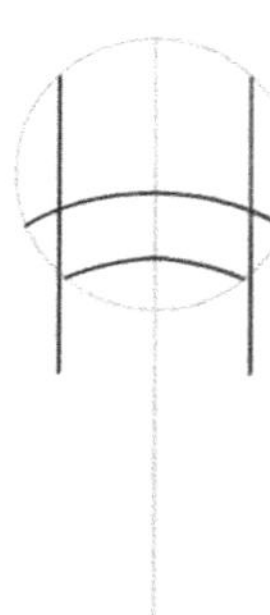

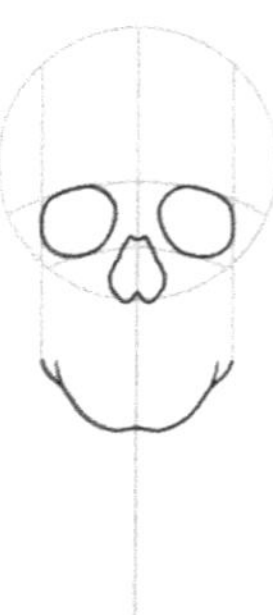

04

05

06

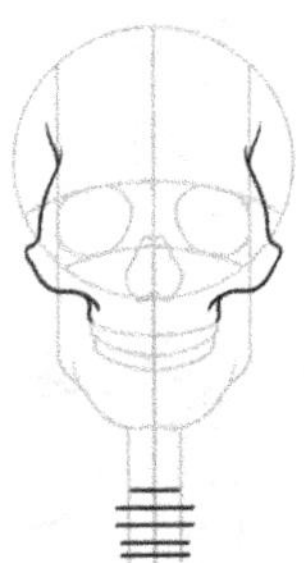

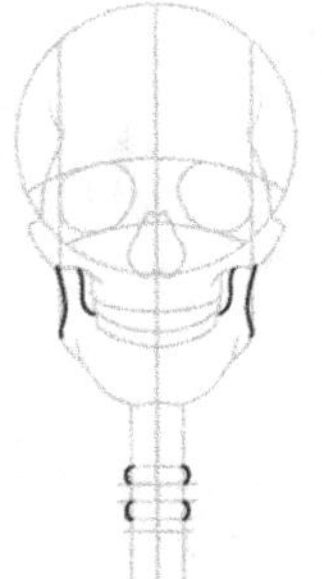

07

08

09

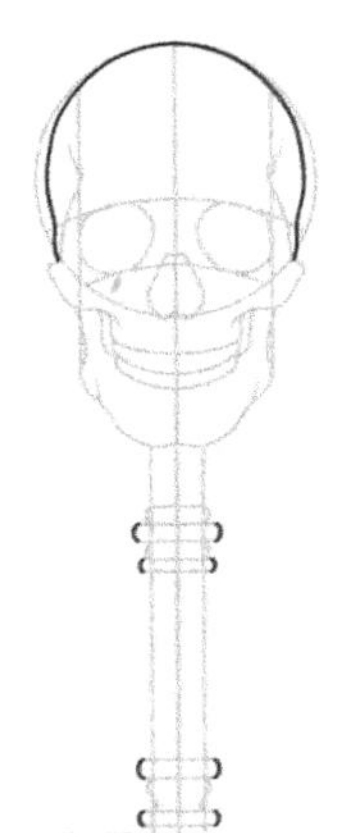

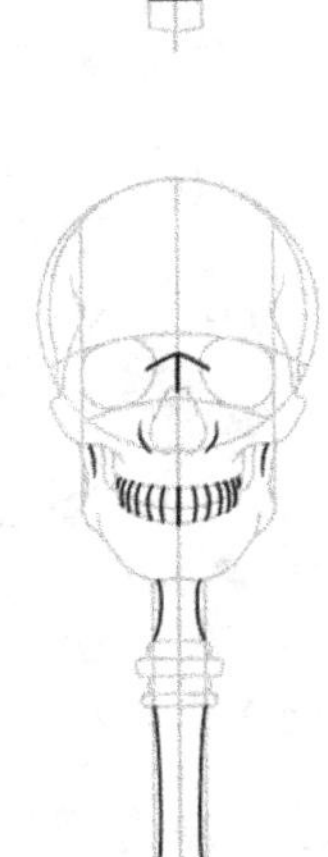

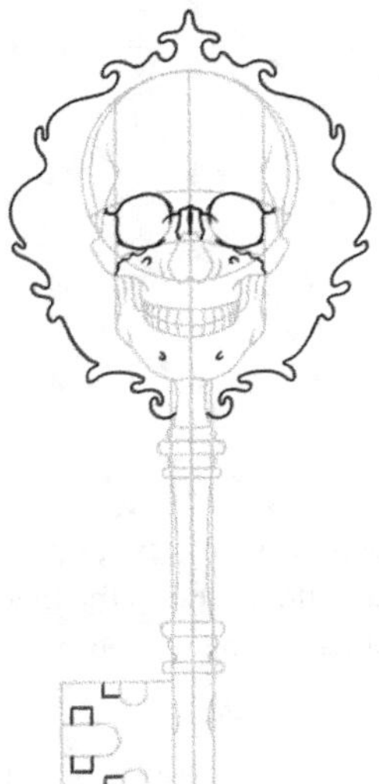

10

11

12

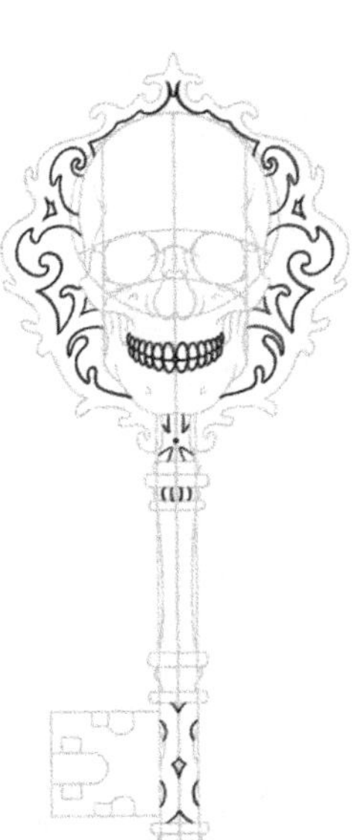

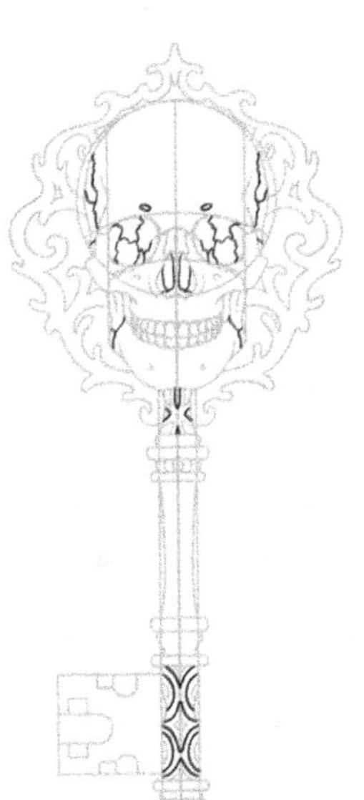

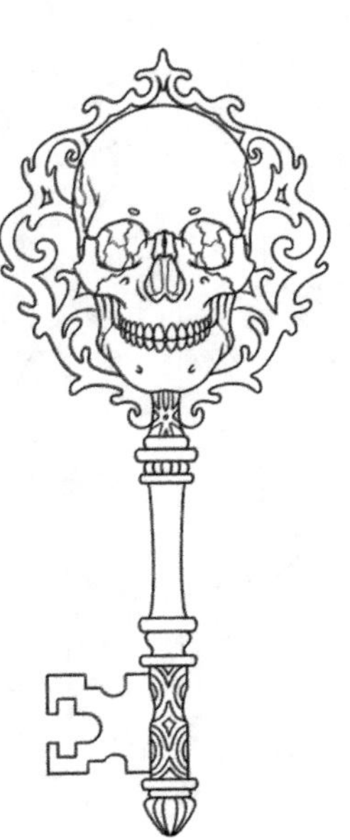

SKULL & SWORD

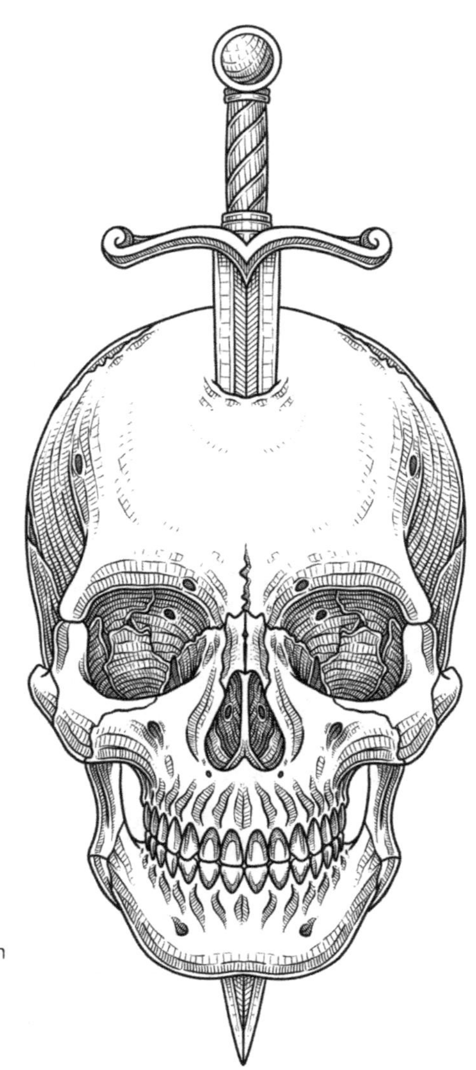

Pro Tip: Use the skull's centreline to align the sword perfectly. Keep the blade, hilt, and tip balanced to match the skull's vertical axis.

01

02

03

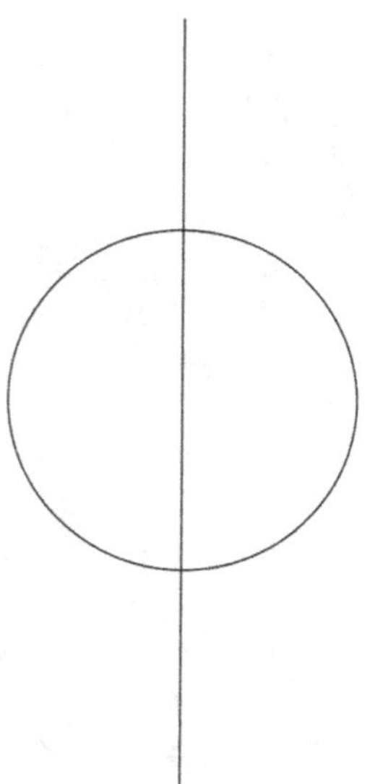

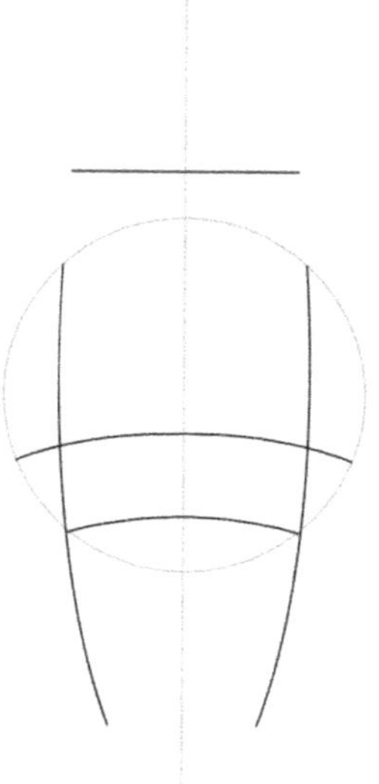

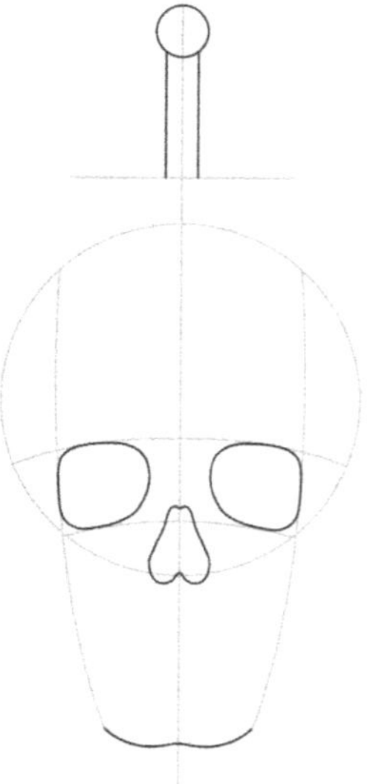

04

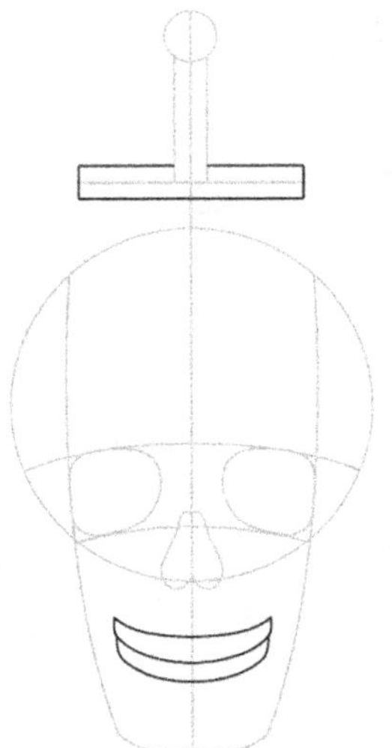

05

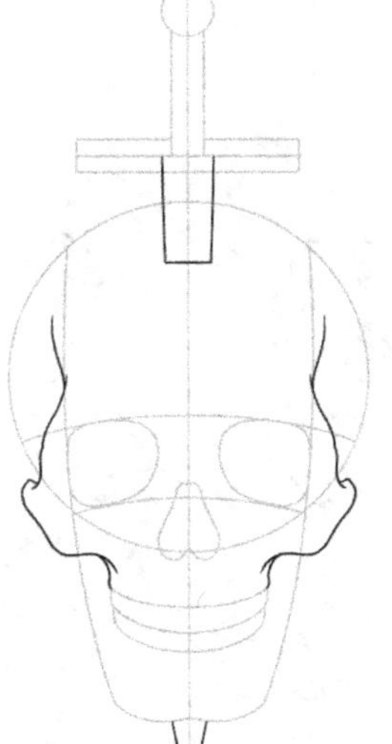

06

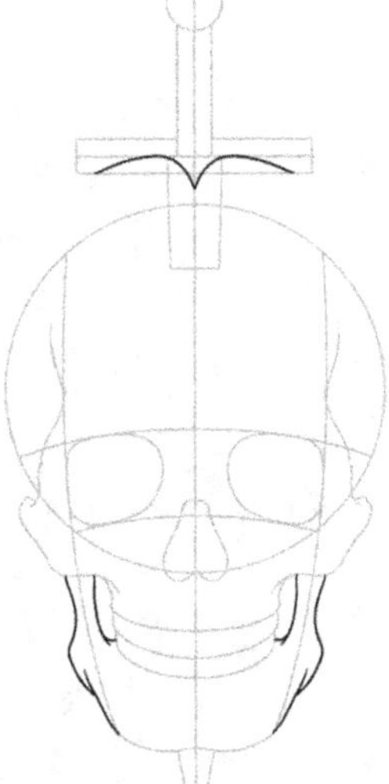

07

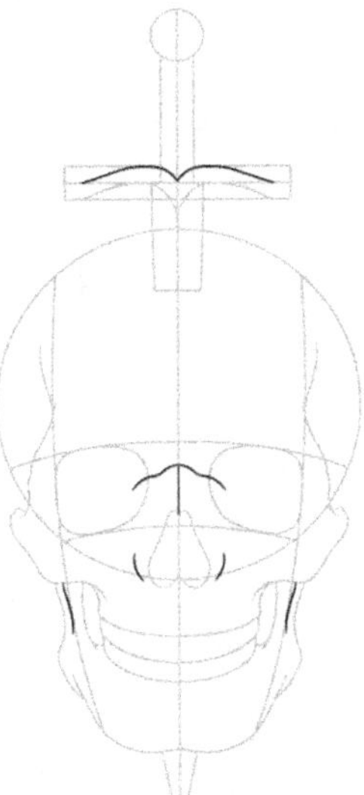

08

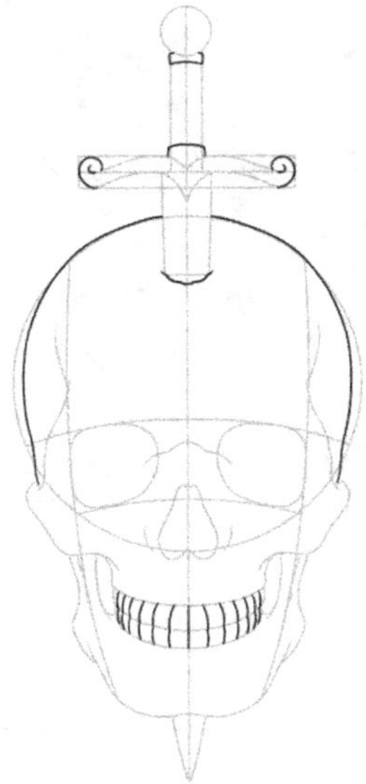

09

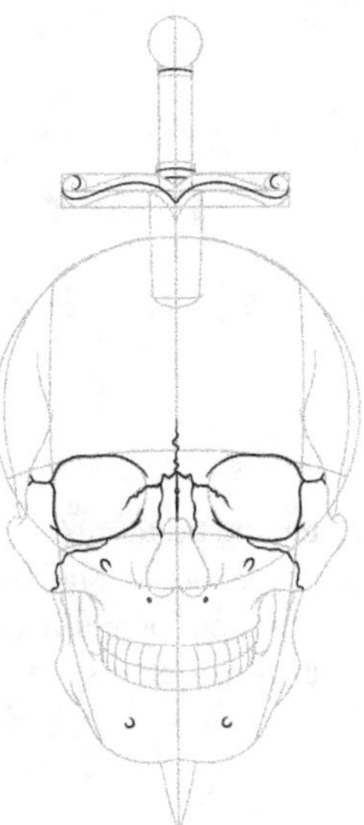

10

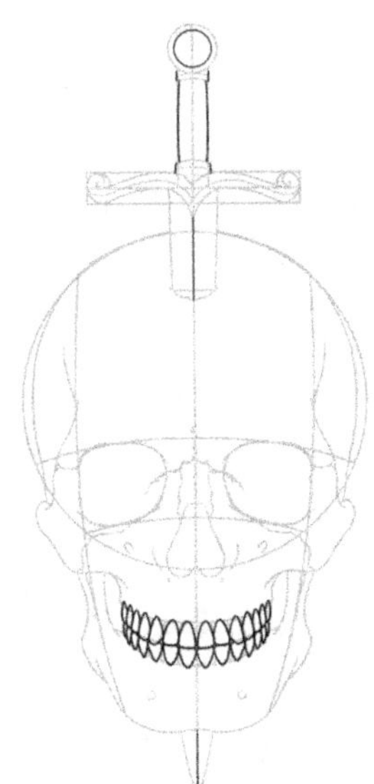

11

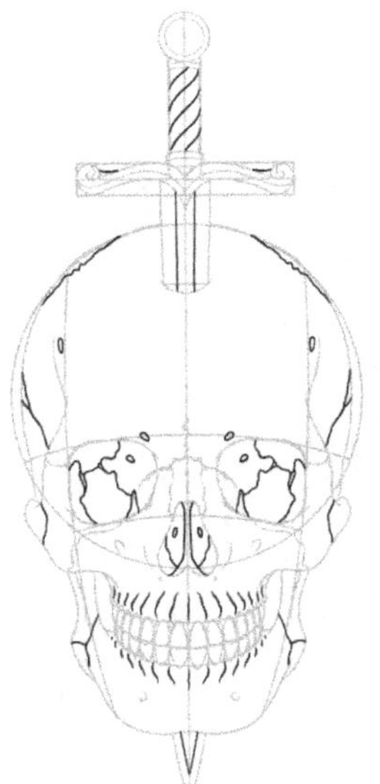

12

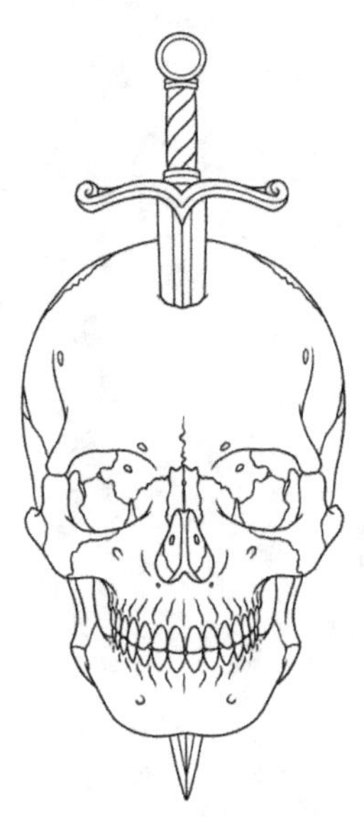

BUTTERFLY SKULL

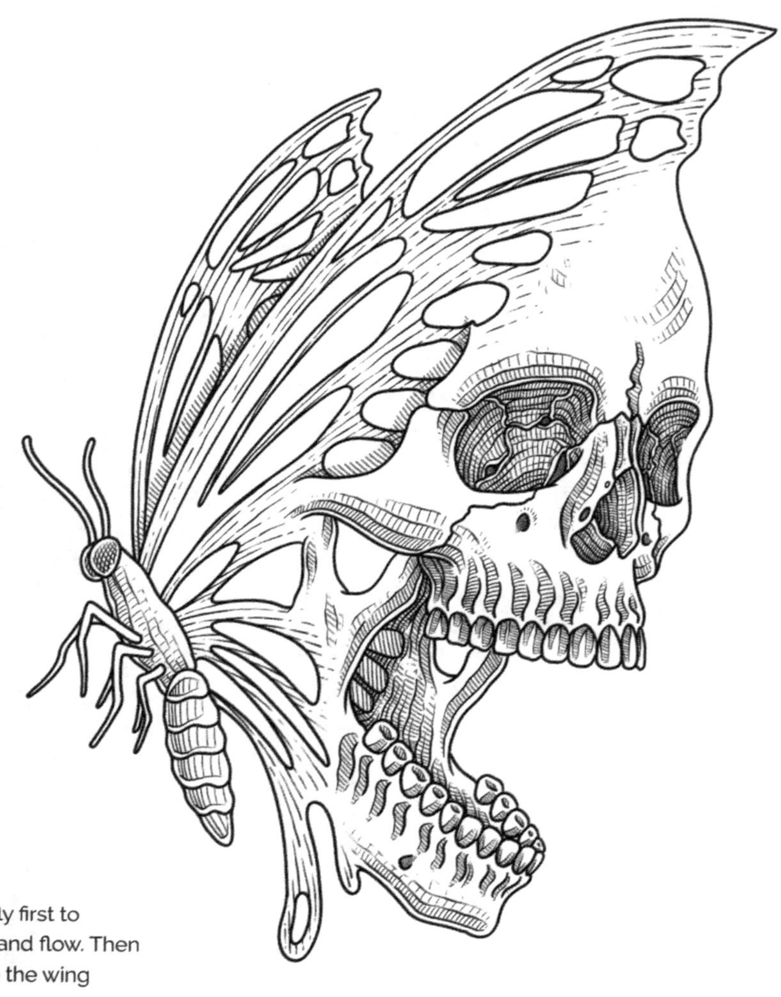

Pro Tip: Sketch the butterfly first to establish wing placement and flow. Then build the skull's profile into the wing shape, aligning key features.

01

02

03

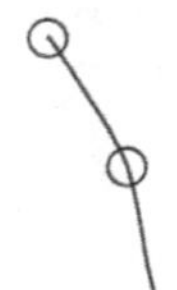

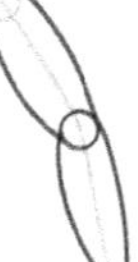

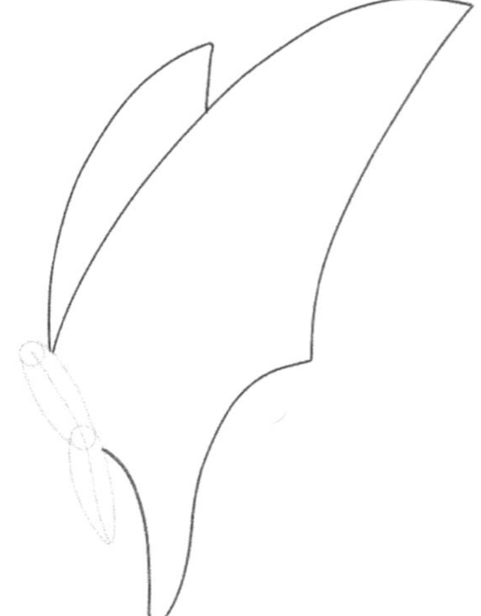

04

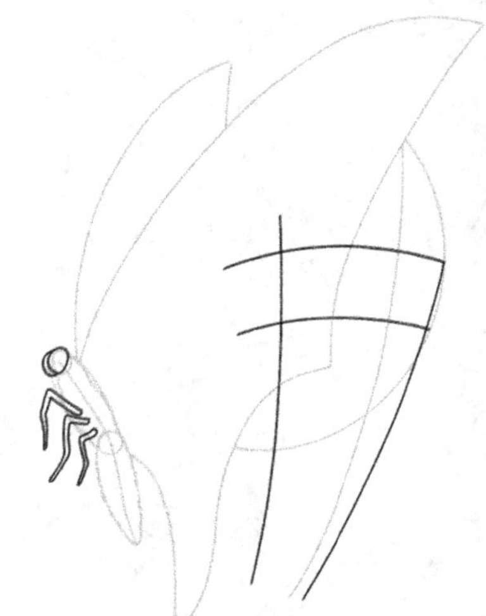

05

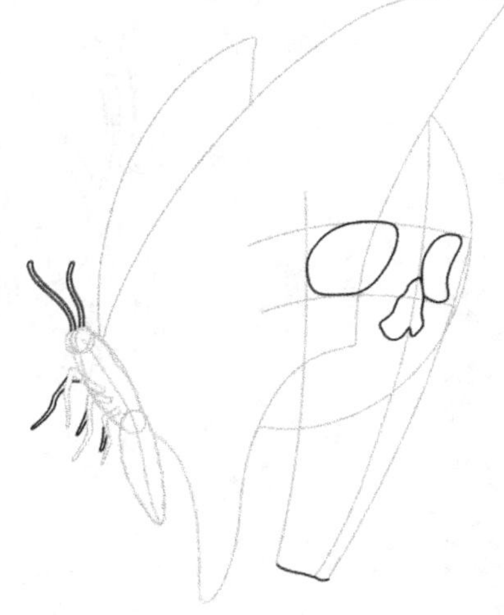

06

07

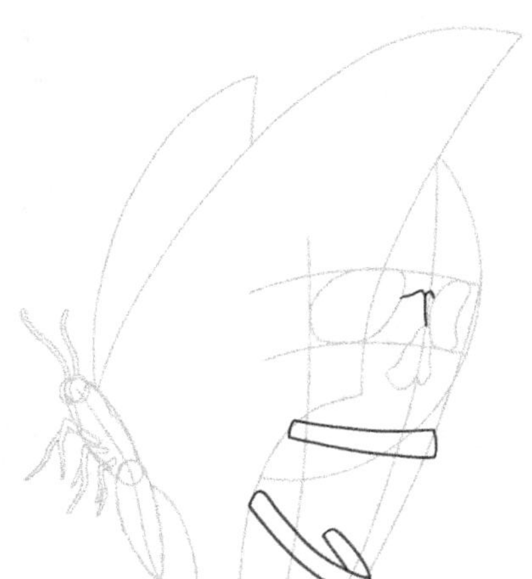

08

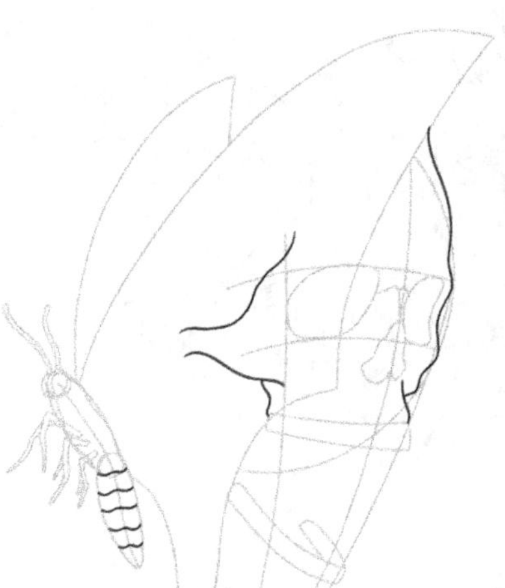

09

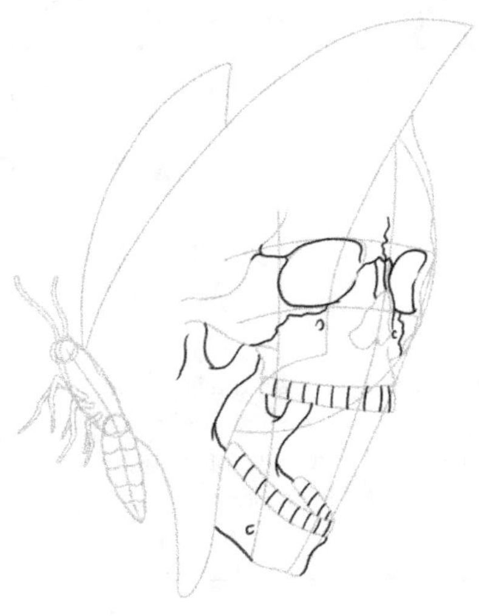

10

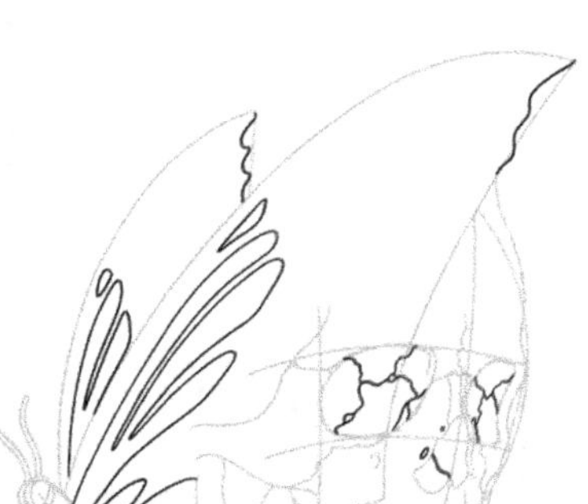

11

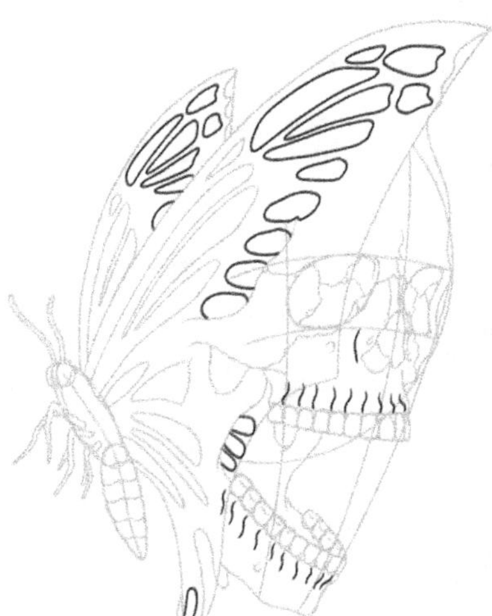

12

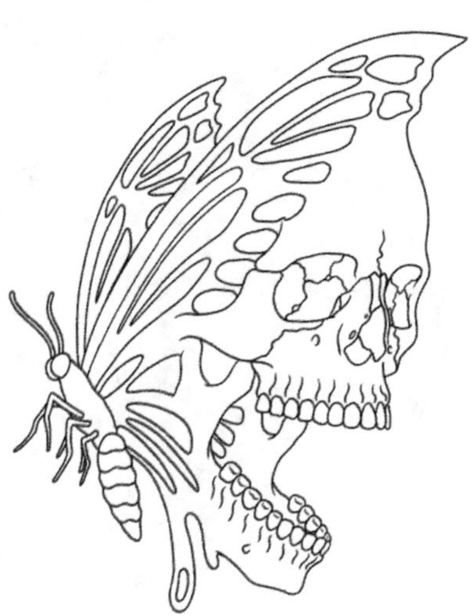

CROWNED SKULL

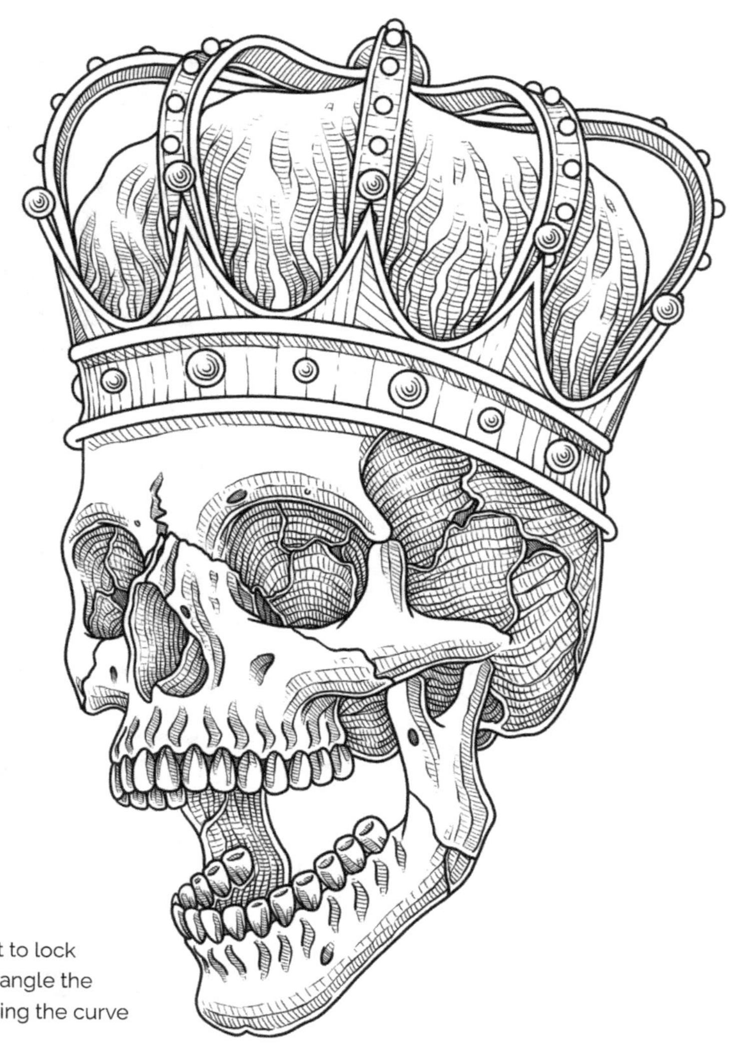

Pro Tip: Sketch the skull first to lock in proportions and tilt. Then angle the crown to sit naturally, following the curve of the brow and cranium.

01

02

03

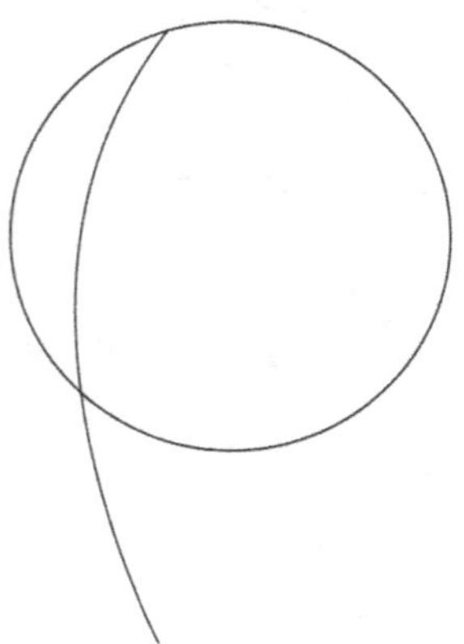

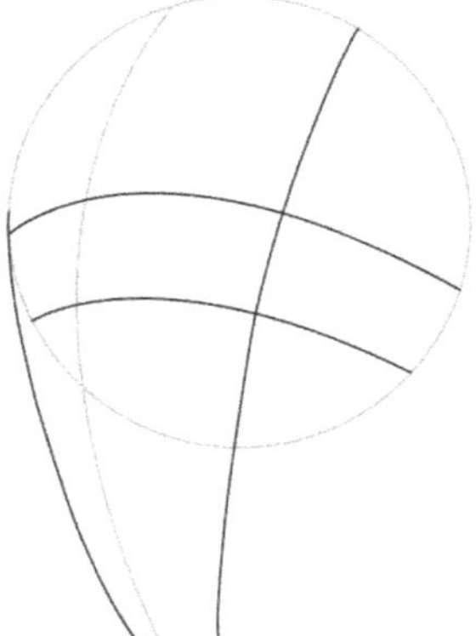

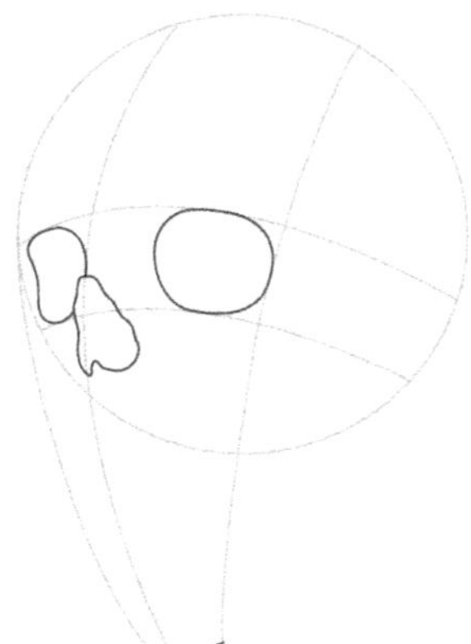

04

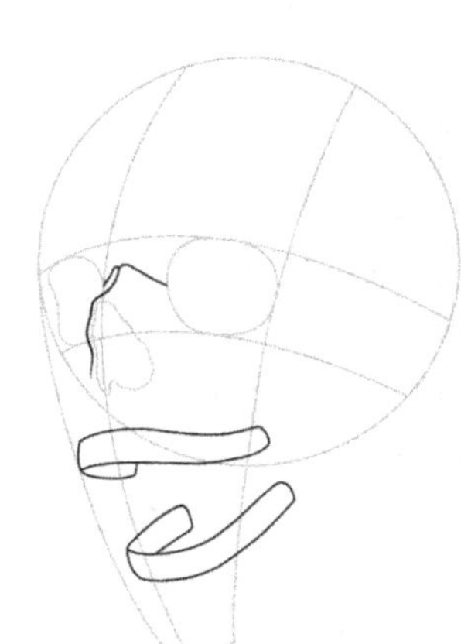

05

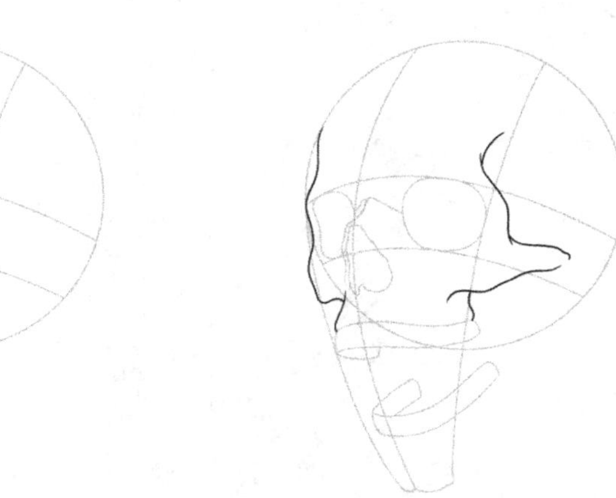

06

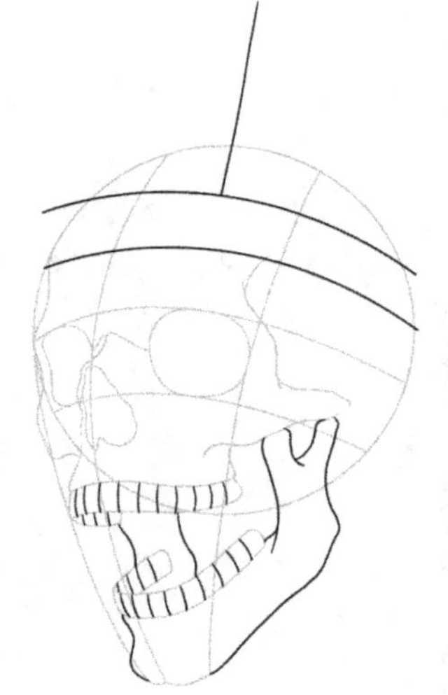

07

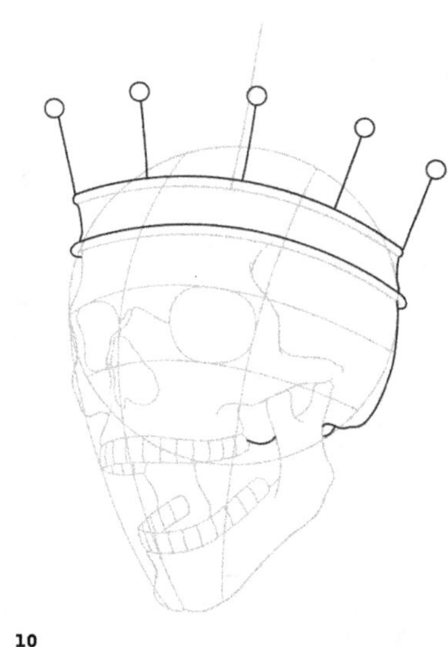

08

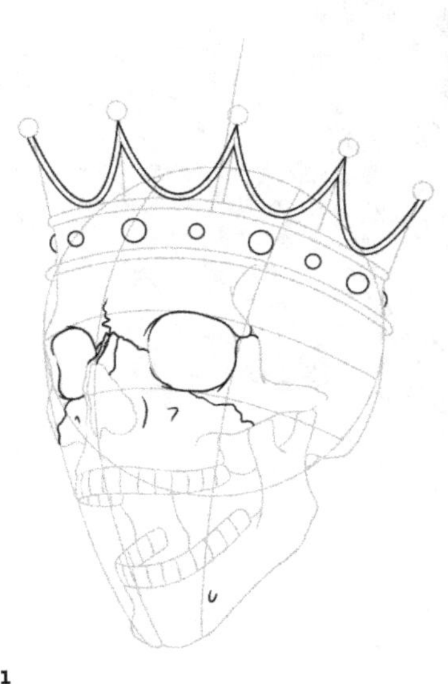

09

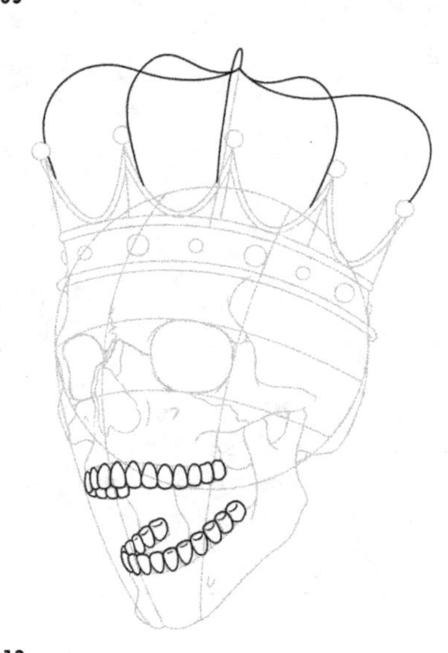

10

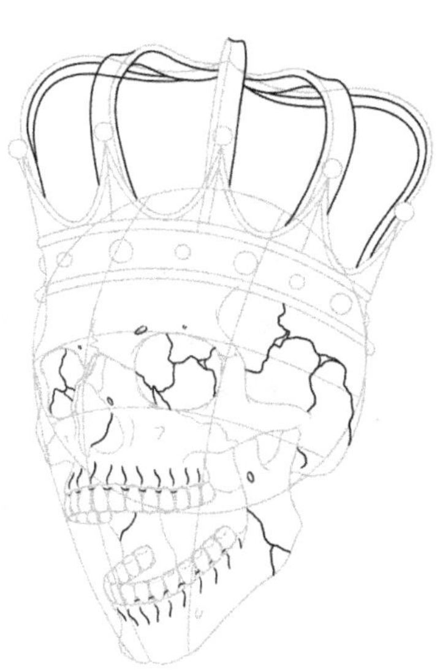

11

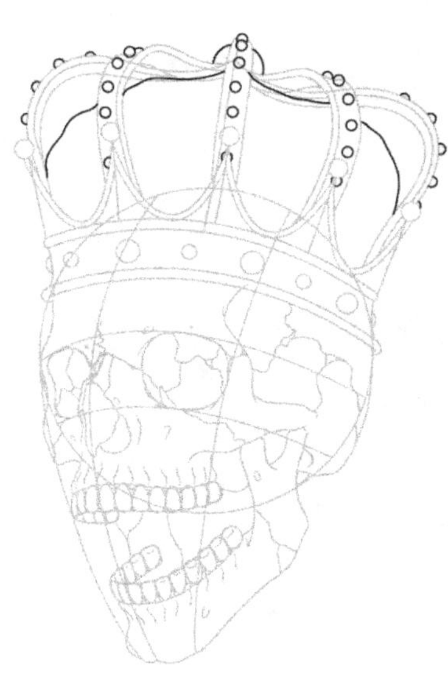

12

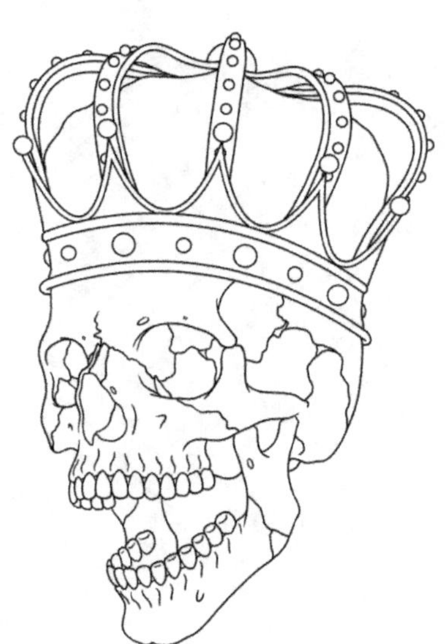

SKULL FLOWER

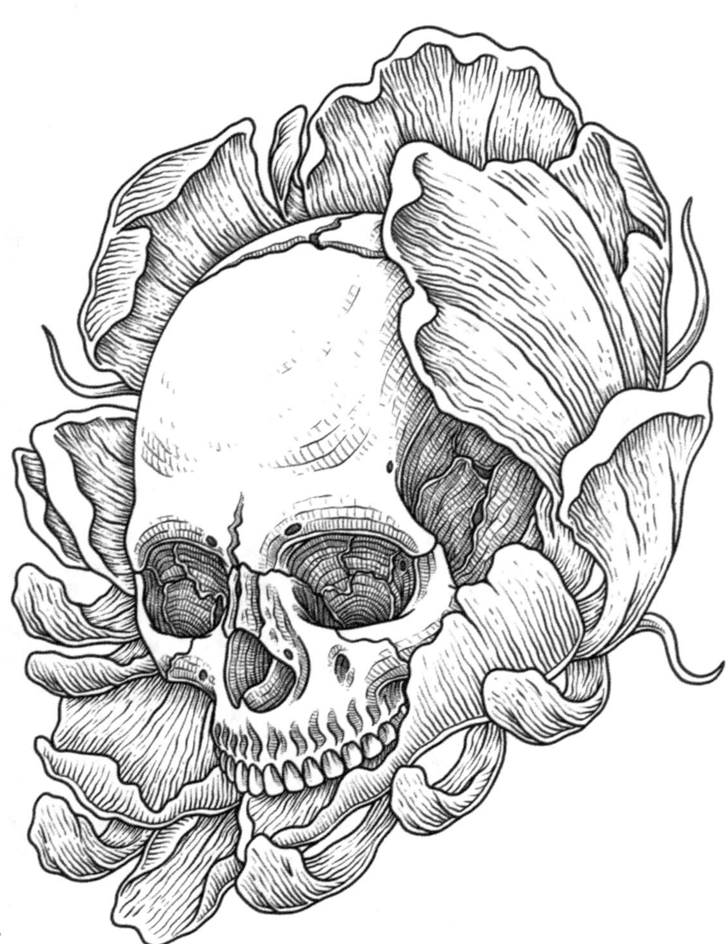

Pro Tip: Start with the skull's form. Then shape the petals to frame the cheekbones, jaw, and cranium for a balanced floral composition.

01

02

03

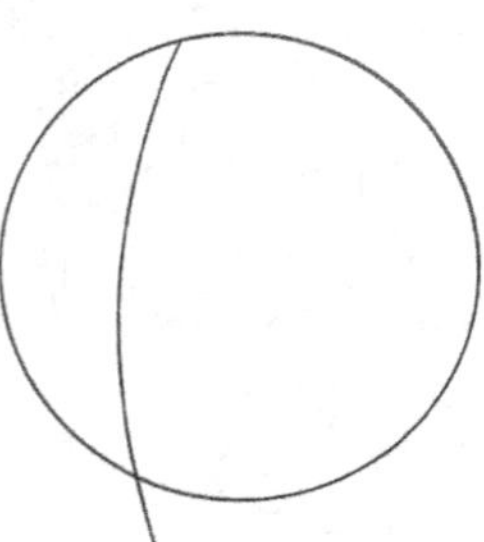

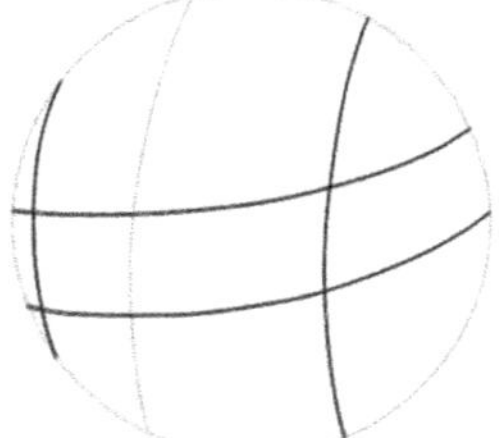

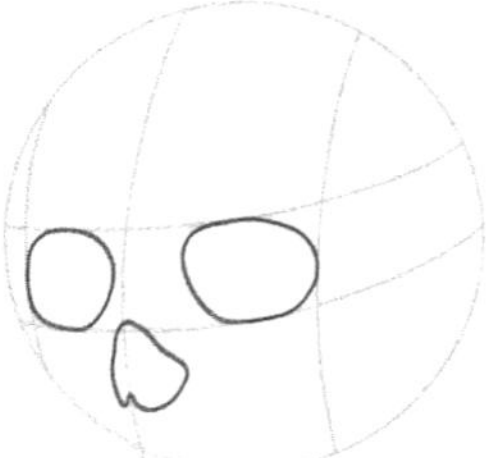

04

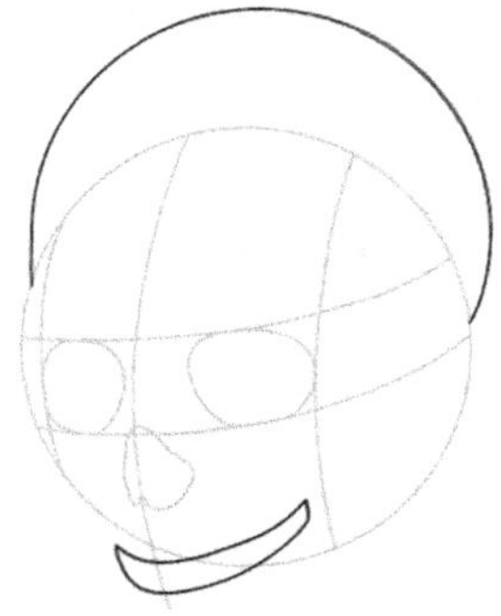

05

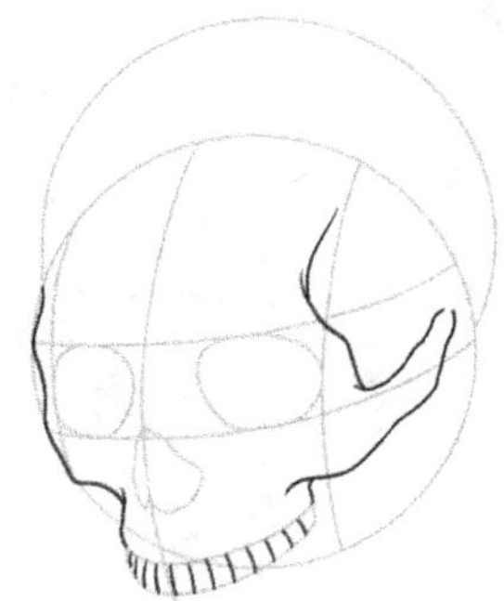

06

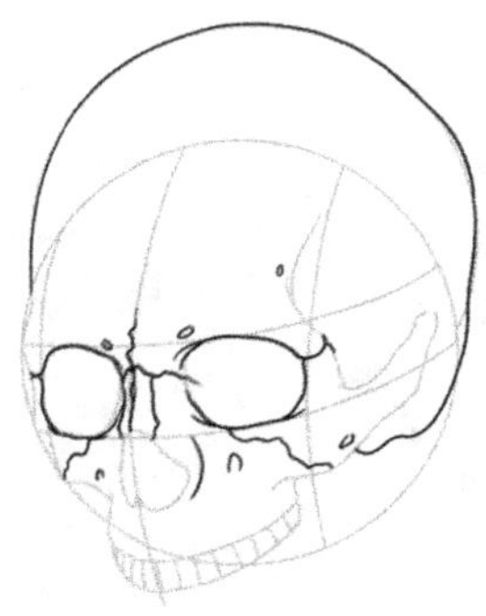

07

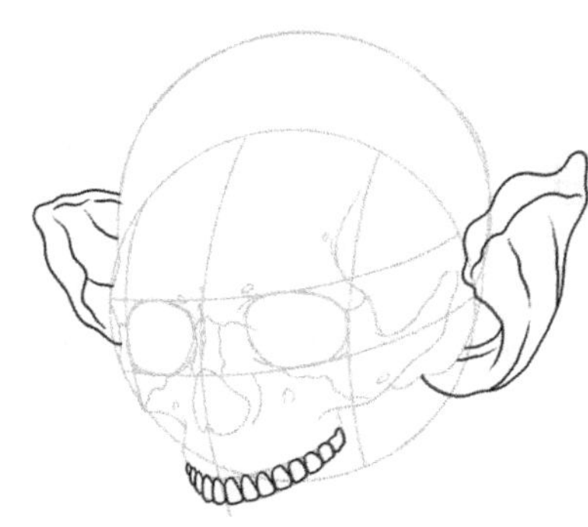

08

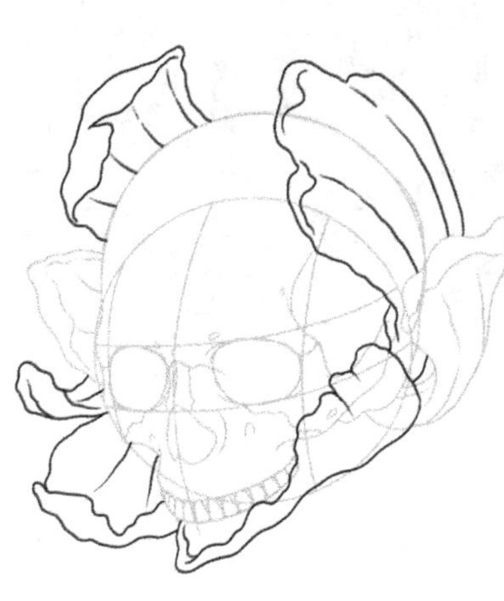

09

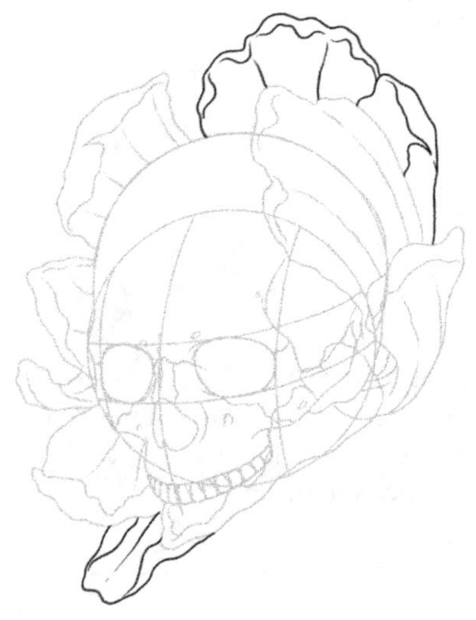

10

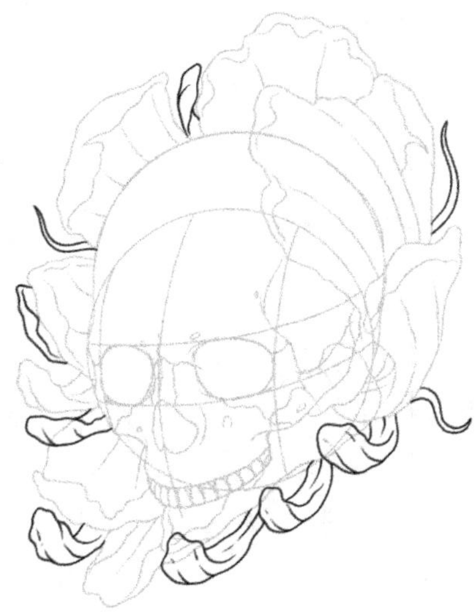

11

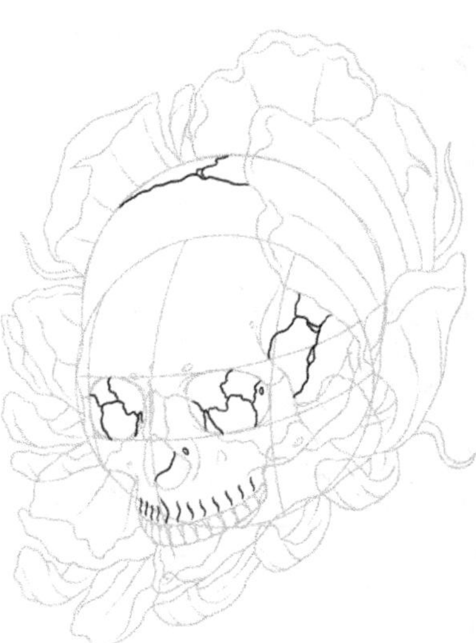

12

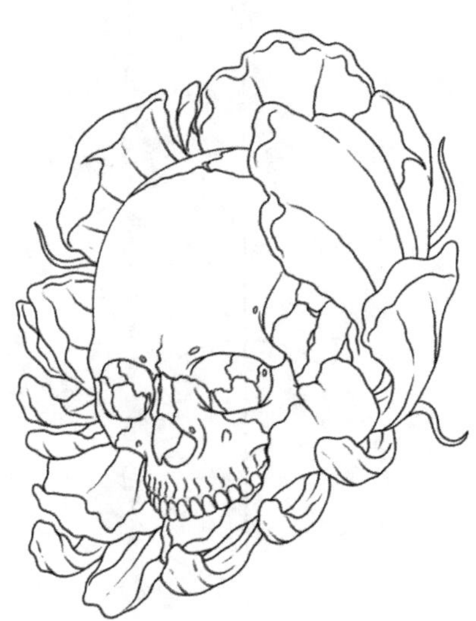

HOW TO DRAW SKULLS

MEMENTO MORI

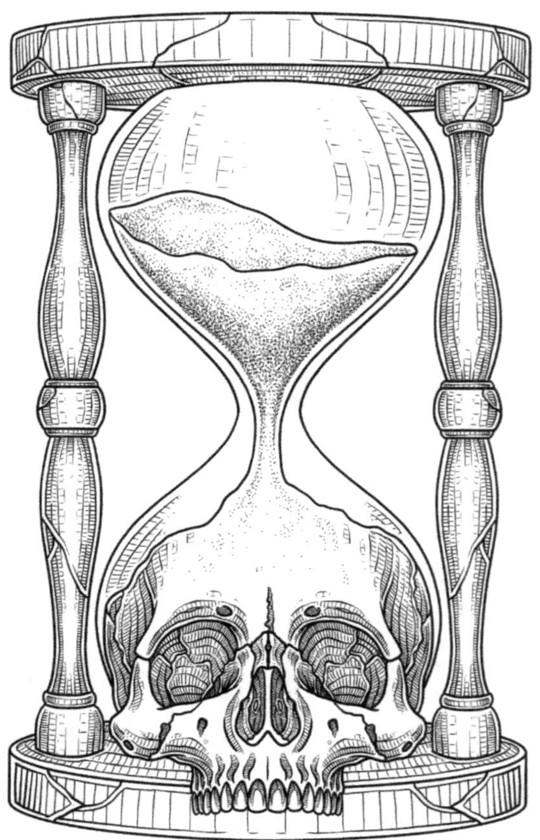

Pro Tip: Draw the hourglass frame first to lock in proportions. Then nest the skull at the base, aligning it with the curve of the glass and bottom rim.

01

02

03

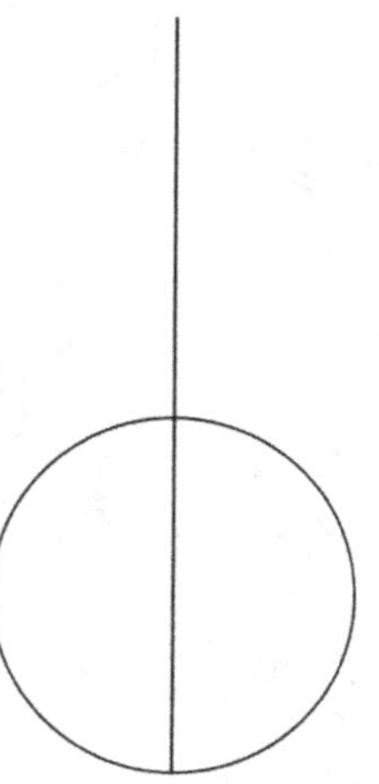

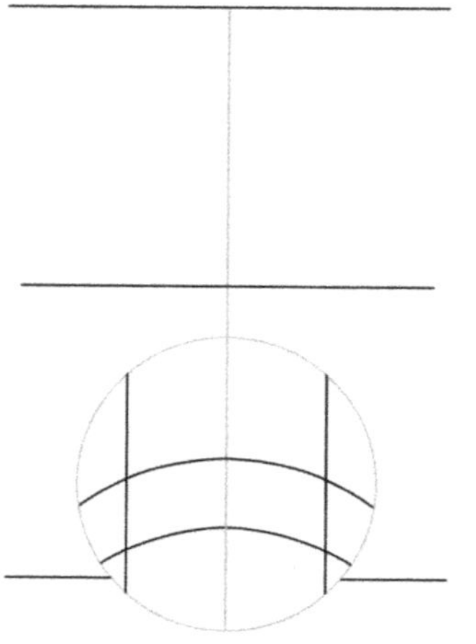

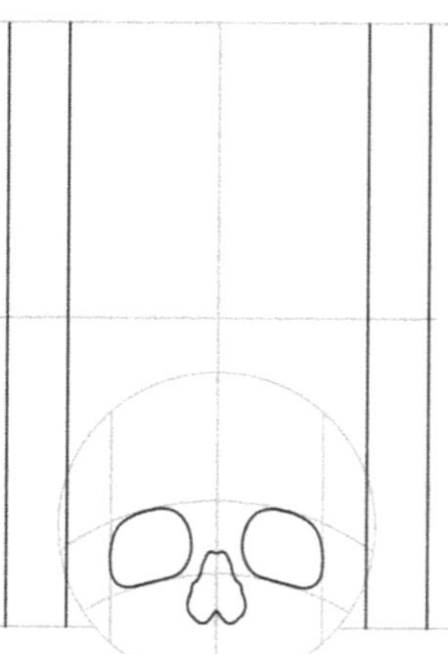

04

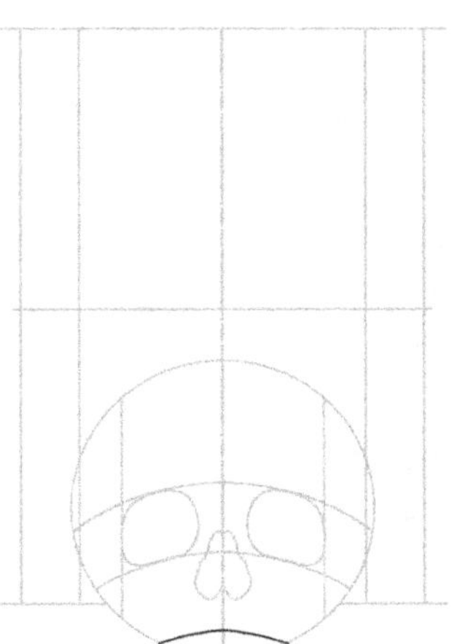

05

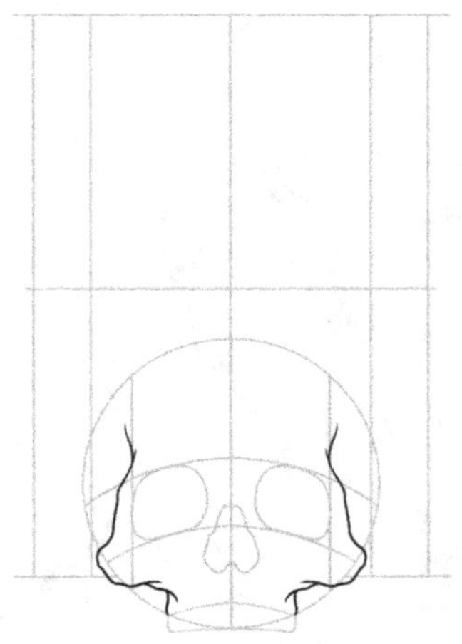

06

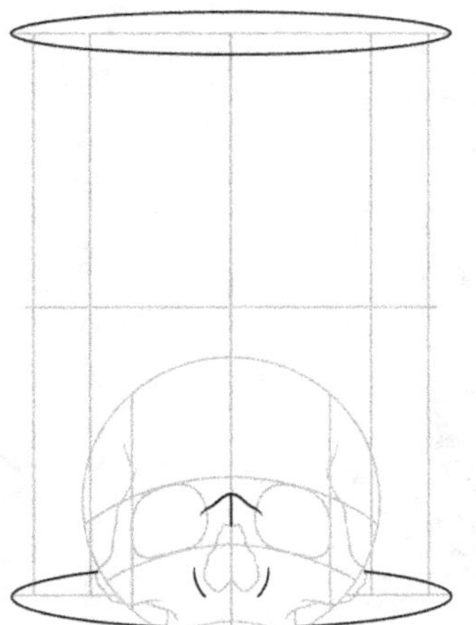

07

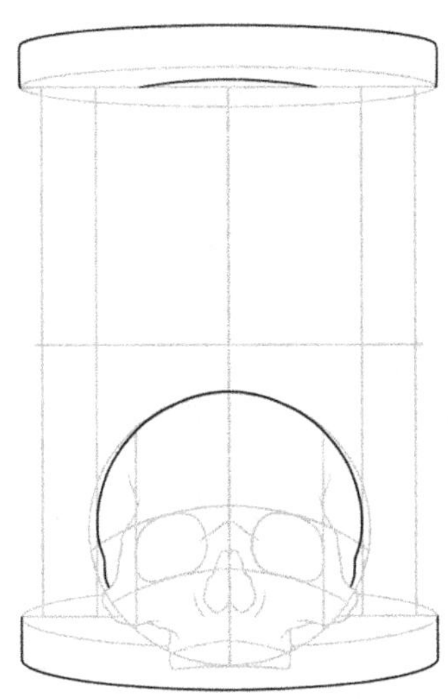

08

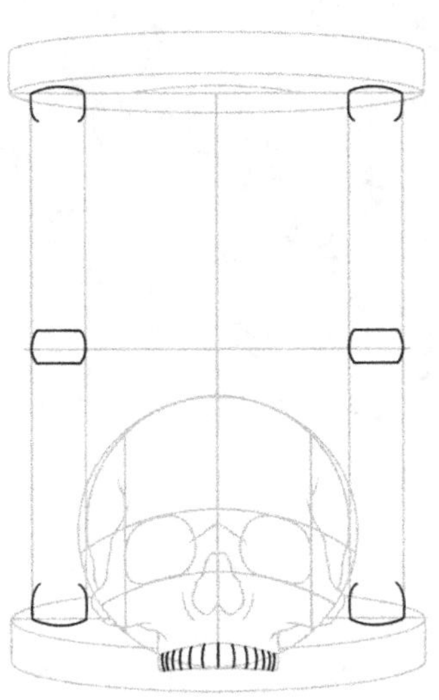

09

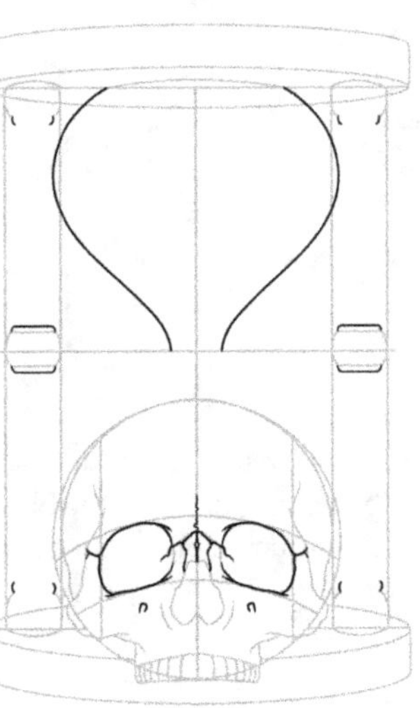

10

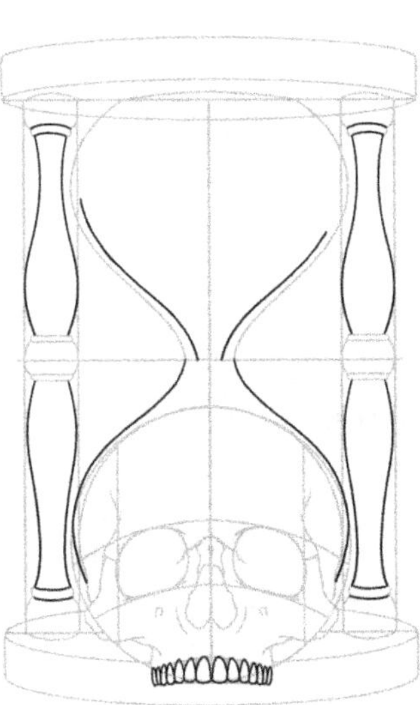

11

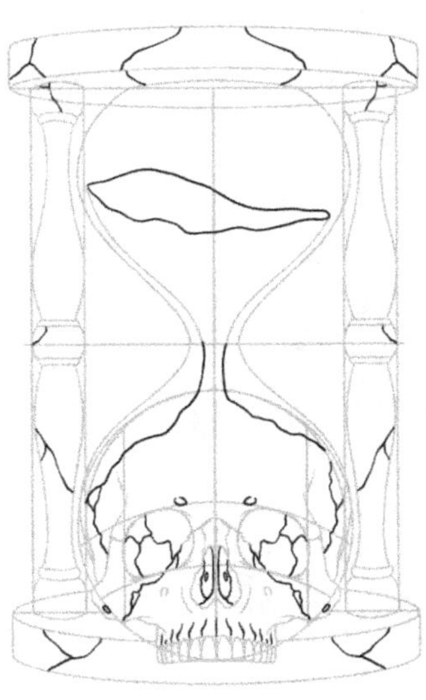

12

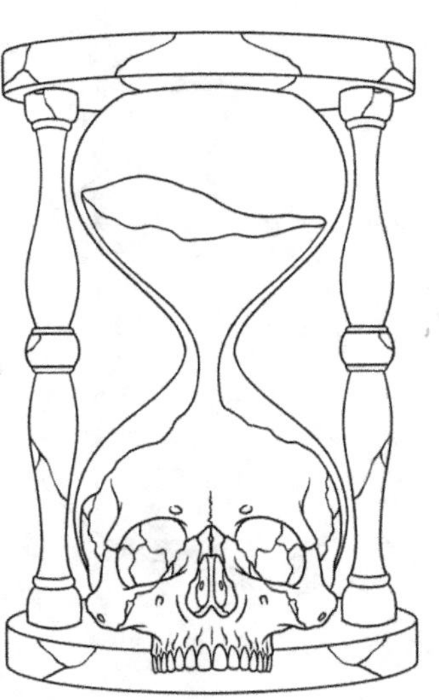

SKULL IN MEDIEVAL HELMET

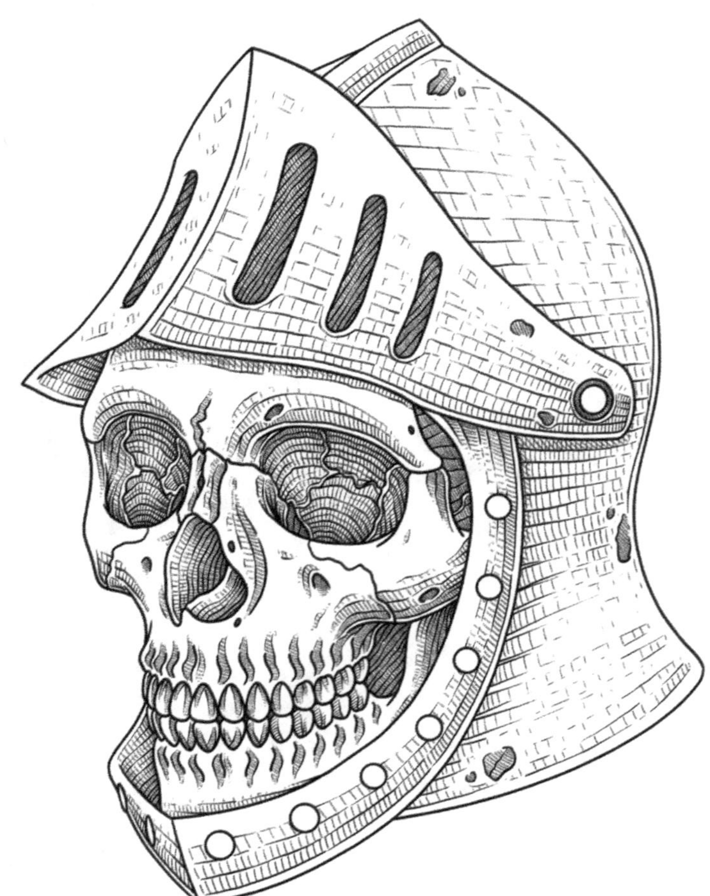

Pro Tip: Block in the skull first. Then shape the helmet to follow the brow ridge, jawline, and cranium for a natural, balanced fit.

01

02

03

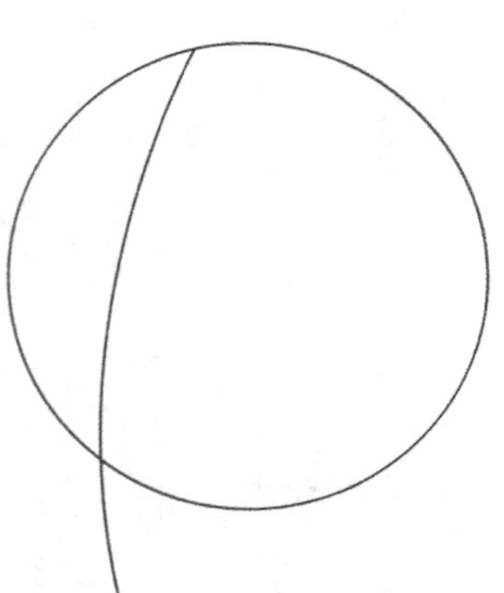

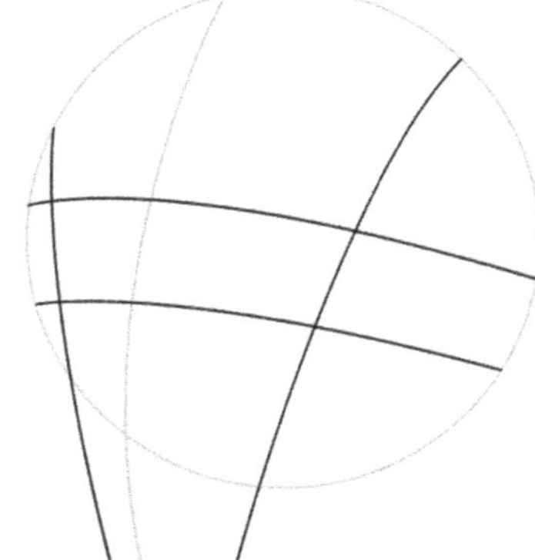

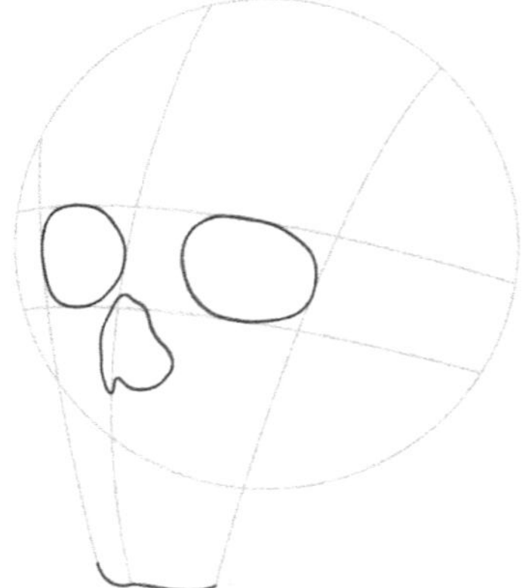

04

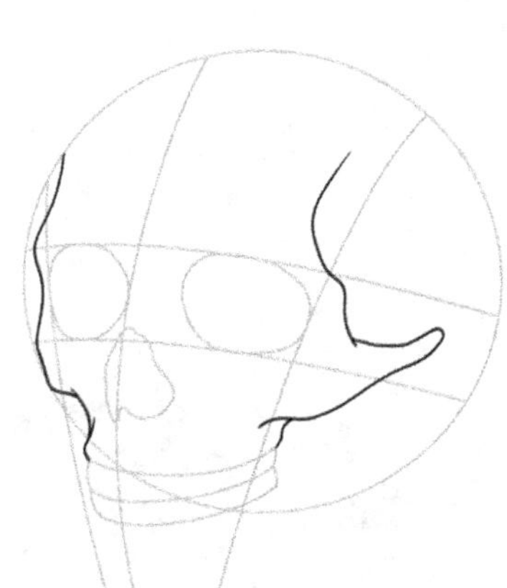

05

06

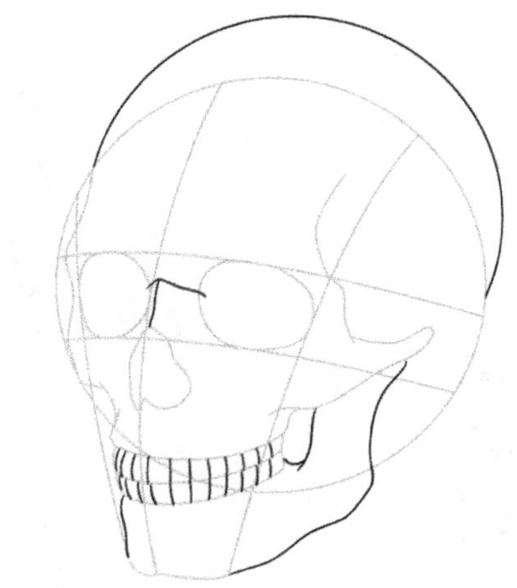

07

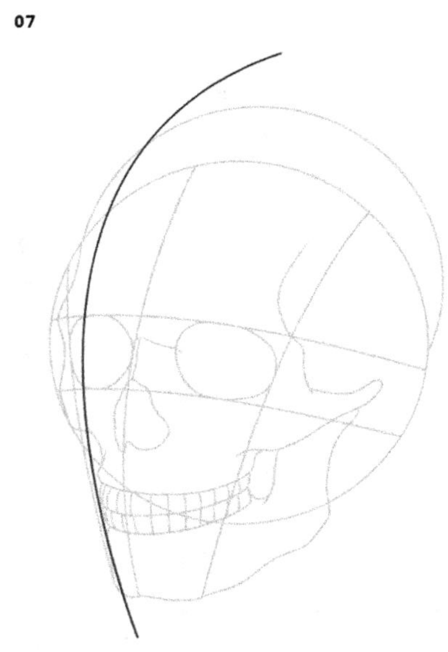

08

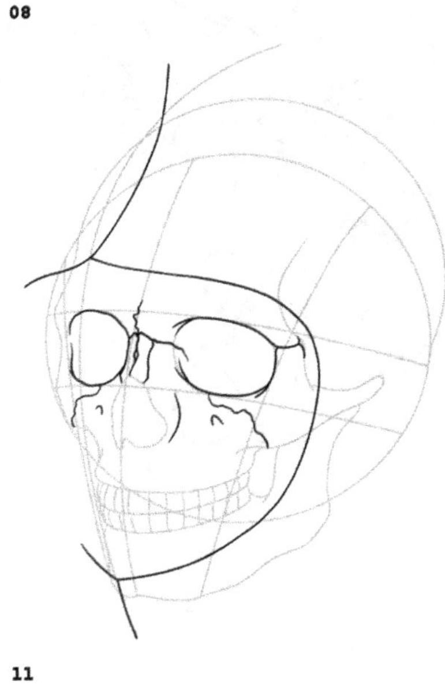

09

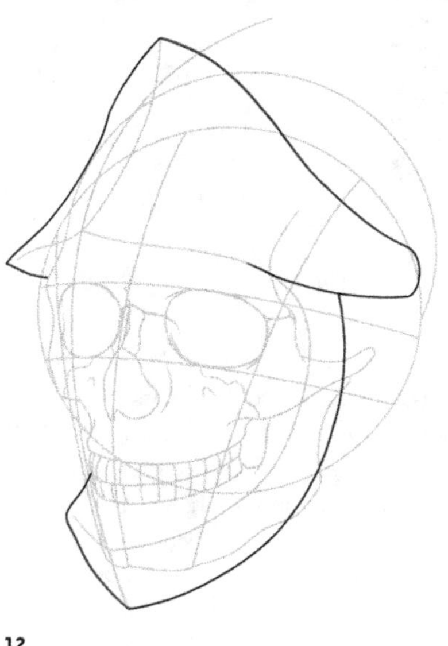

10

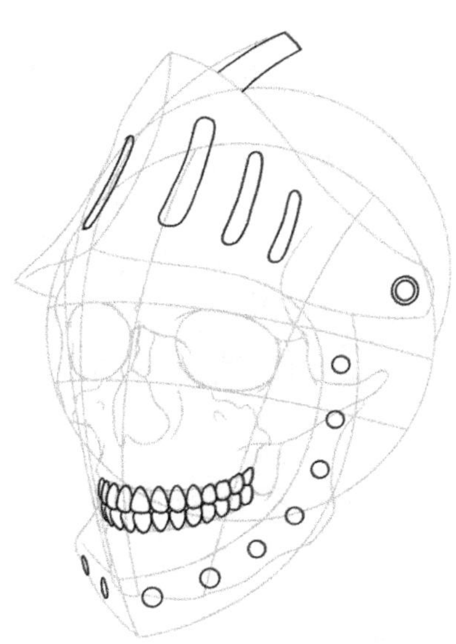

11

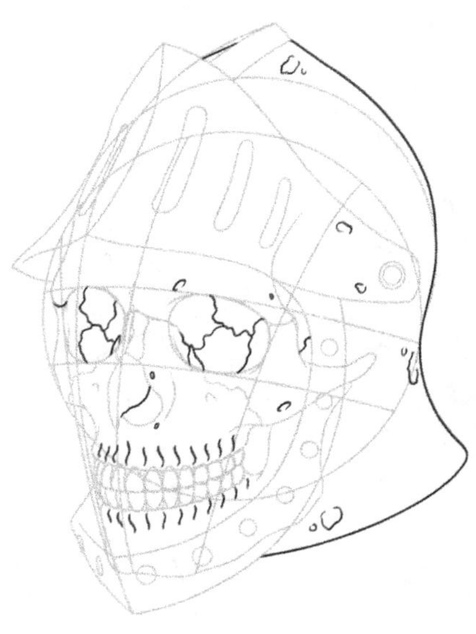

12

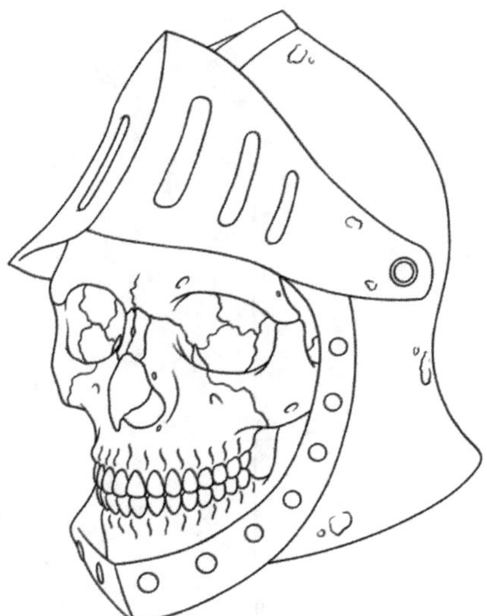

HOW TO DRAW SKULLS

DECAYING SKULL

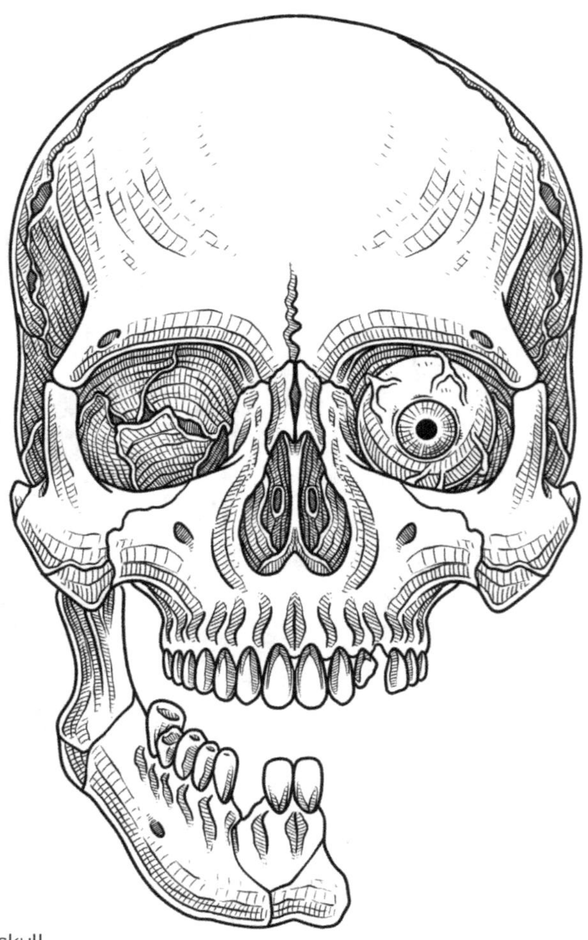

Pro Tip: Use construction lines that would allow you to draw a complete skull first. Then erase sections to create the broken jaw, missing teeth, and decay.

01

02

03

04

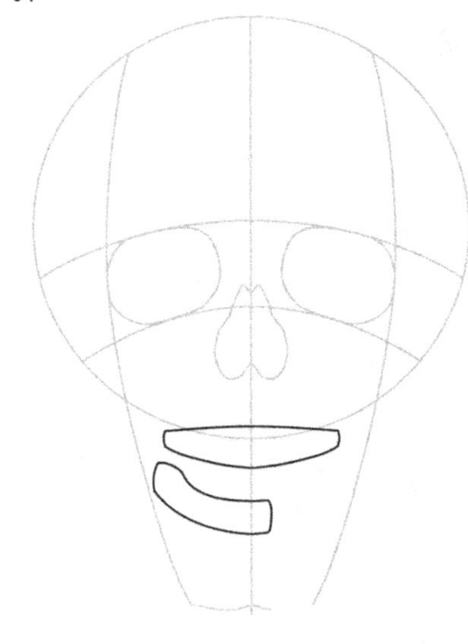

05

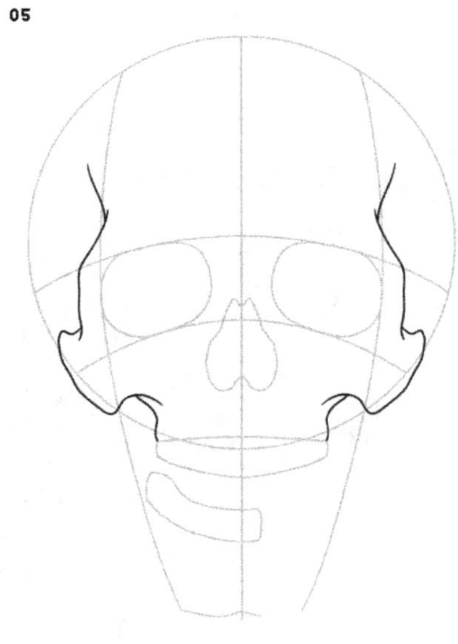

06

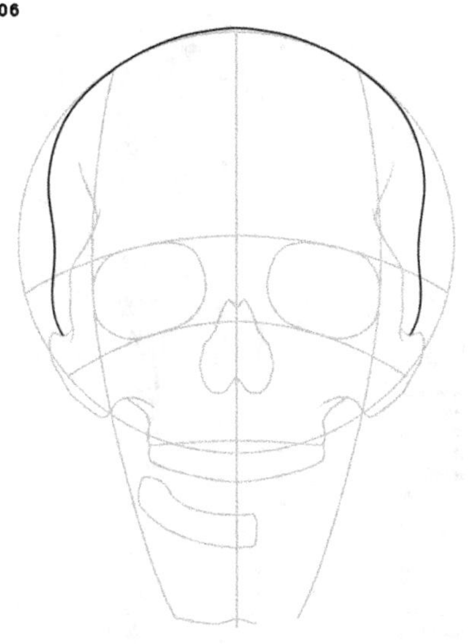

07

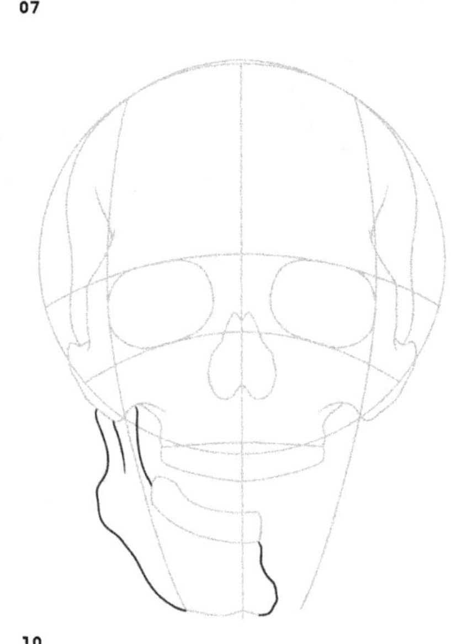

08

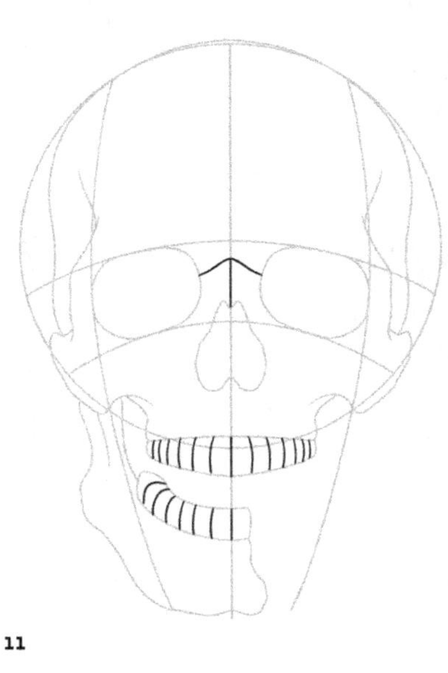

09

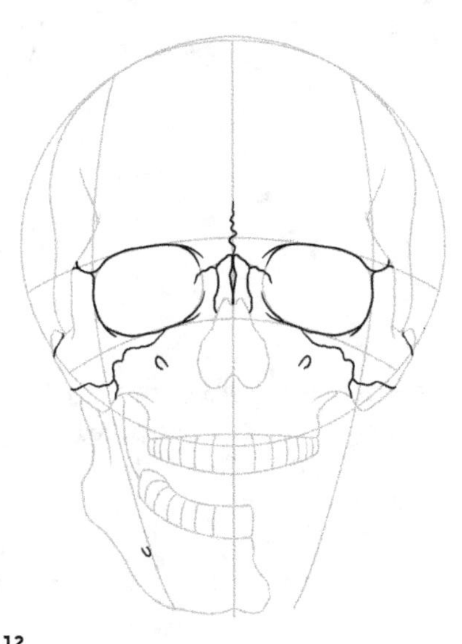

10

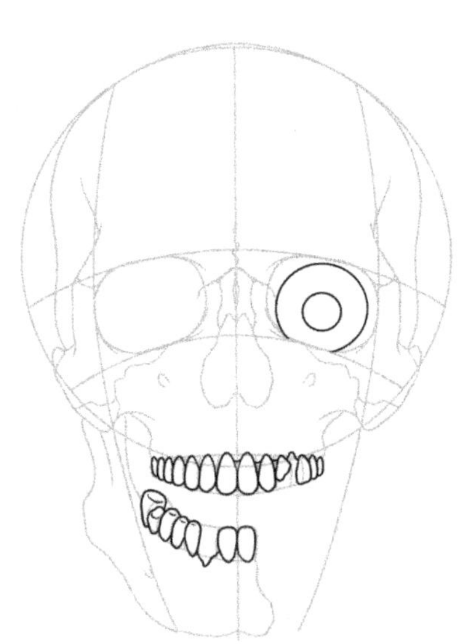

11

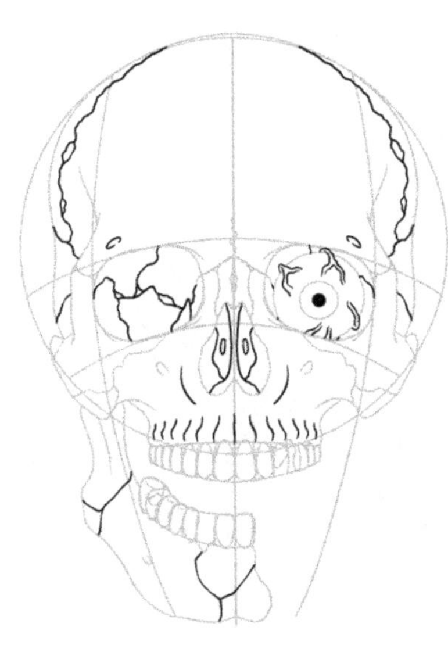

12

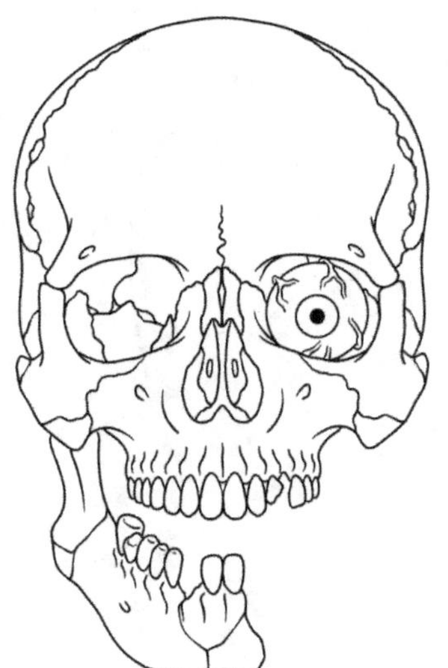

SKULL SPIDER

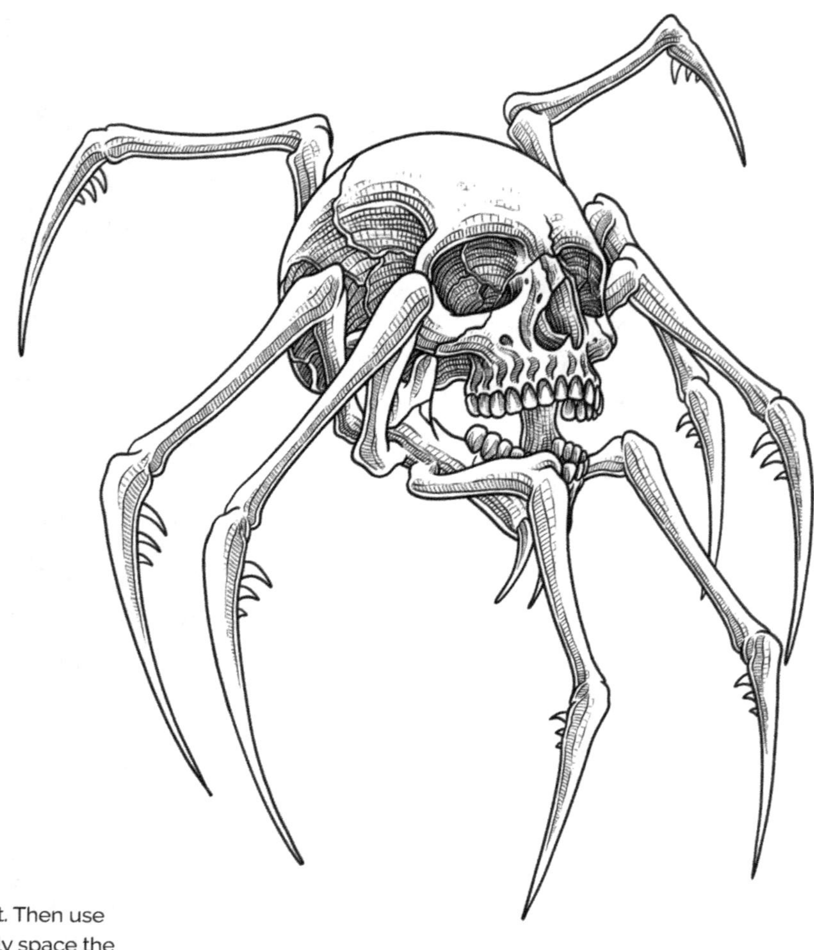

Pro Tip: Draw the skull first. Then use construction lines to evenly space the legs, adjusting their angle for balance, movement, and flow.

01

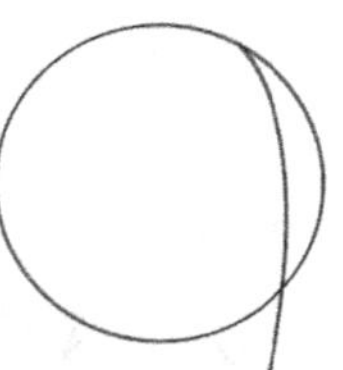

02

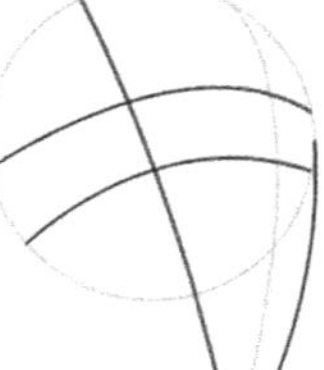

03

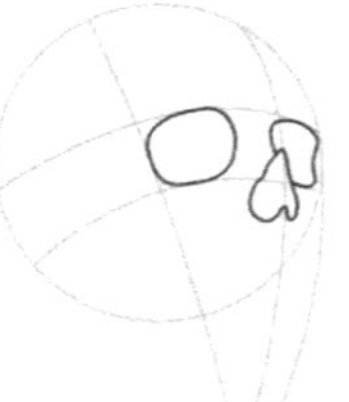

04

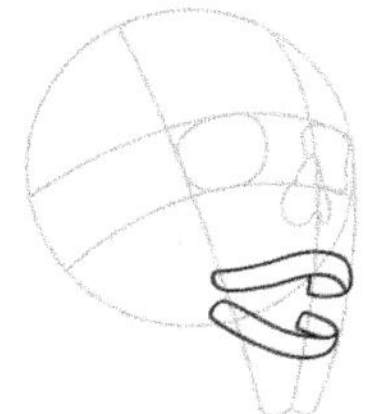

05

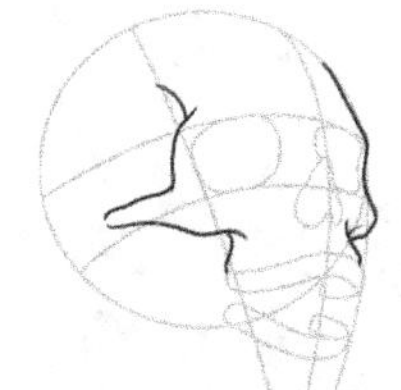

06

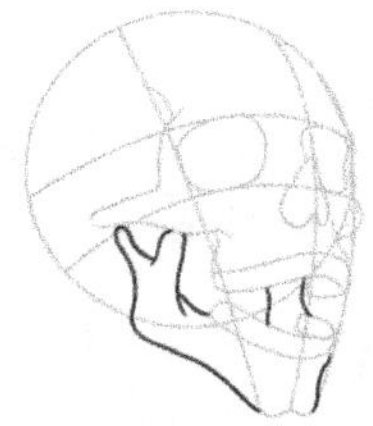

07

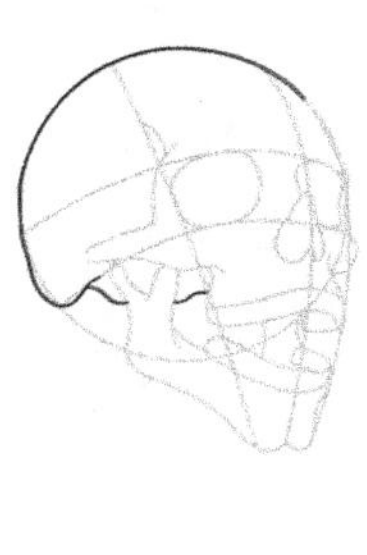

08

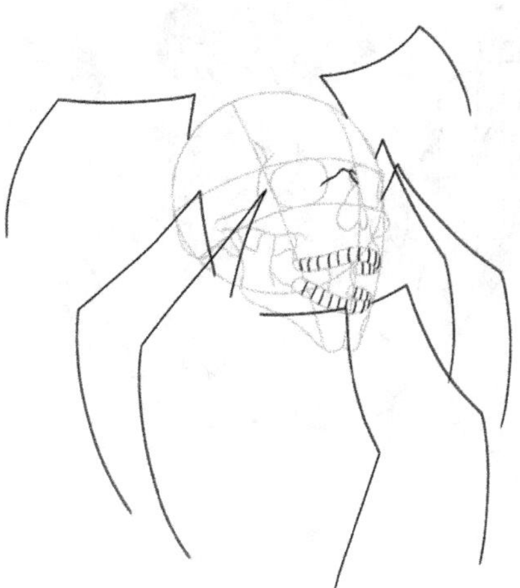

09

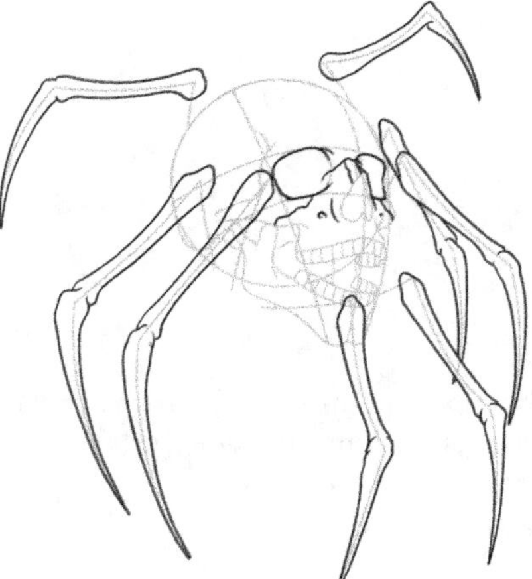

HOW TO DRAW SKULLS

10

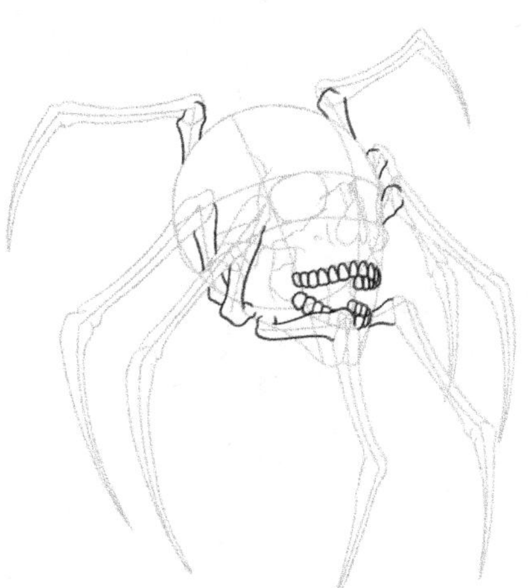

11

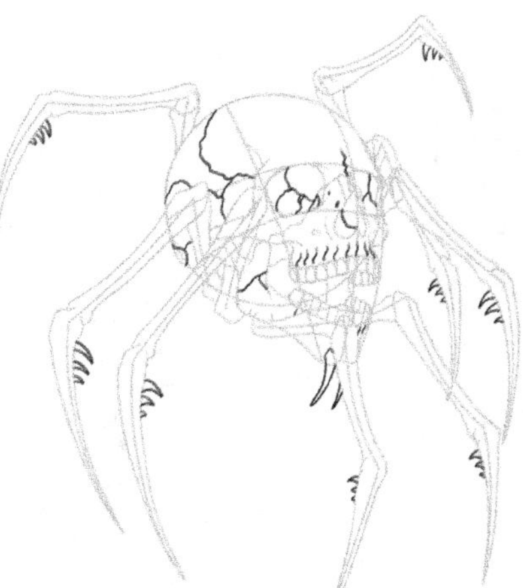

12

SUGAR SKULL

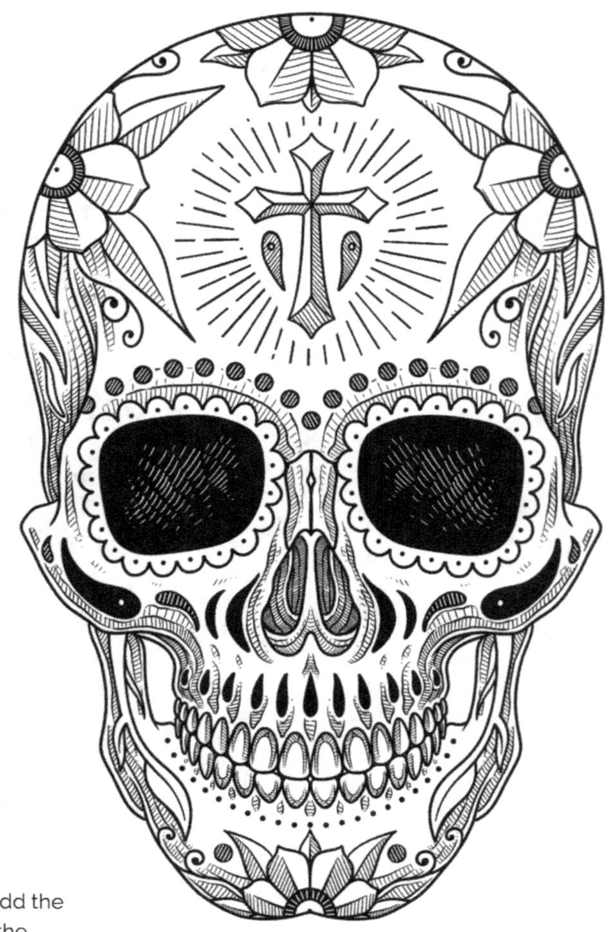

Pro Tip: Draw the skull first. Then add the decorative elements starting with the cross and flowers.

01

02

03

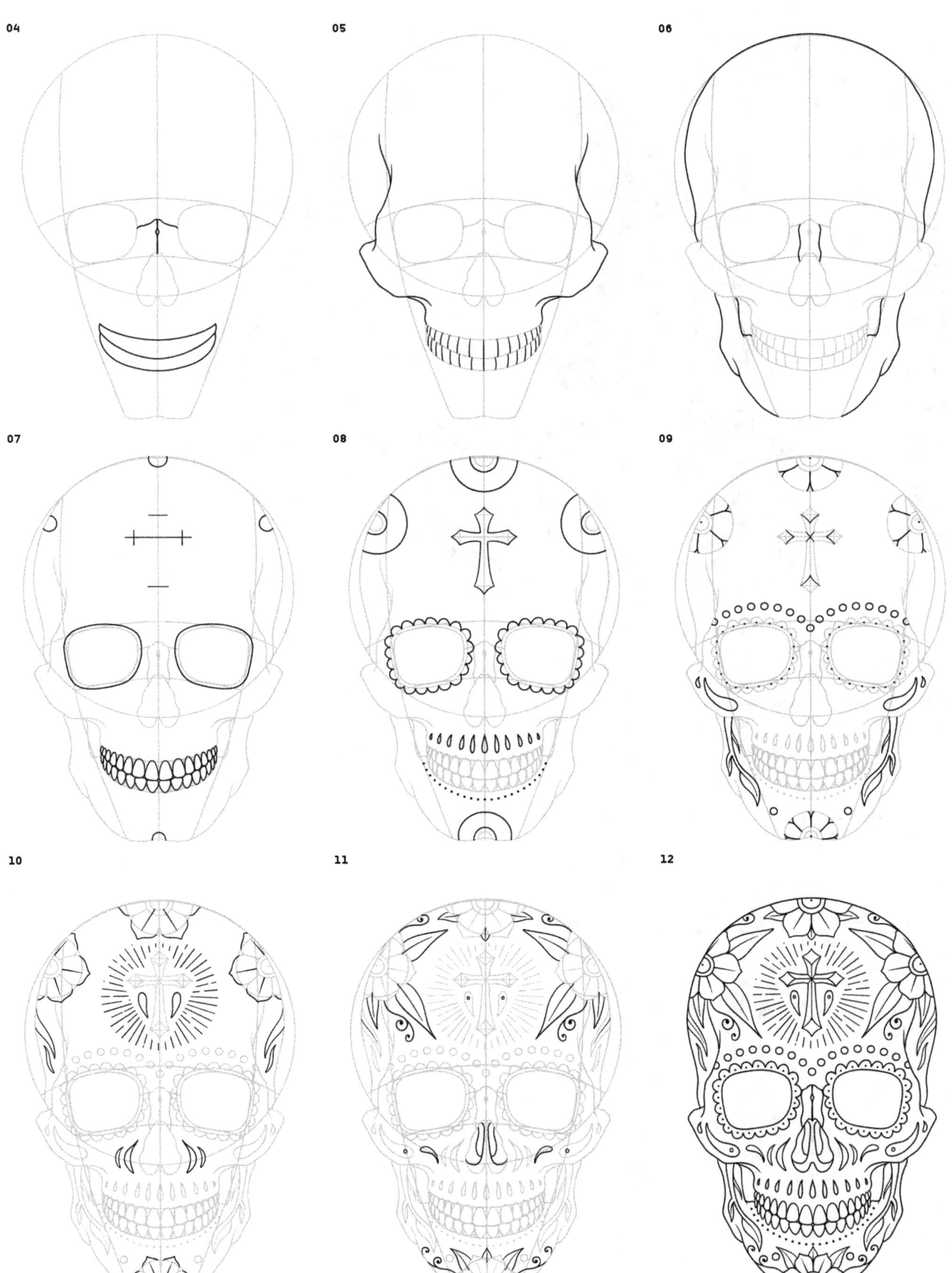

04
05
06
07
08
09
10
11
12
HOW TO DRAW SKULLS

SKULL & BAT WINGS

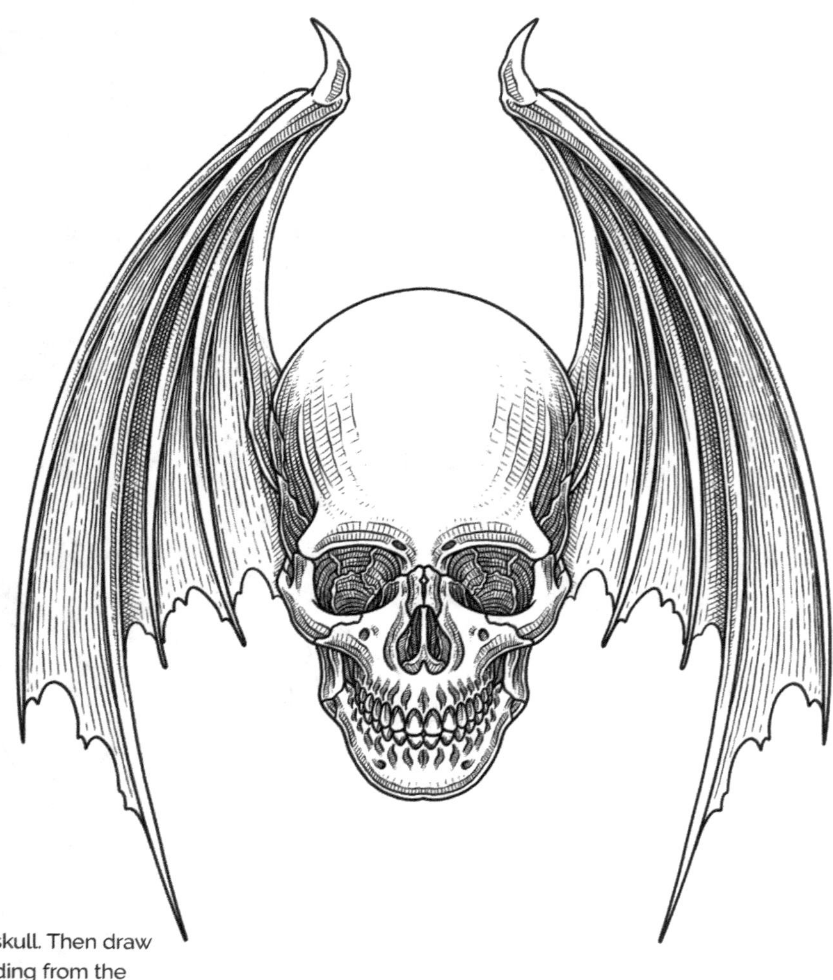

Pro Tip: Start with the skull. Then draw the wing frames extending from the cheekbones, curving outward to create height, balance, and flow.

01

02

03

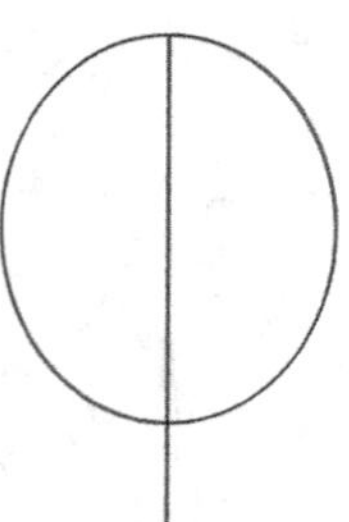

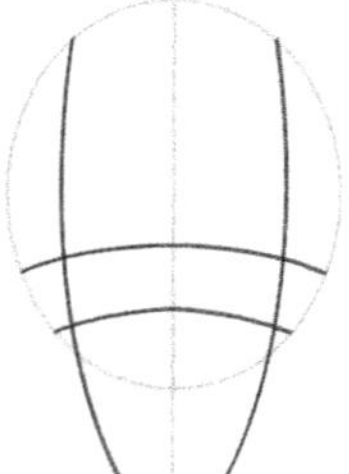

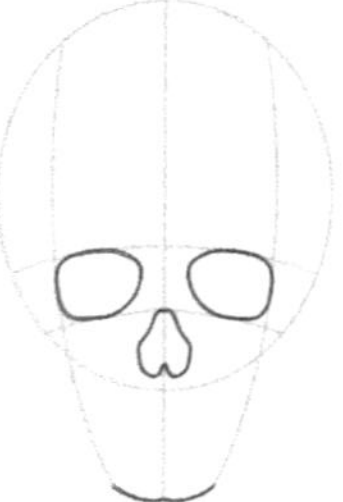

04

05

06

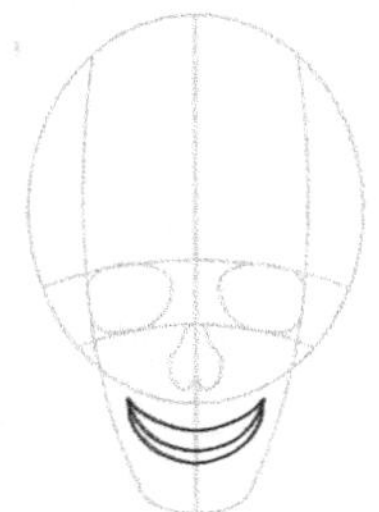

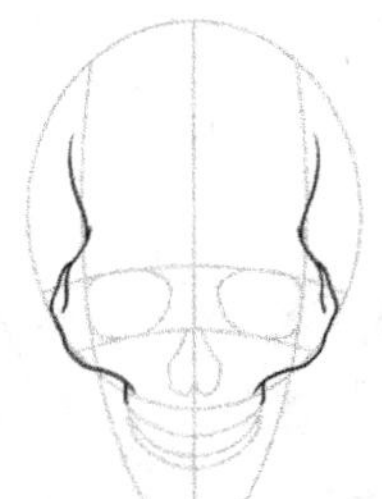

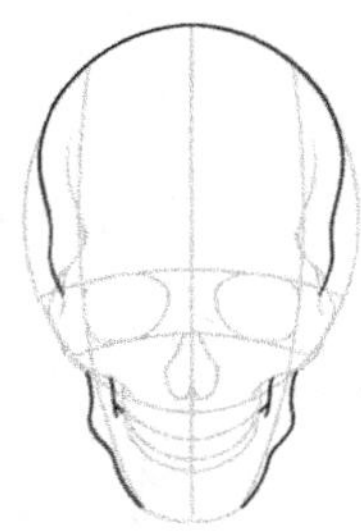

07

08

09

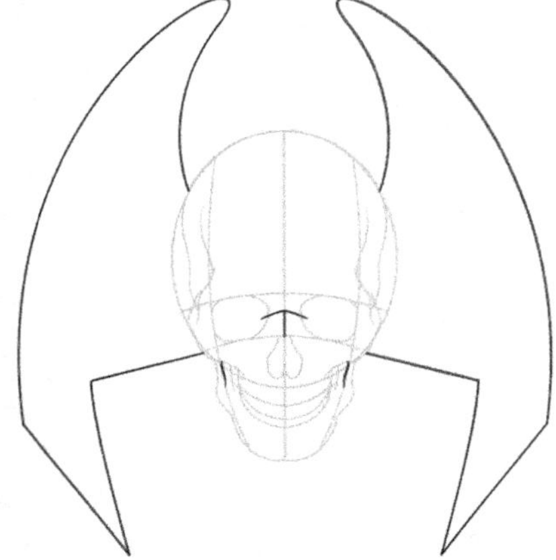

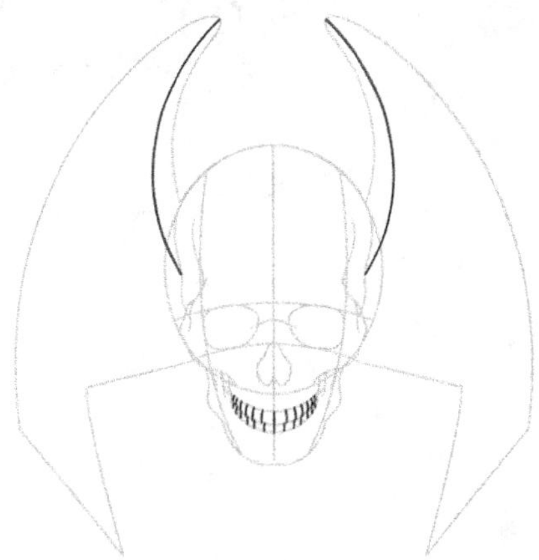

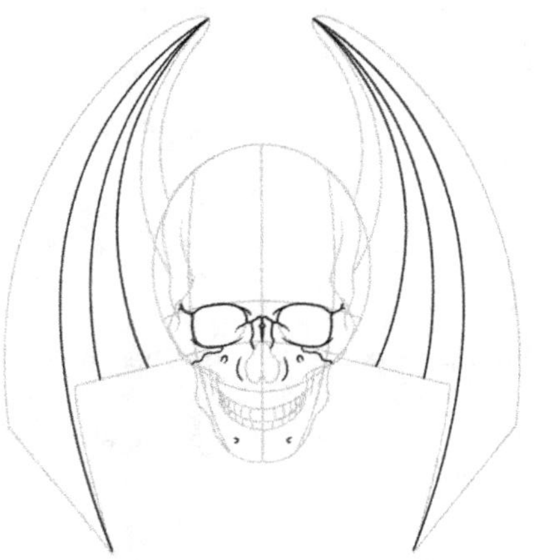

10

11

12

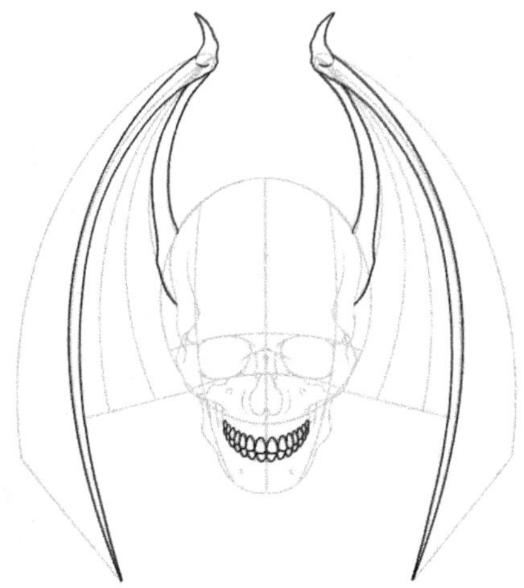

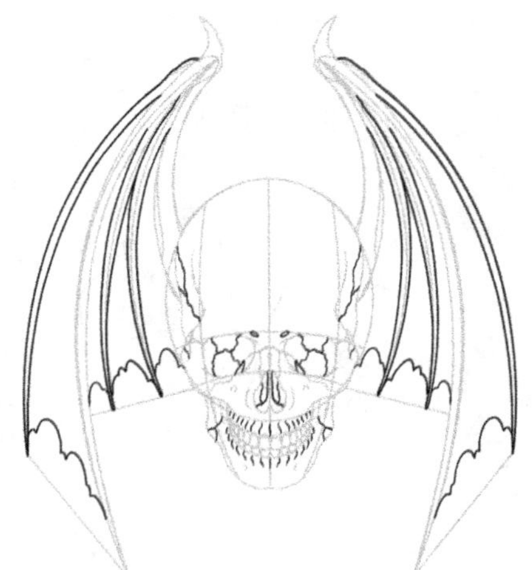

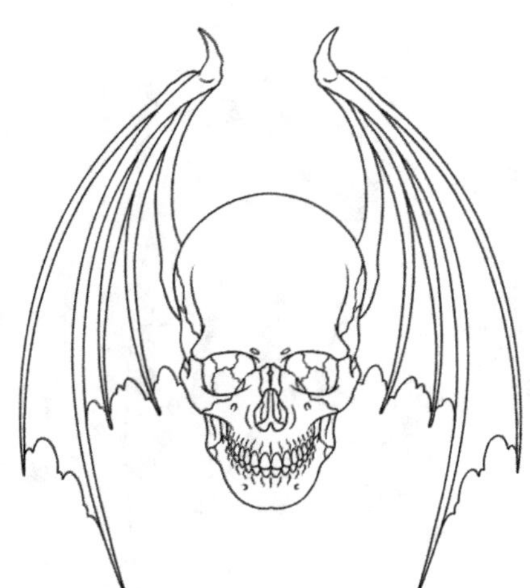

HOW TO DRAW SKULLS

SKULL & ARROWS

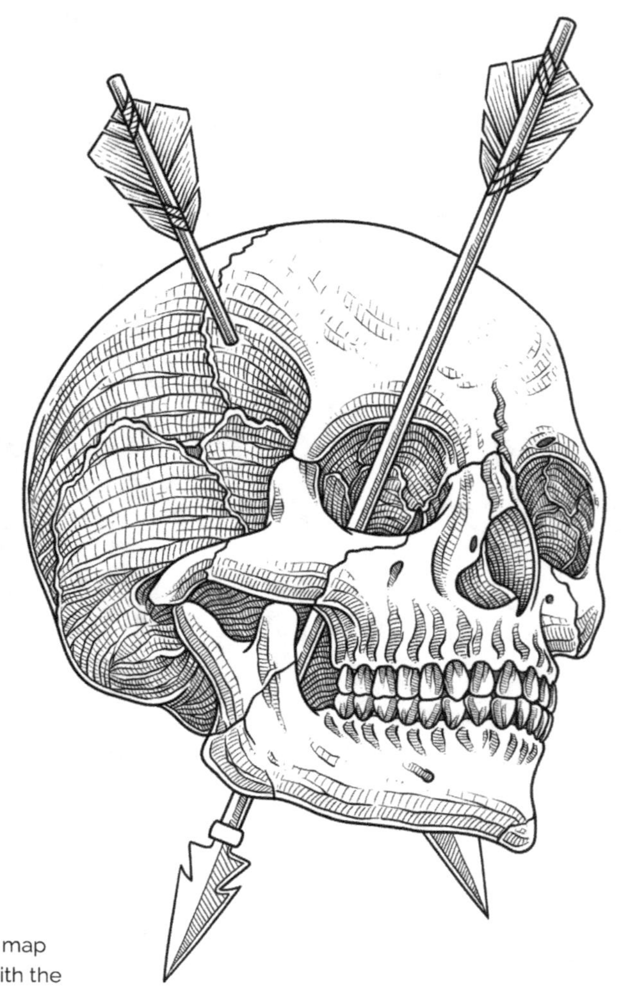

Pro Tip: Draw the skull first. Then map the arrows, aligning their angle with the curves of the cranium for a natural and dynamic flow.

01

02

03

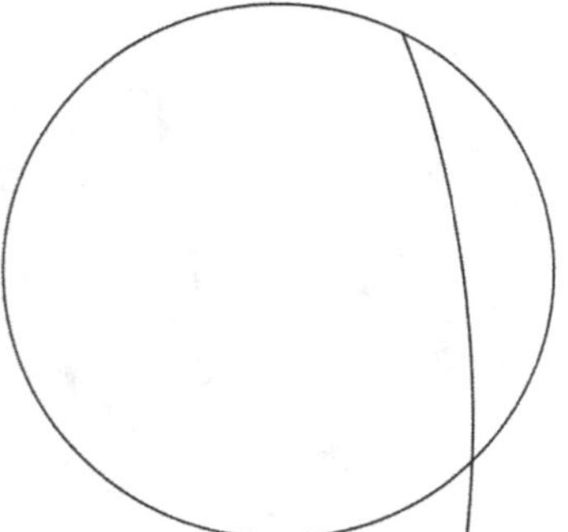

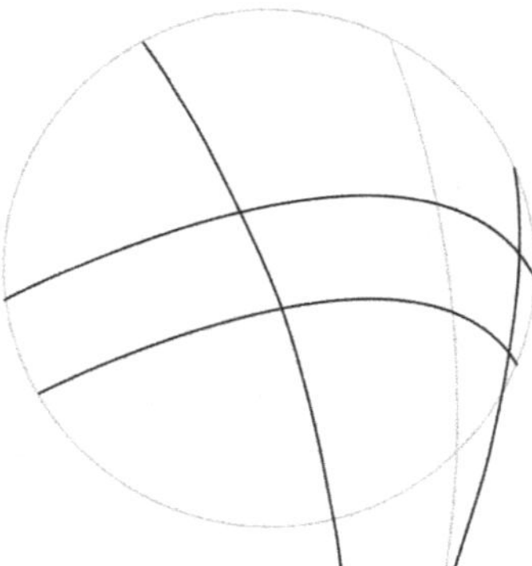

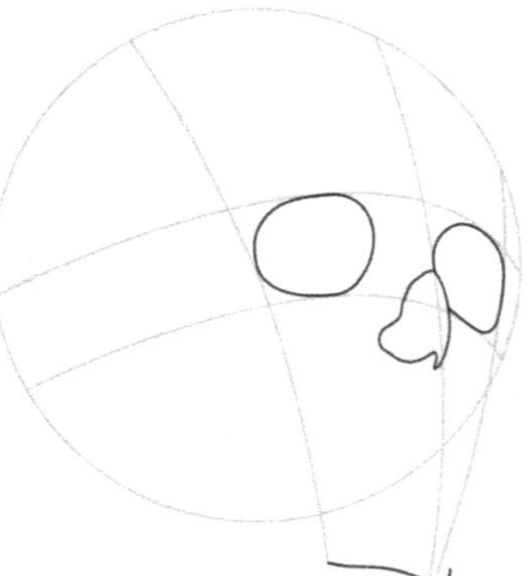

04

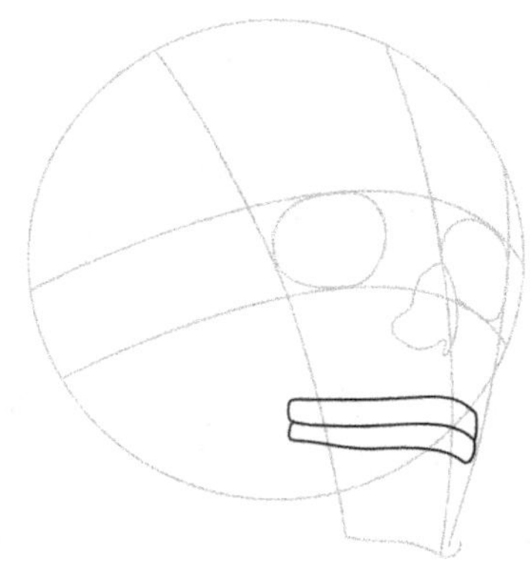

05

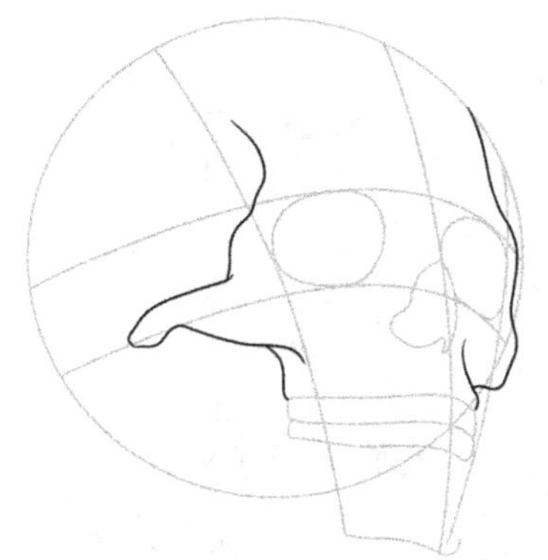

06

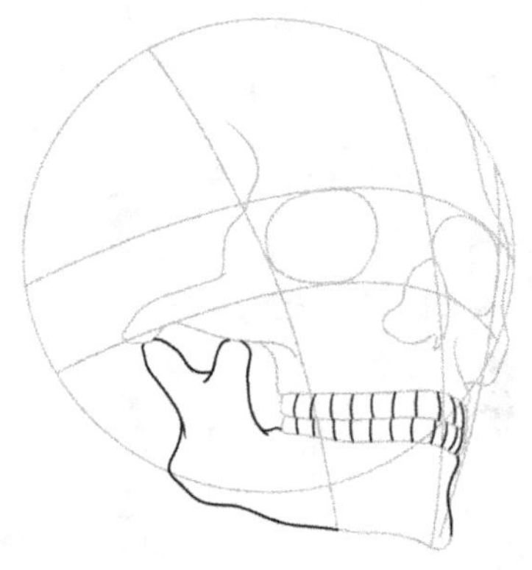

07

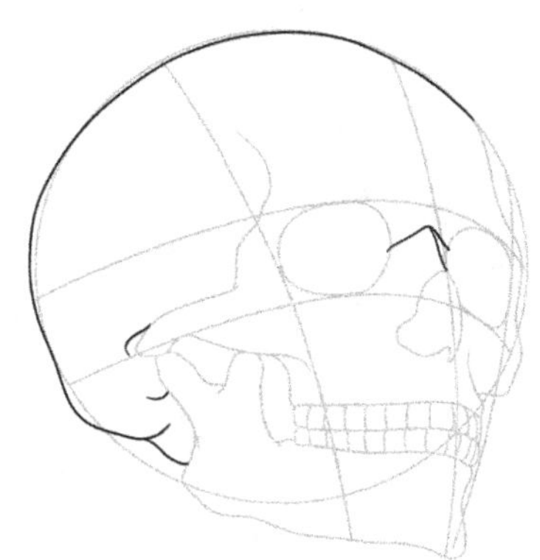

08

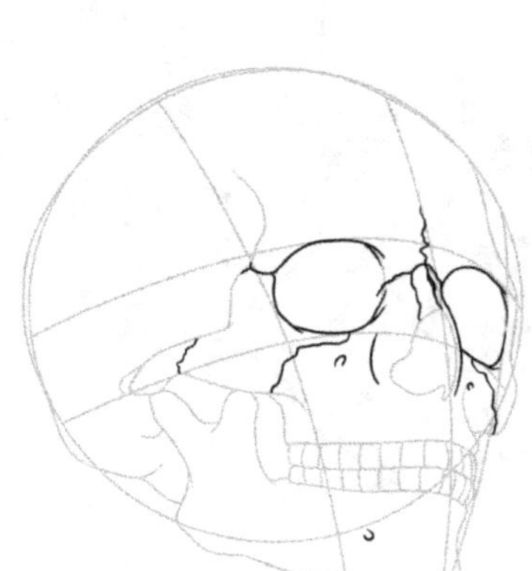

09

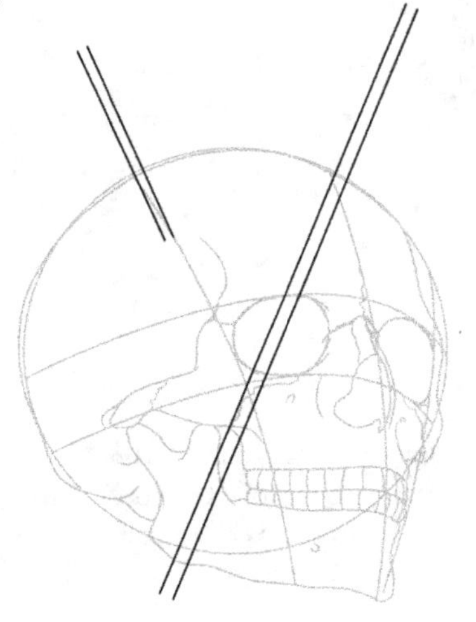

10

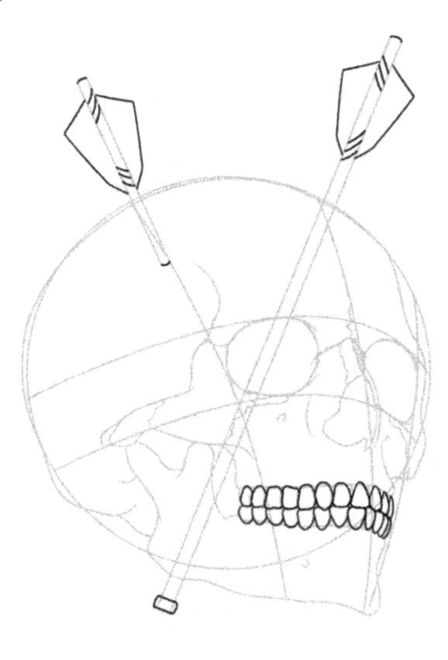

11

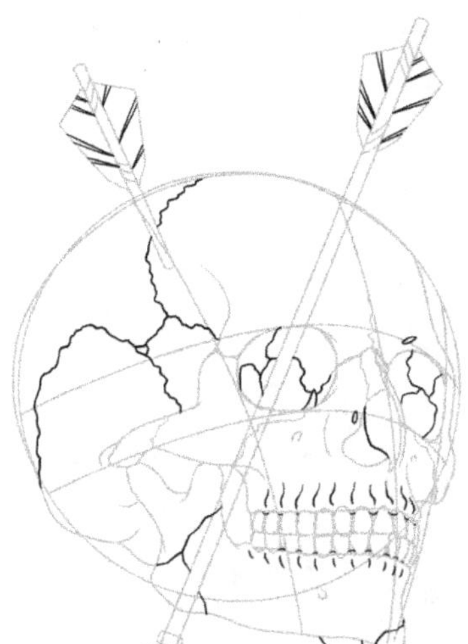

12

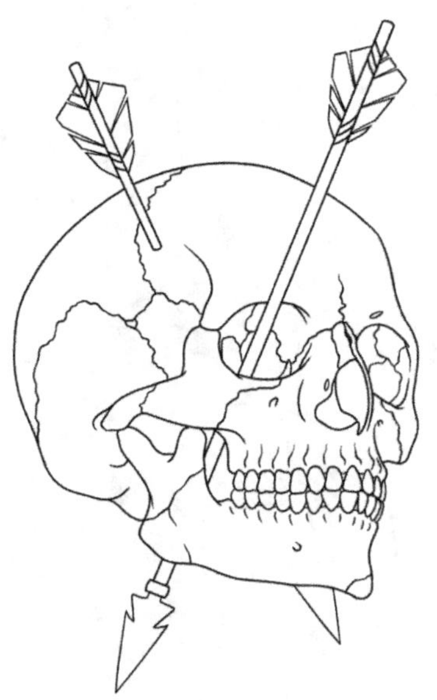

SKULL & CANDLE

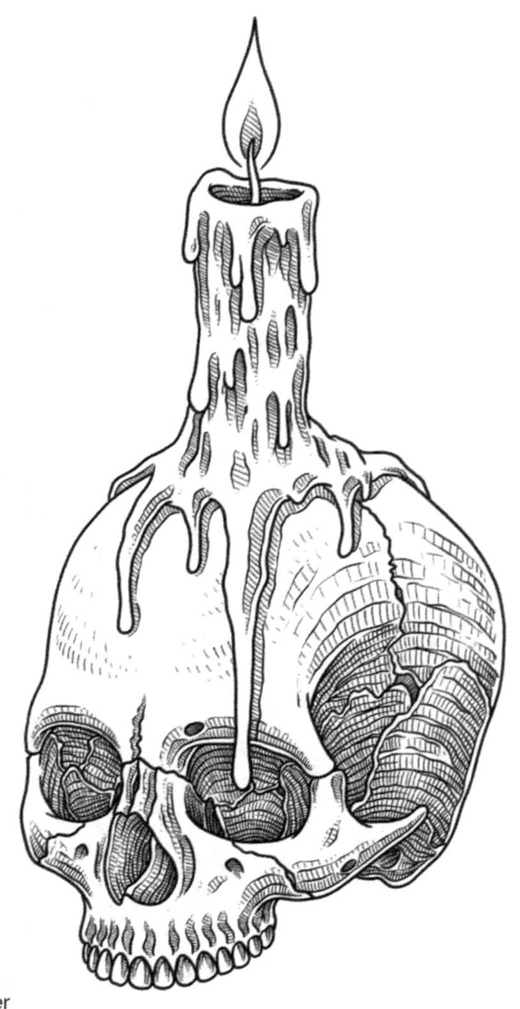

Pro Tip: Draw the skull first. Then map the candle's base to fit the curve of the cranium, adding wax drips that flow over natural bone contours.

01

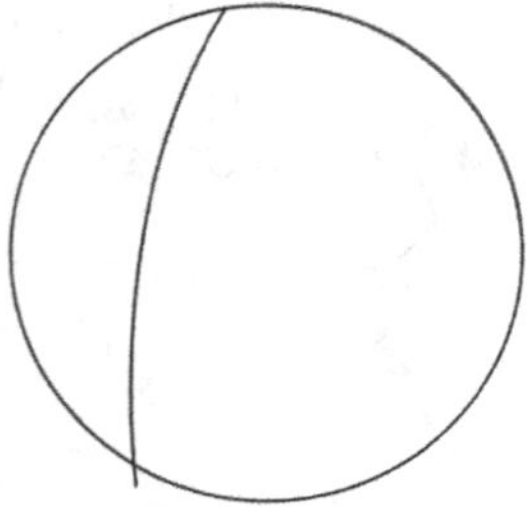

02

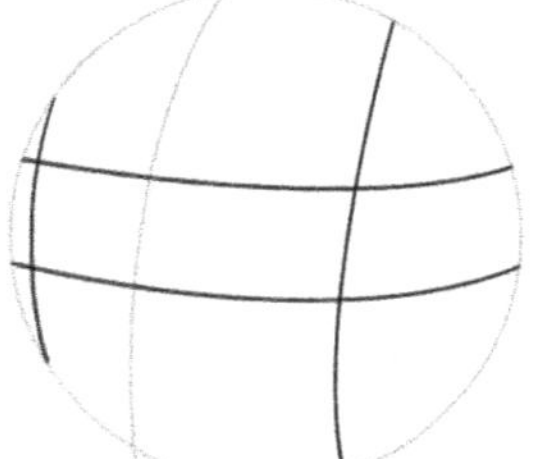

03

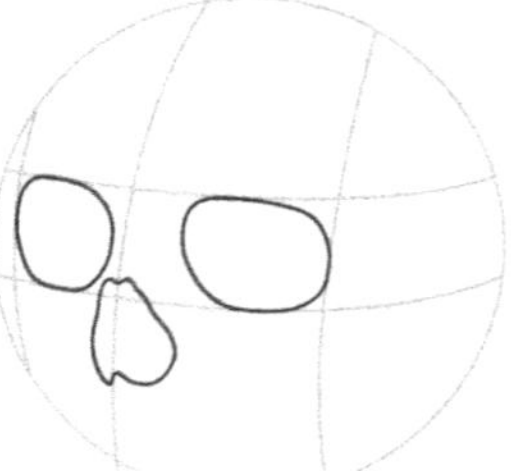

04

05

06

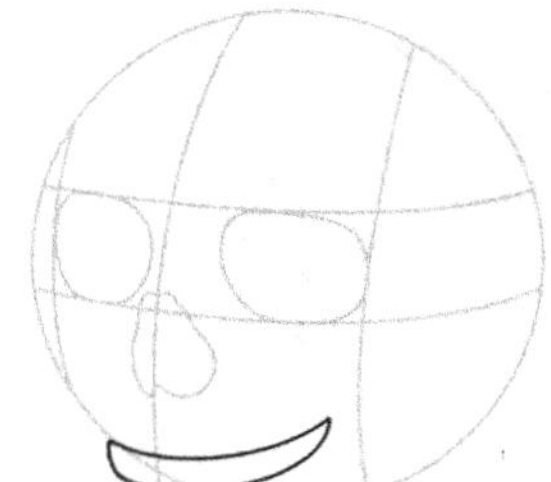

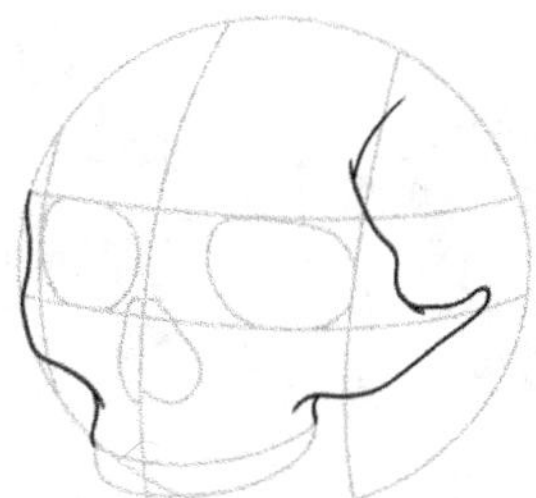

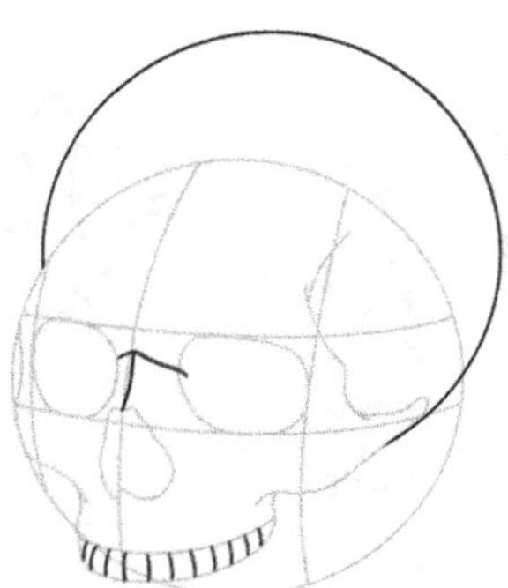

07

08

09

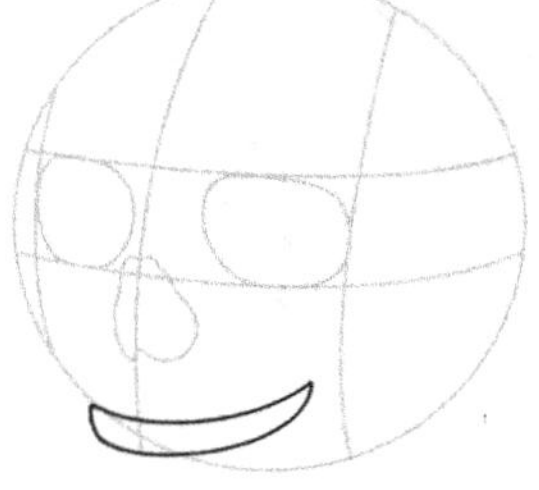

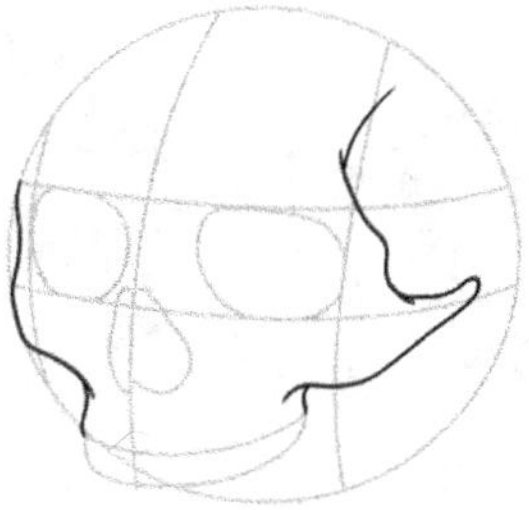

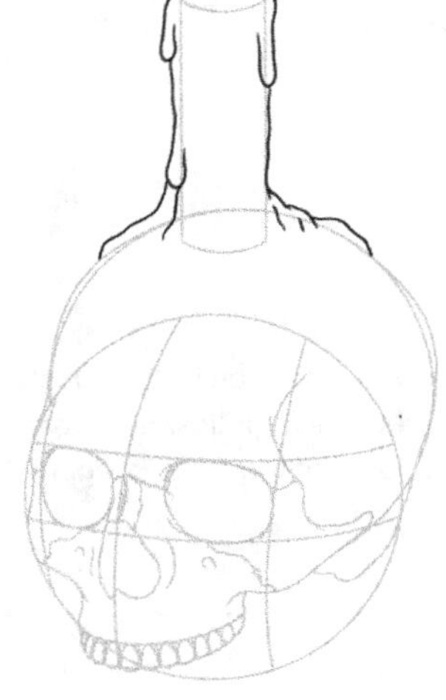

10

11

12

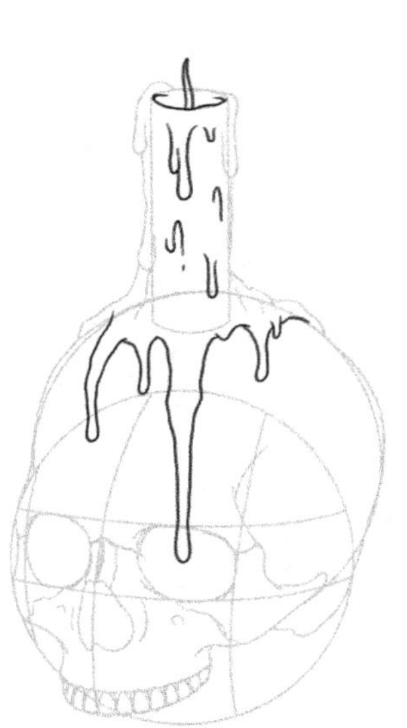

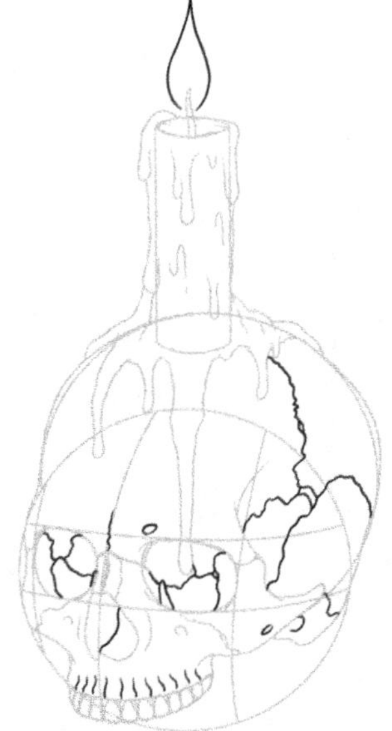

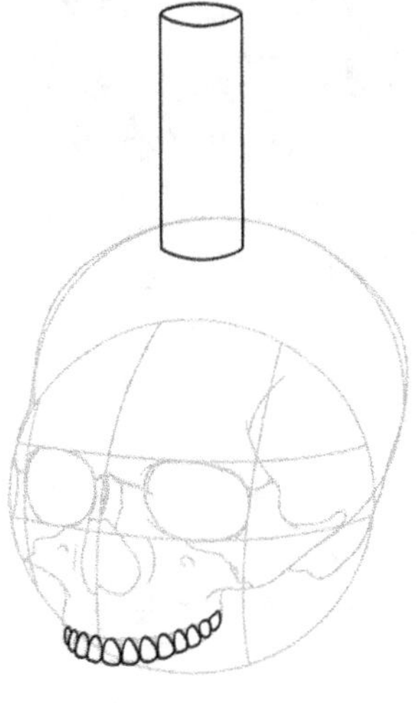

HOW TO DRAW SKULLS

SKULL WITH CROWN OF THORNS

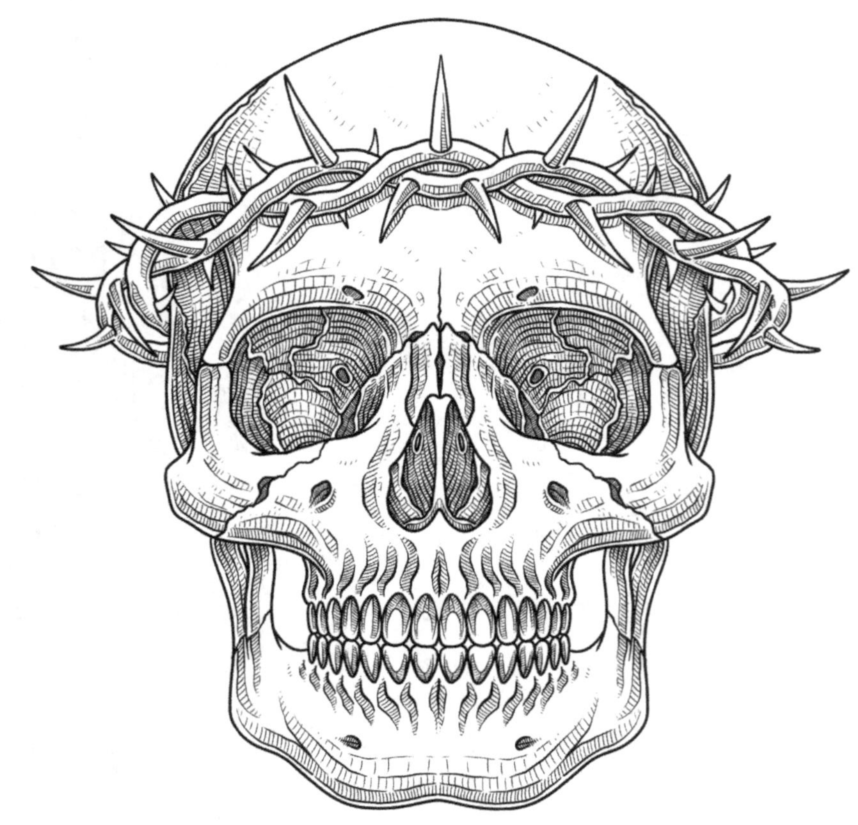

Pro Tip: Draw the skull first. Then shape the thorned vine to follow the brow line and curve of the skull, keeping the tension and flow natural.

01

02

03

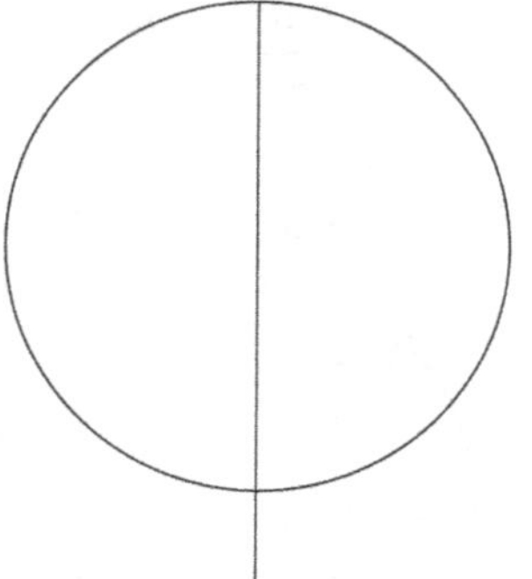

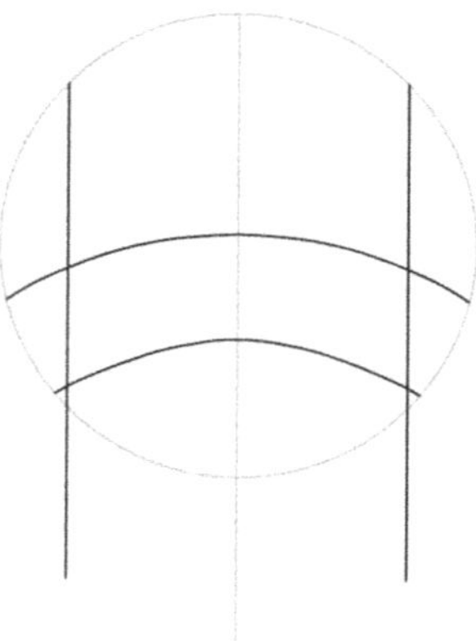

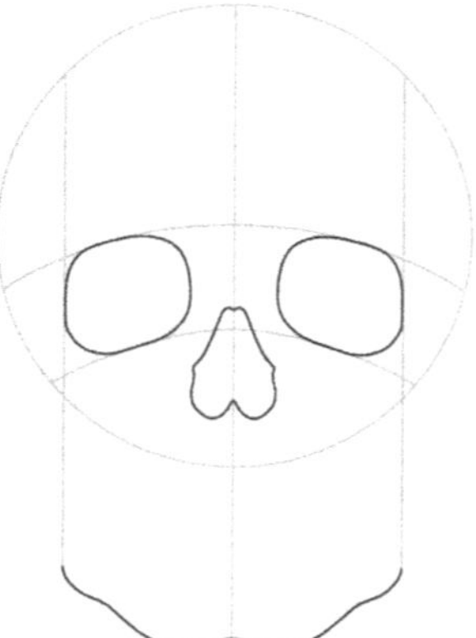

04

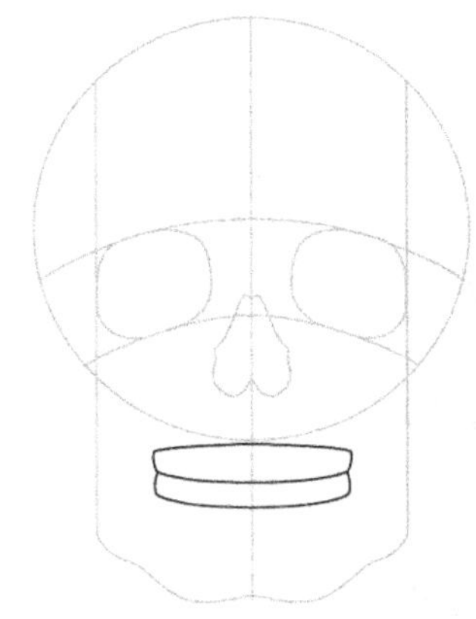

05

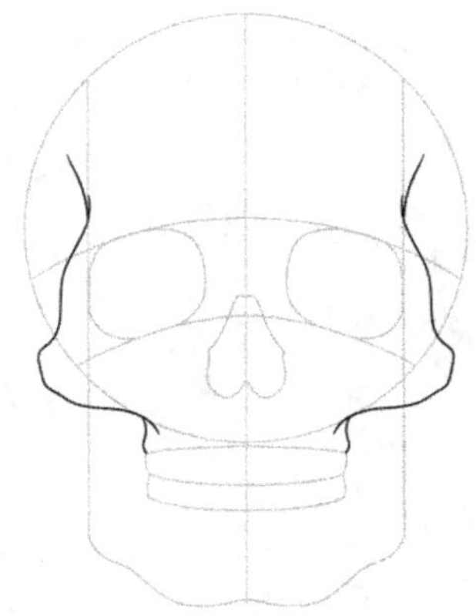

06

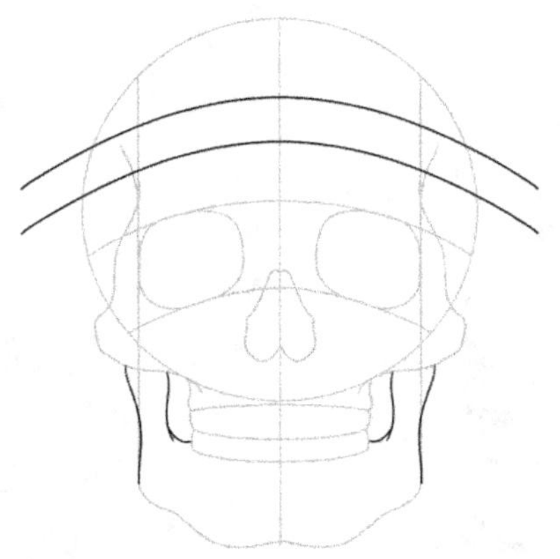

07

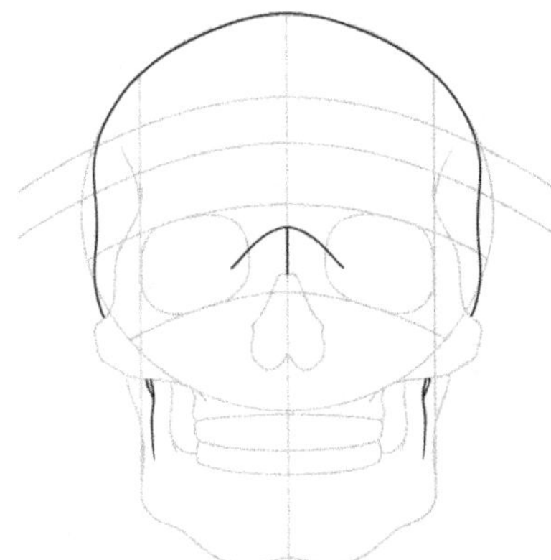

08

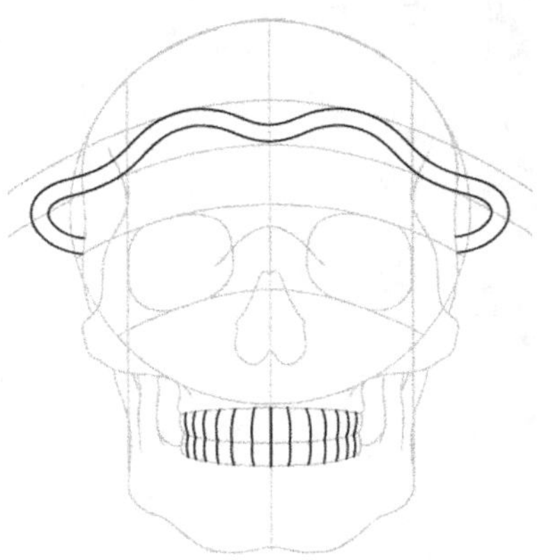

09

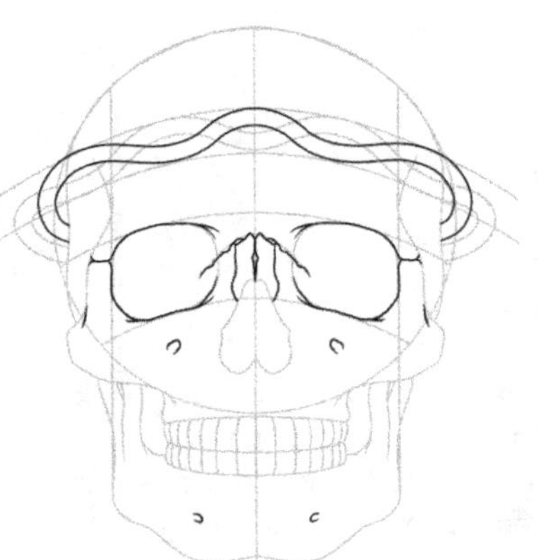

10

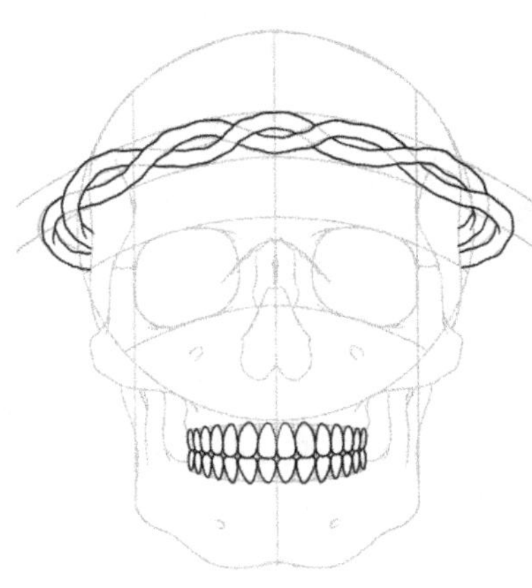

11

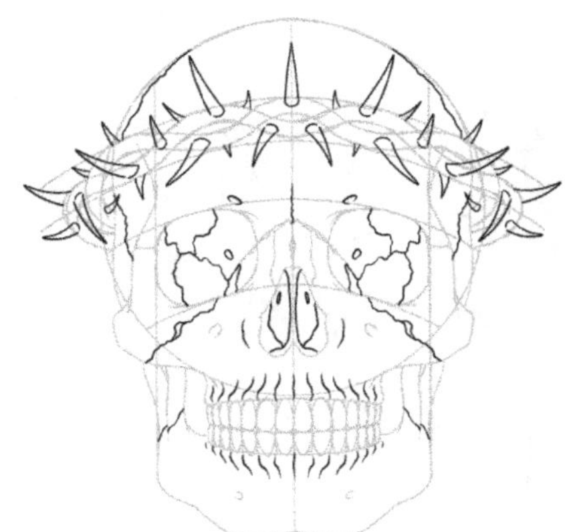

12

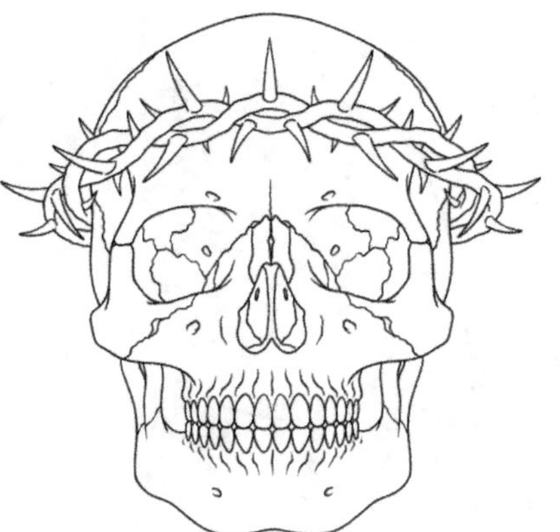

HOW TO DRAW SKULLS

FLAMING SKULL

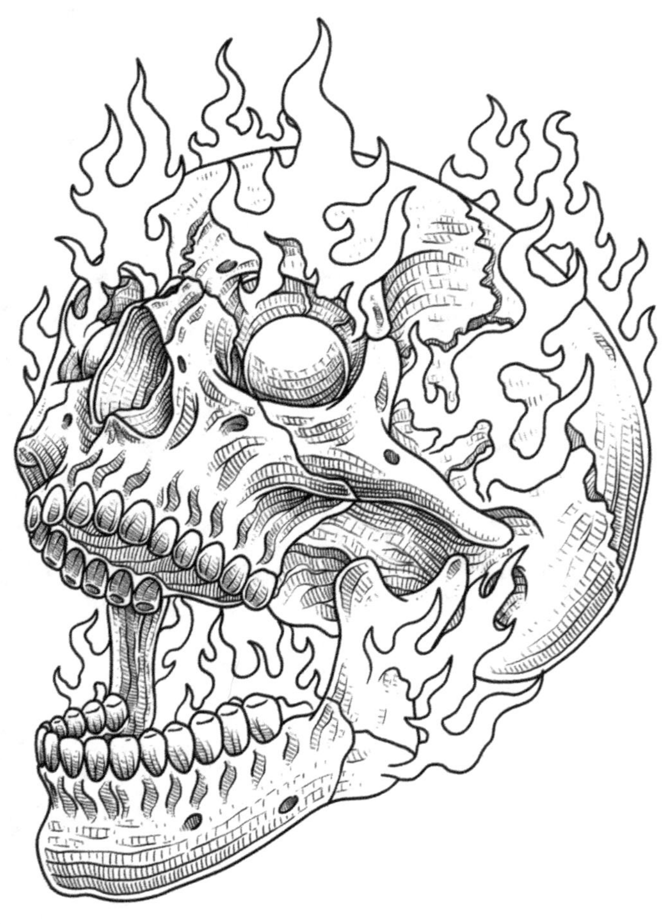

Pro Tip: Start with the skull. Then draw flames wrapping around its contours, using smooth, curved shapes to create a sense of motion and energy.

01

02

03

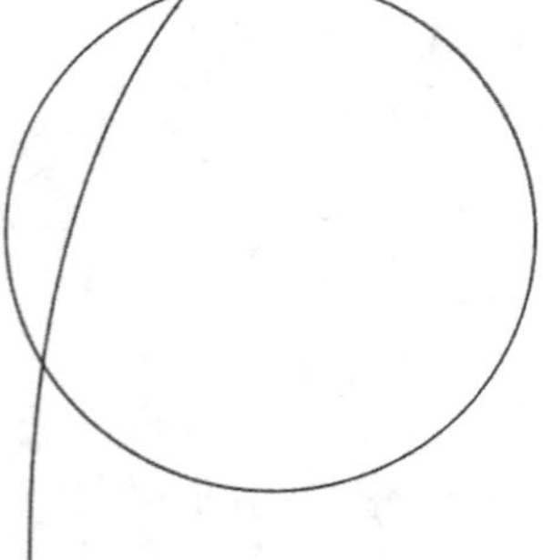

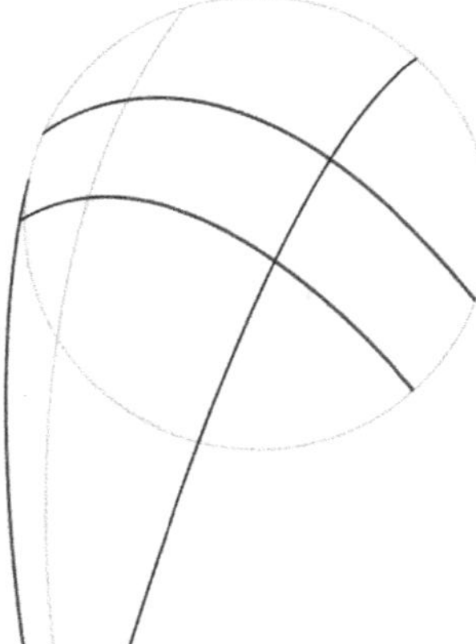

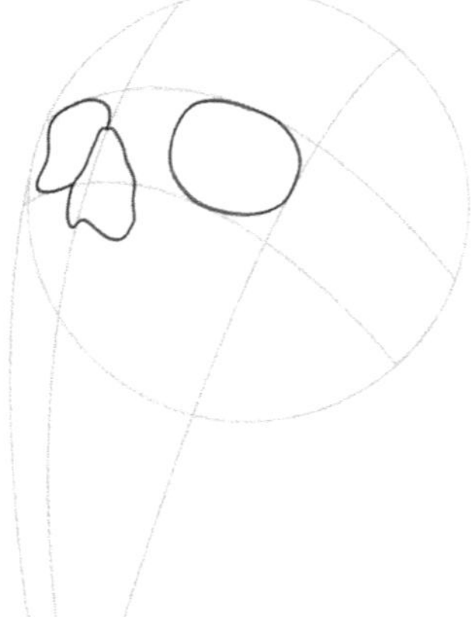

04

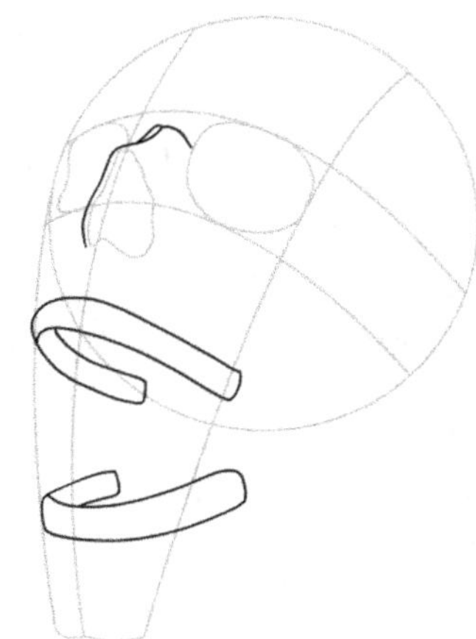

05

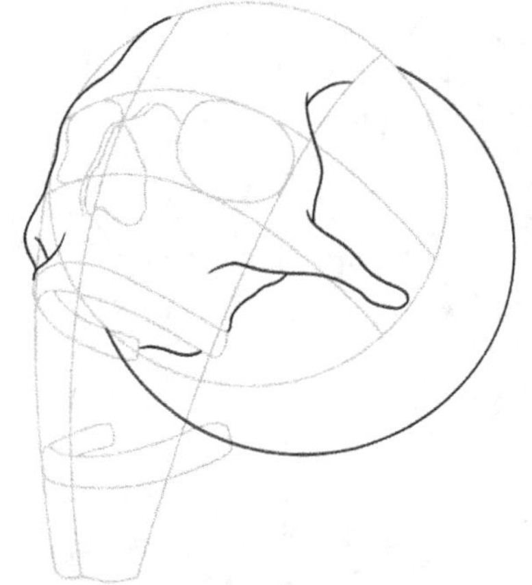

06

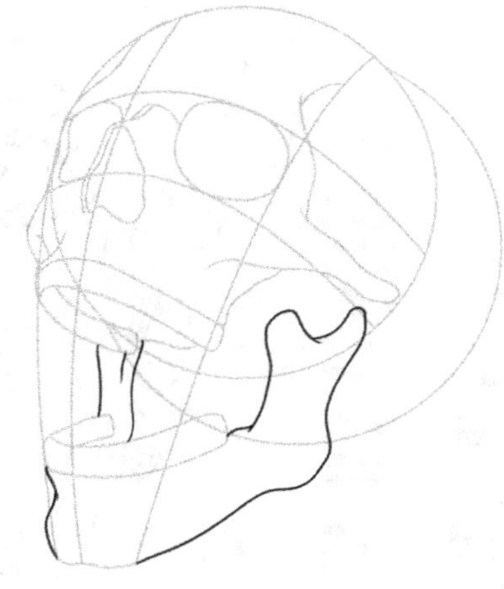

07

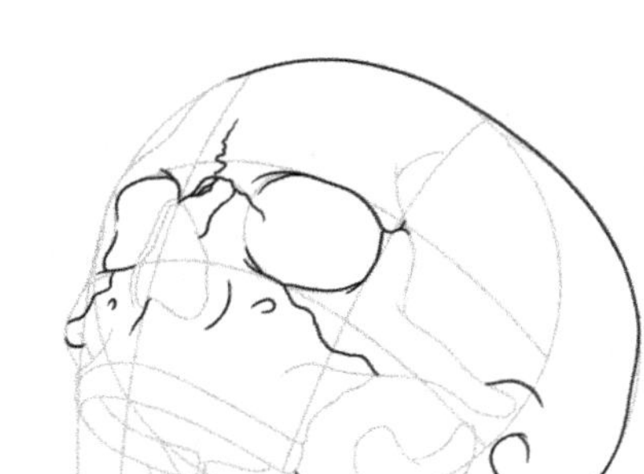

08

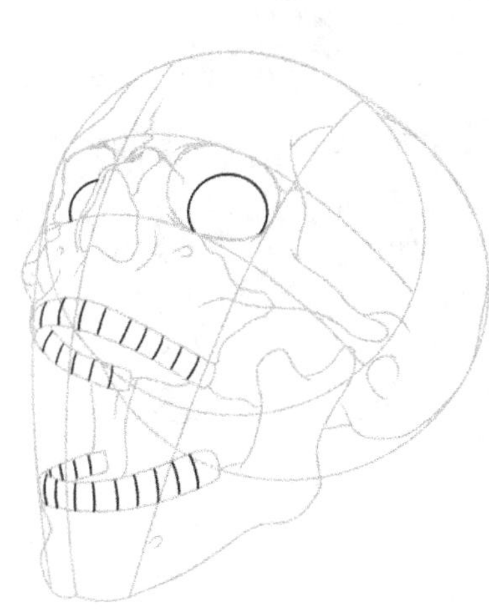

09

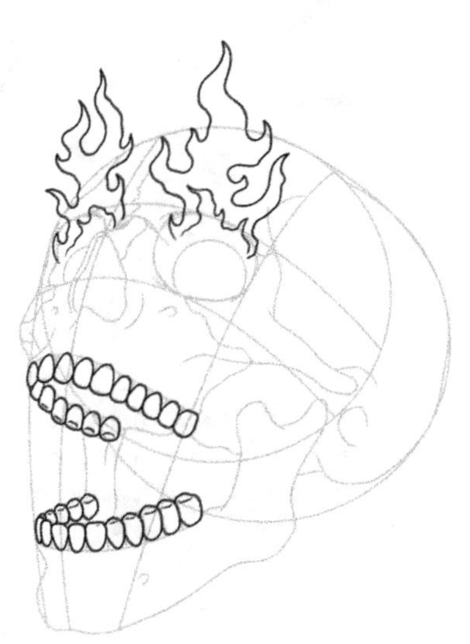

10

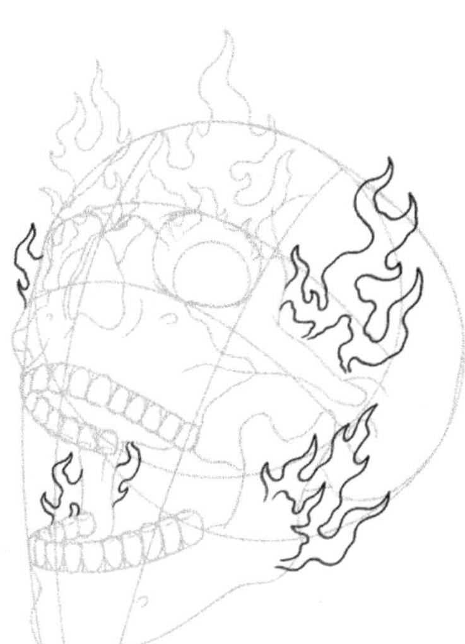

11

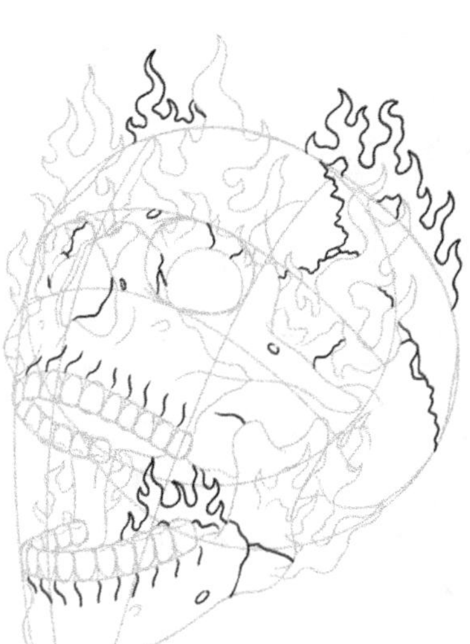

12

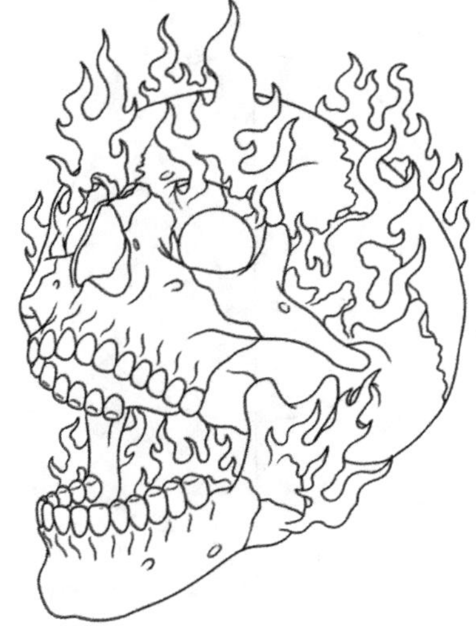

HOW TO DRAW SKULLS

SKULL WITH FLOWER GARLAND

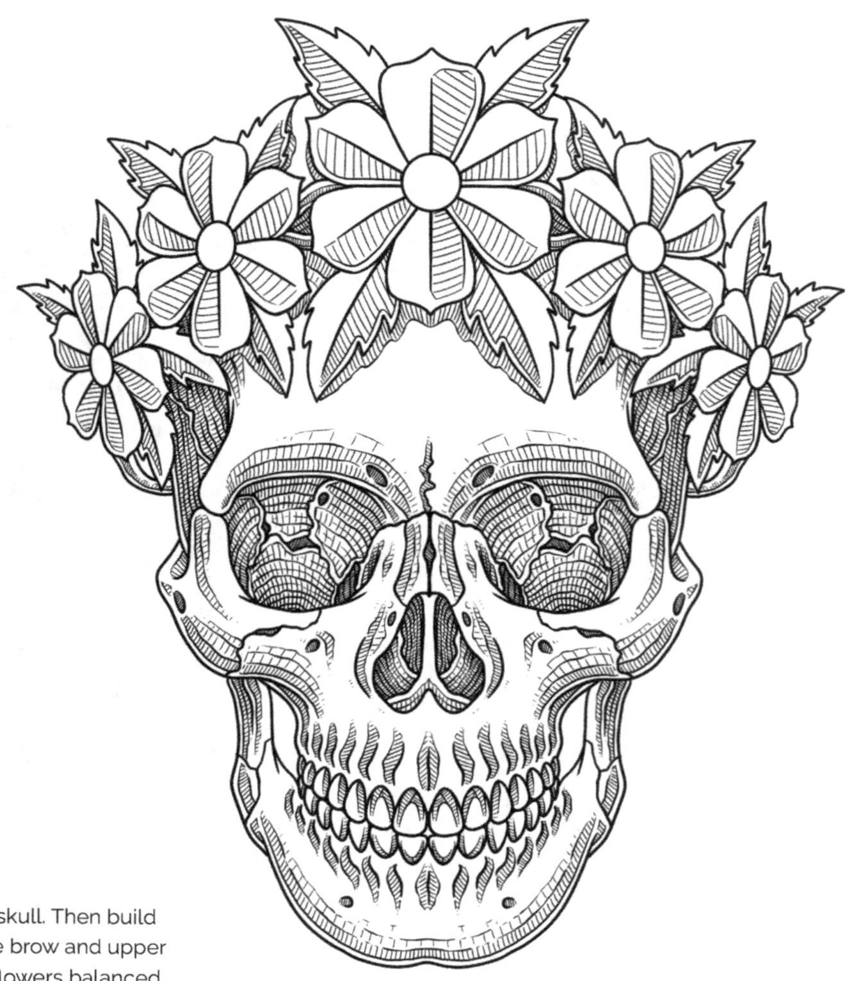

Pro Tip: Start with the skull. Then build the garland around the brow and upper cranium, keeping the flowers balanced and following the skull's curve.

01

02

03

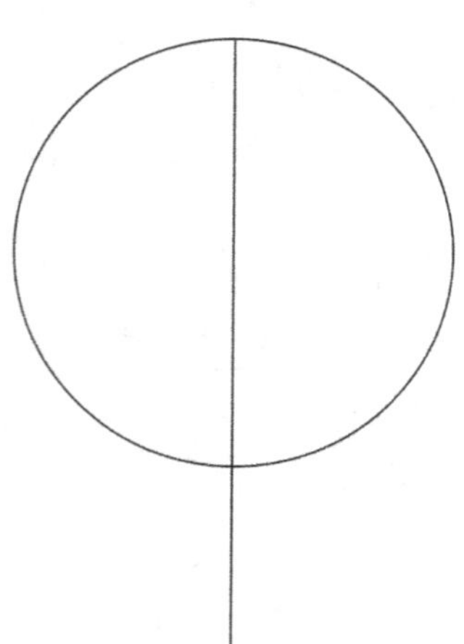

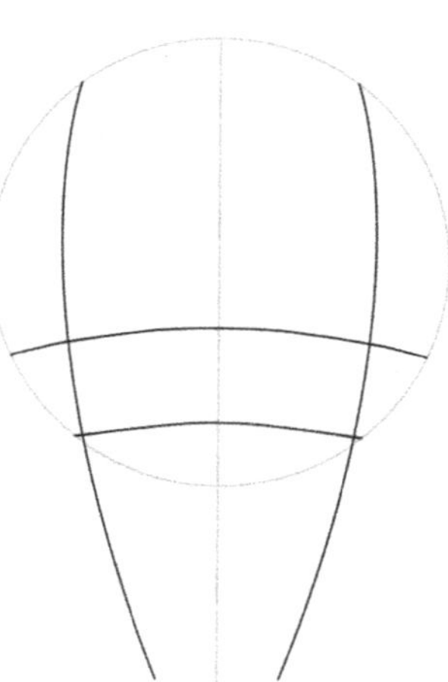

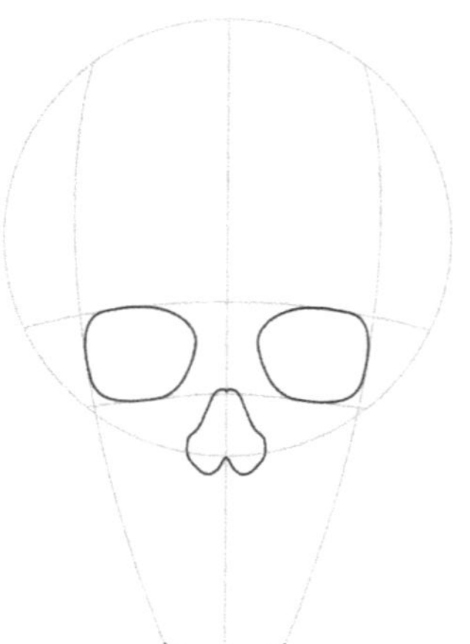

04

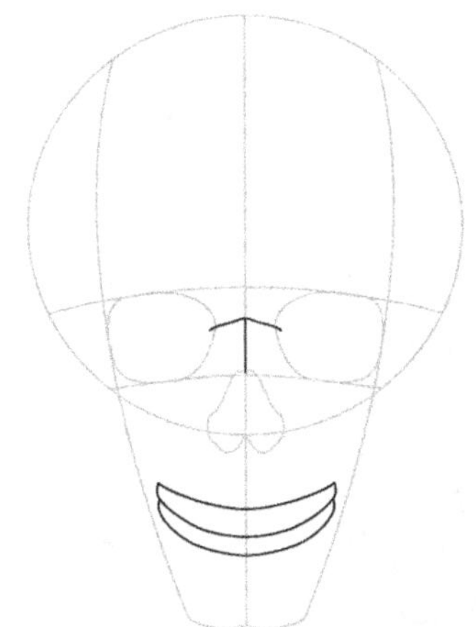

05

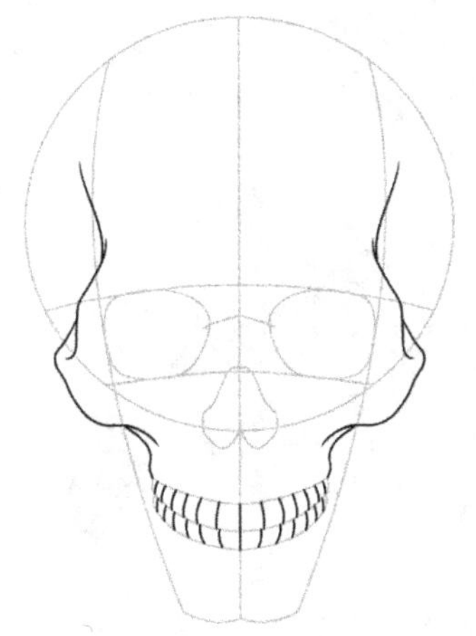

06

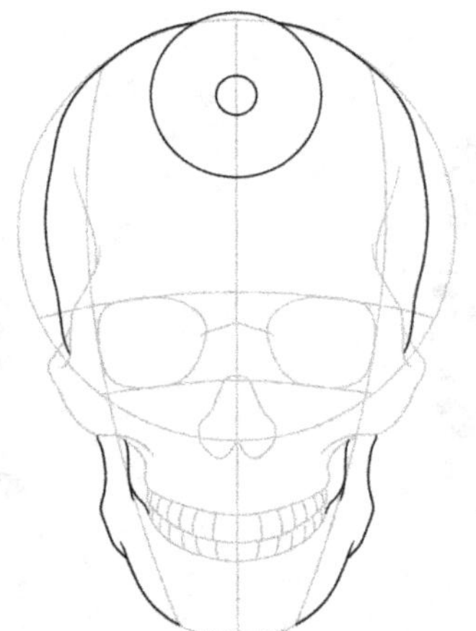

07

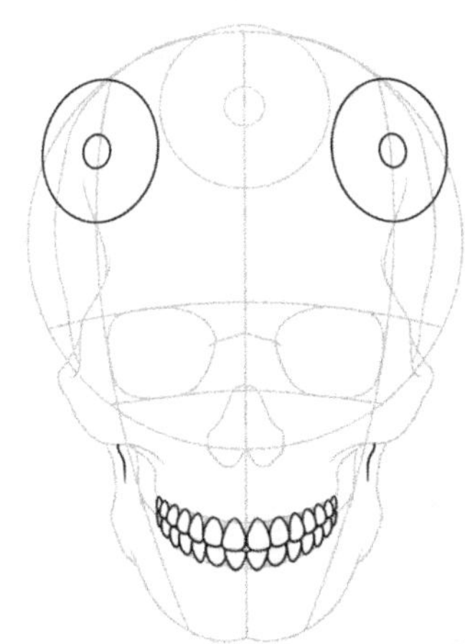

08

09

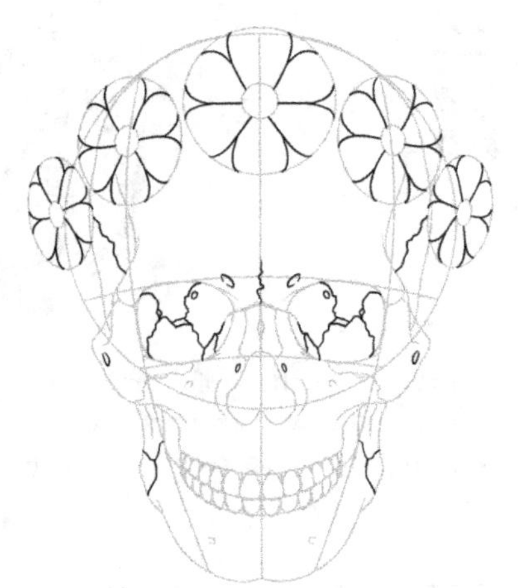

10

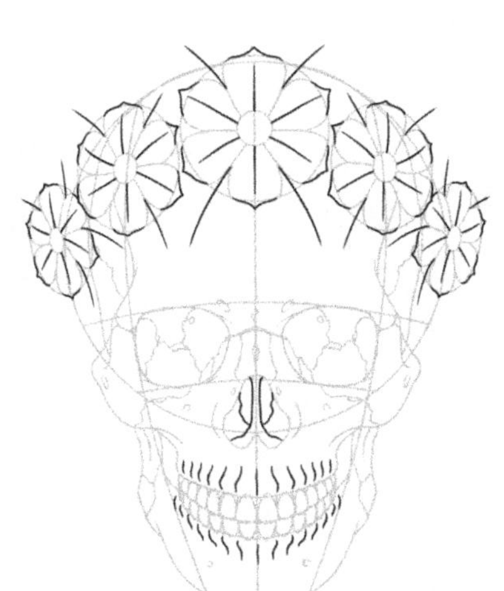

11

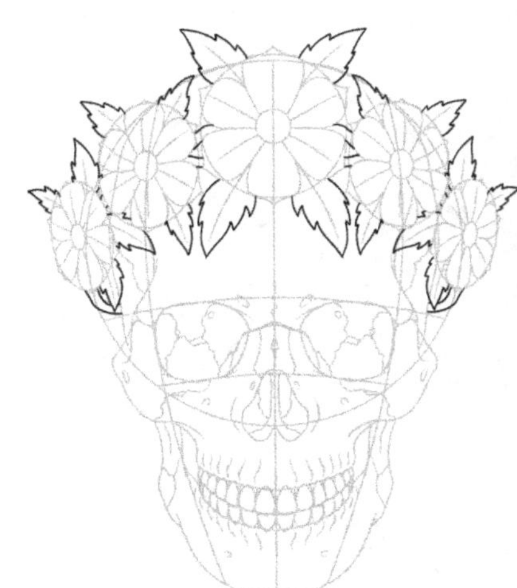

12

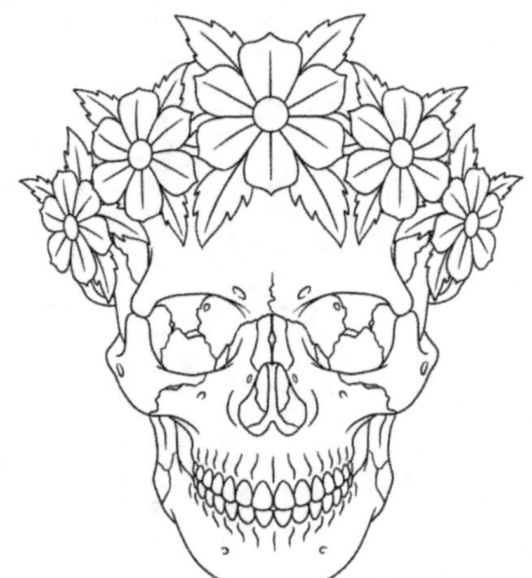

SKULL GRIPPED BY CLAW

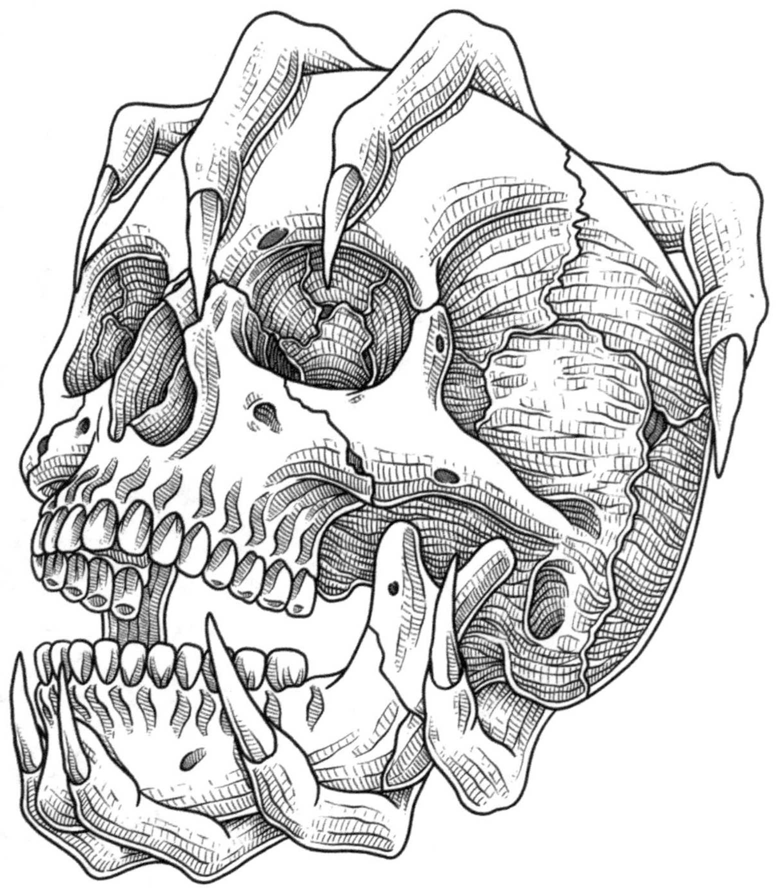

Pro Tip: Start with the skull's structure. Then map the claw placement, using the curve of the cranium and cheekbones to guide where each finger hooks in.

01

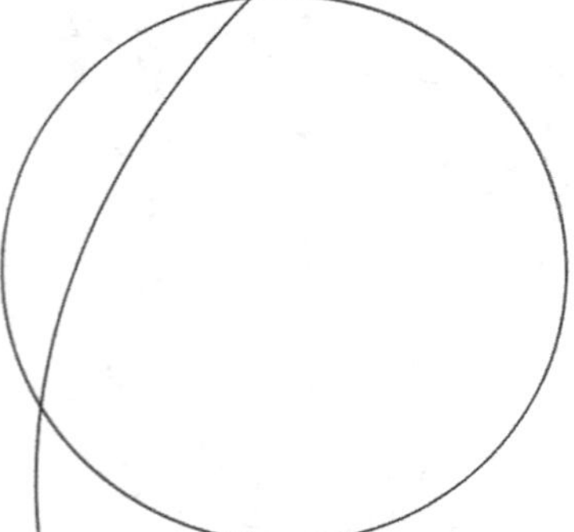

02

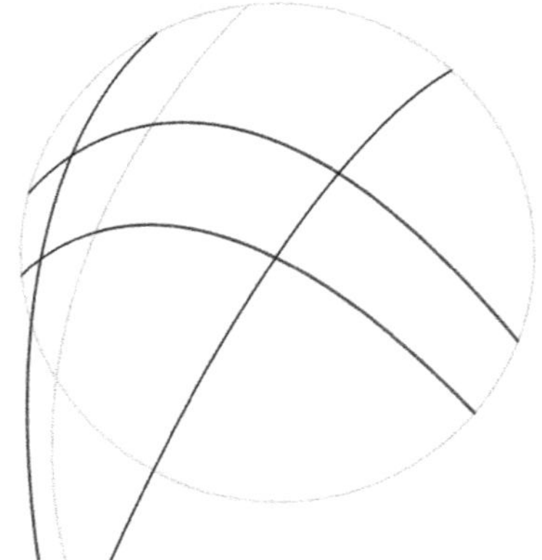

03

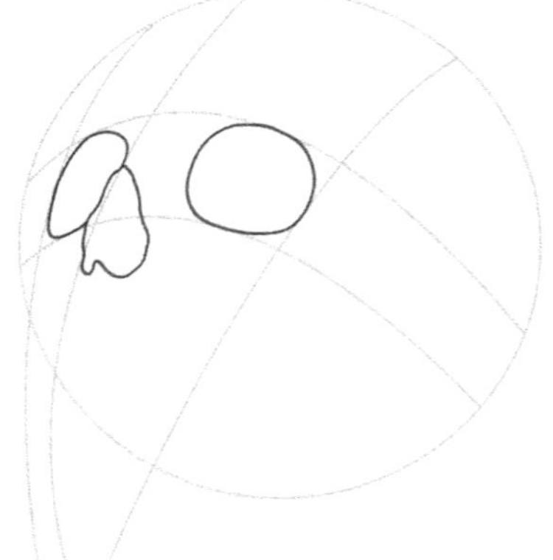

04

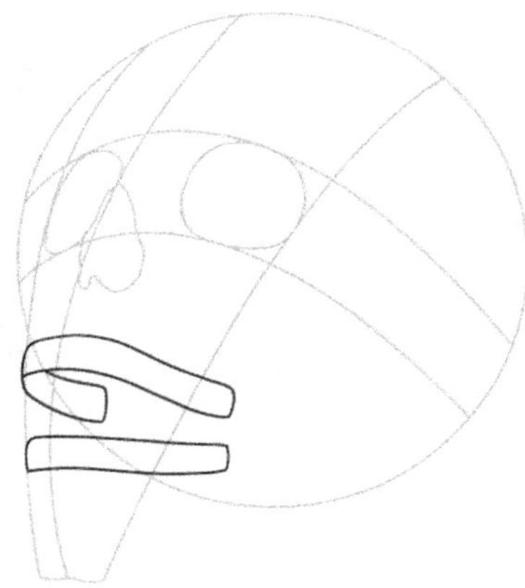

05

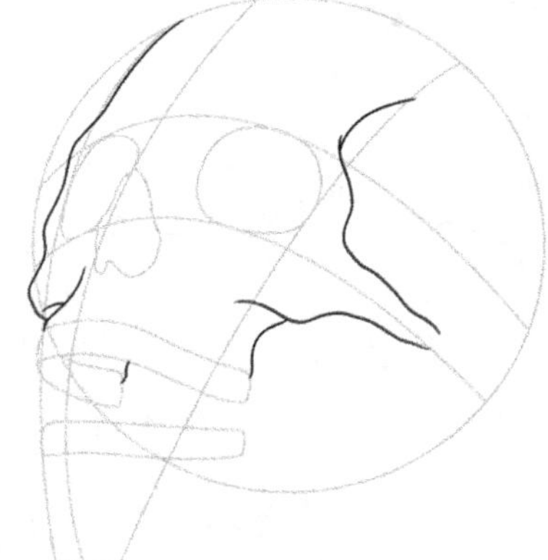

06

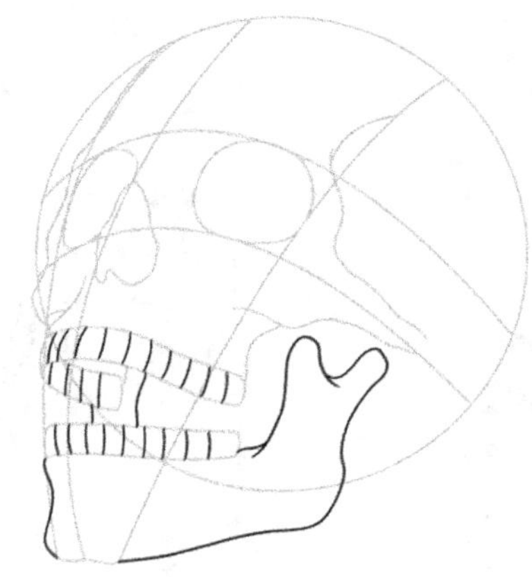

07

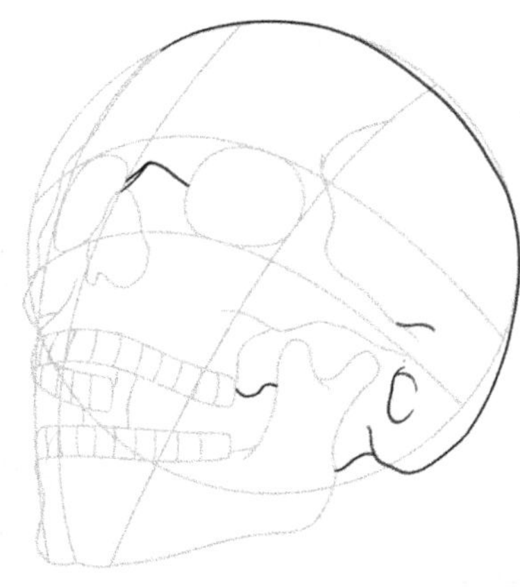

08

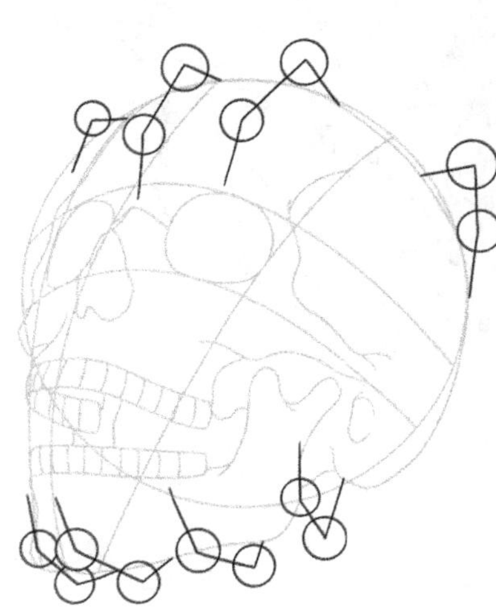

09

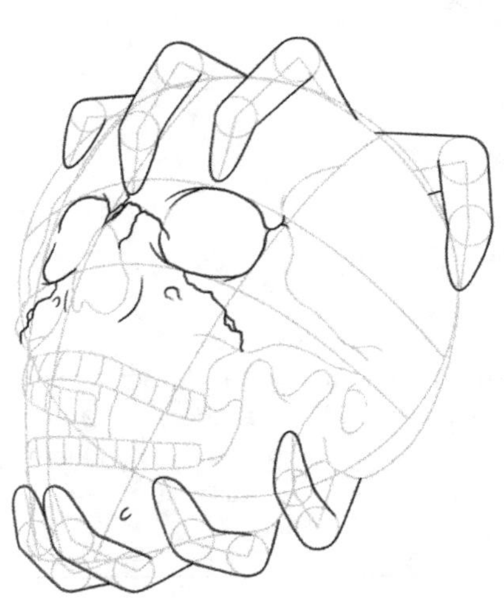

10

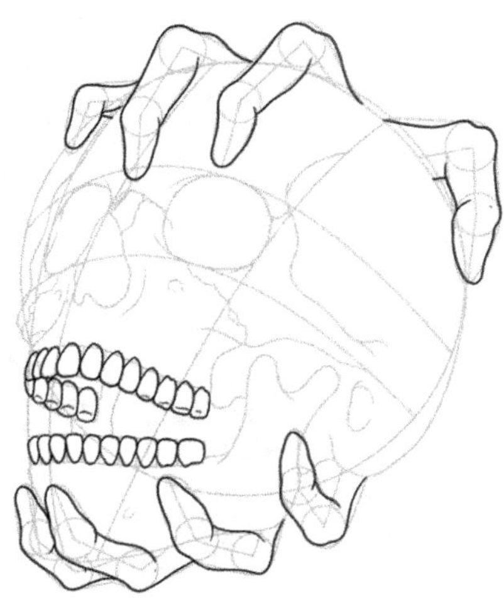

11

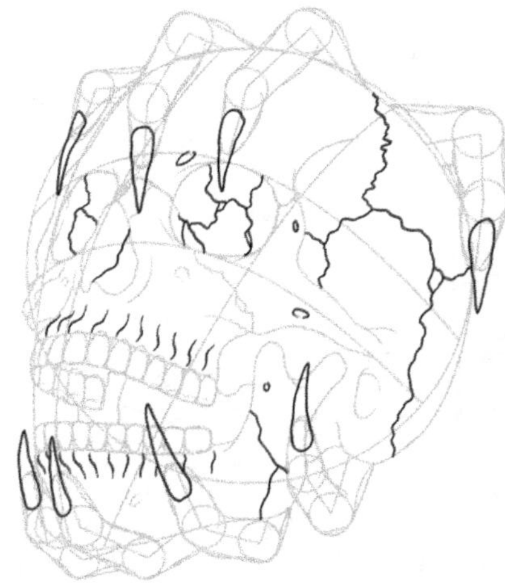

12

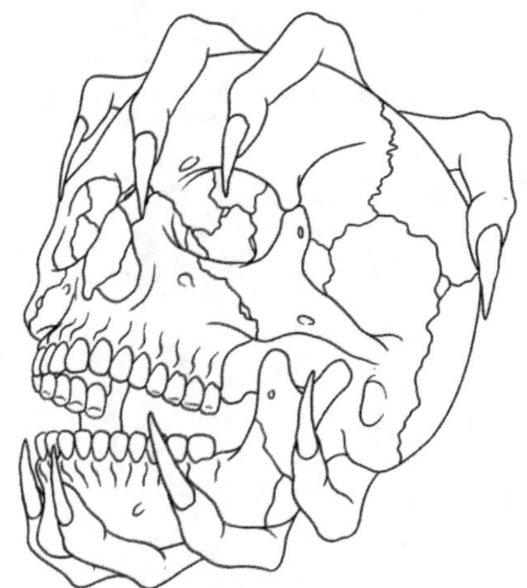

HORNED SKULL

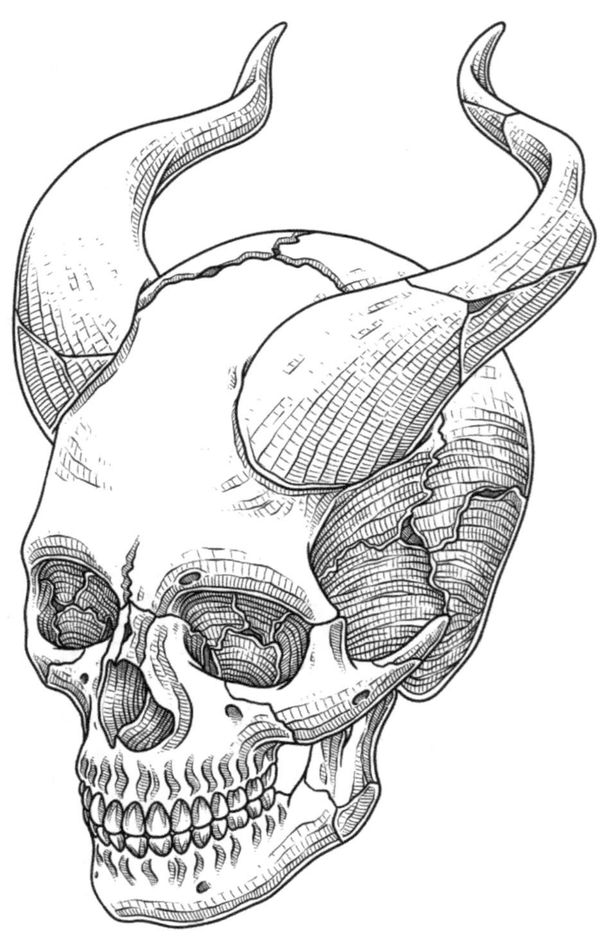

Pro Tip: Draw the skull first. Then map the horn placement, anchoring them just above the brow ridge and curving them to complement the skull's tilt.

01   02   03

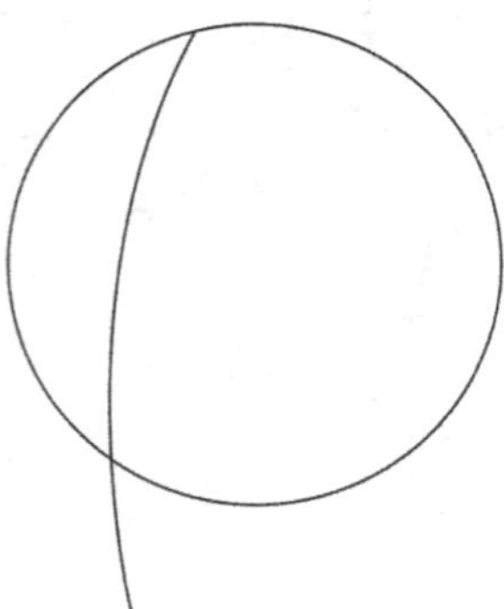
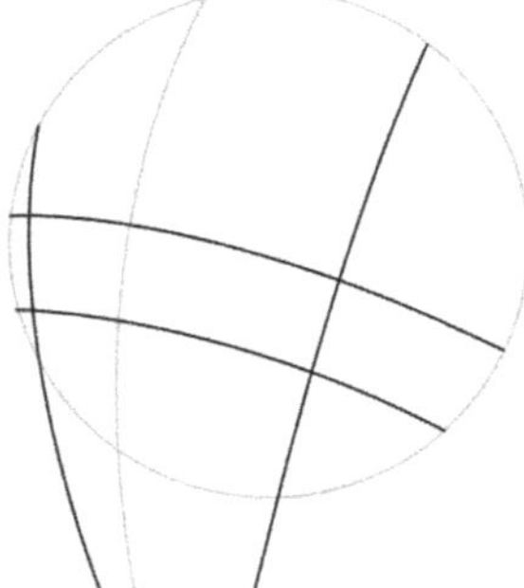
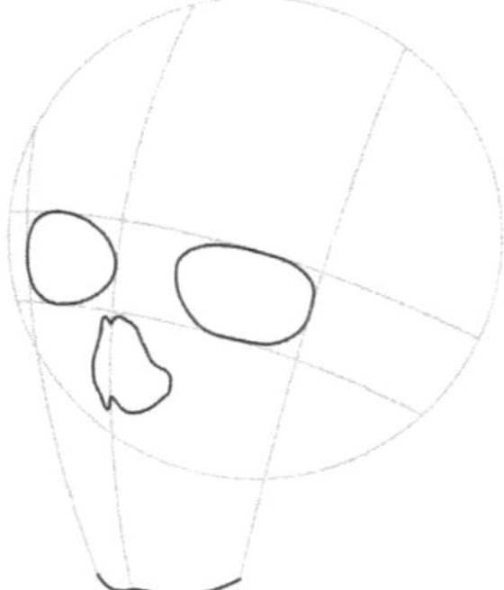

04

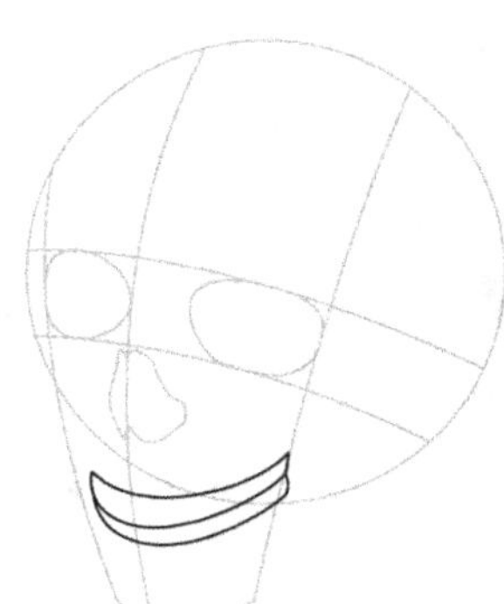

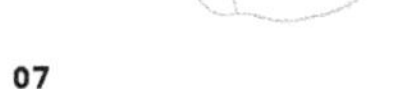

05

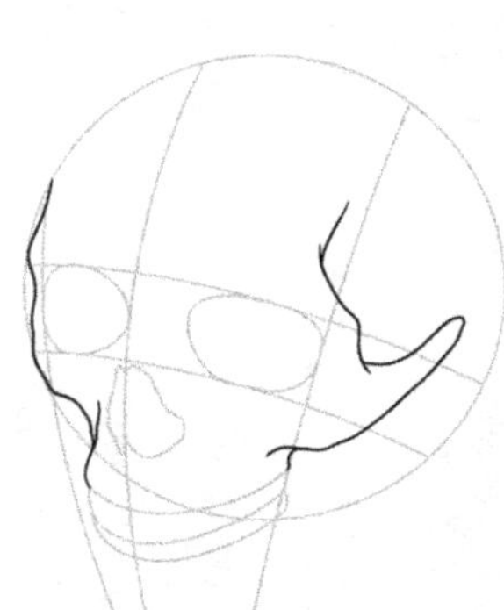

06

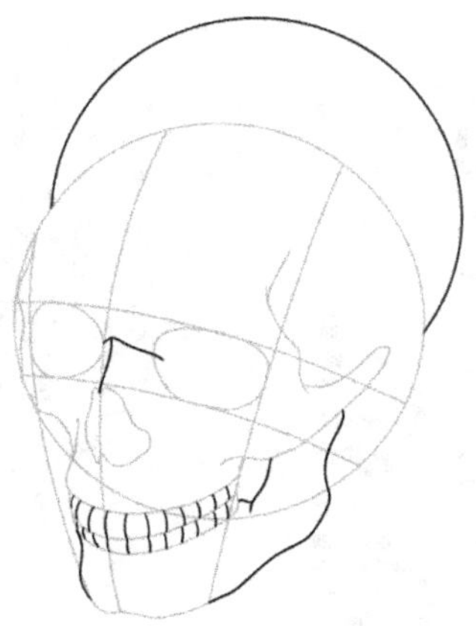

07

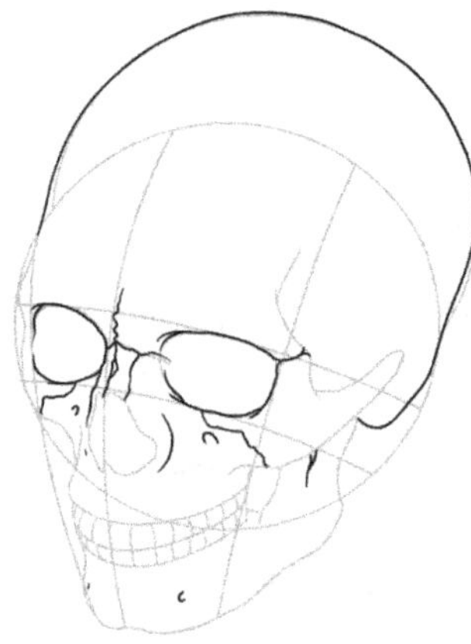

08

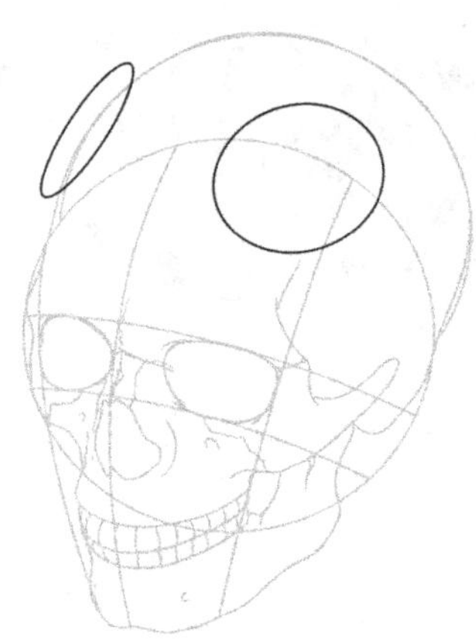

09

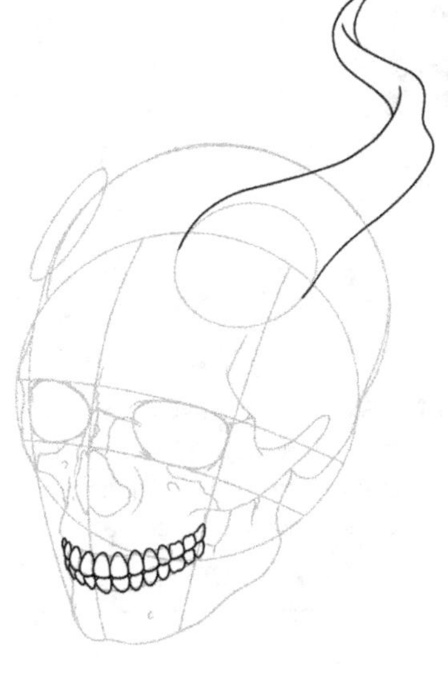

10

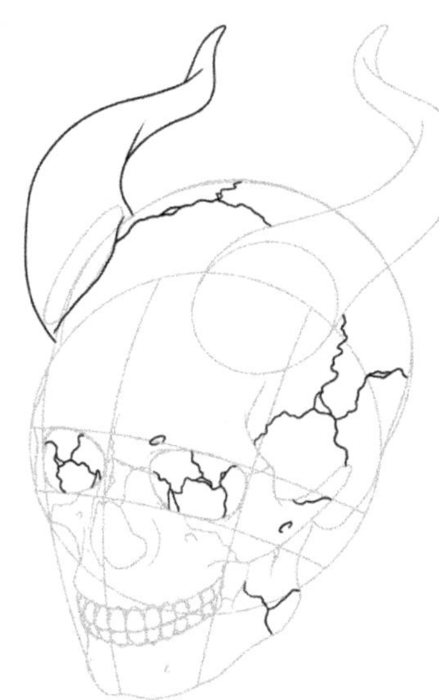

11

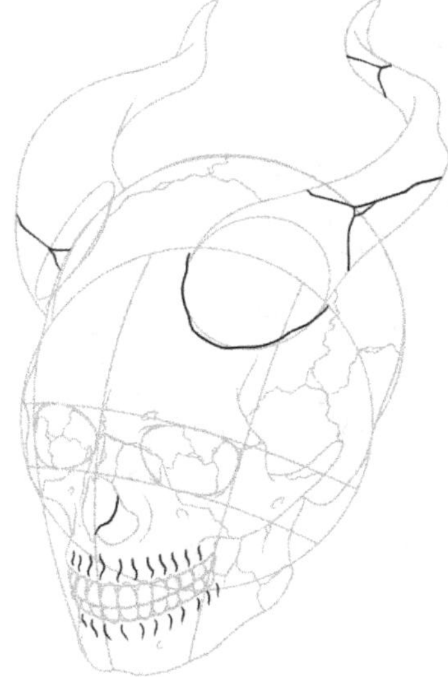

12

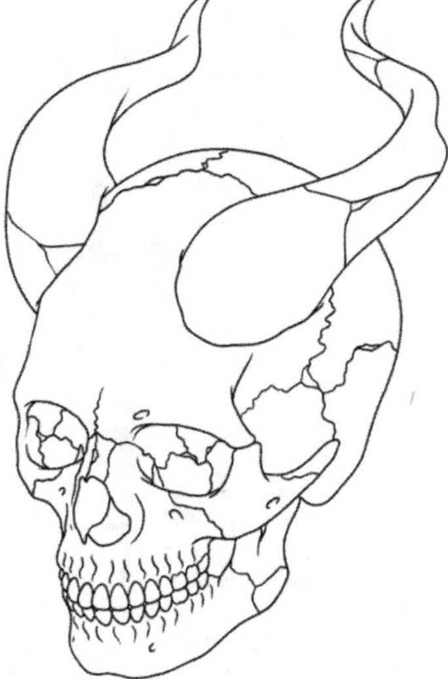

HOW TO DRAW SKULLS

SKULL WITH LAUREL WREATH1

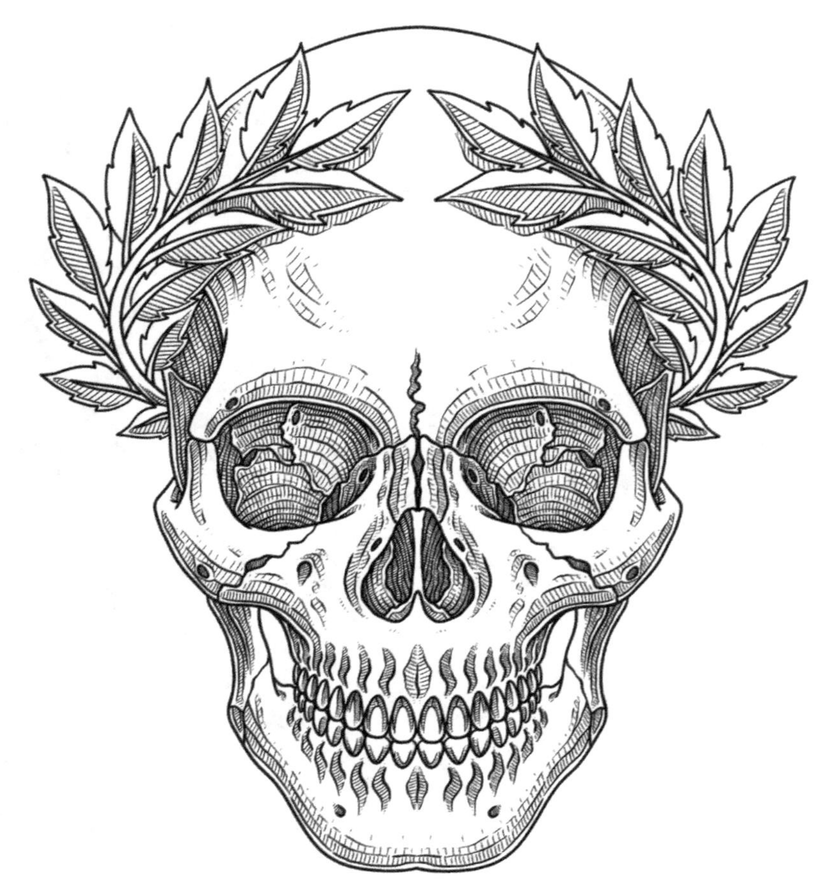

Pro Tip: Start with the skull's form. Then shape the laurel wreath to follow the curve of the brow and upper cranium, keeping the leaves balanced and flowing.

01

02

03

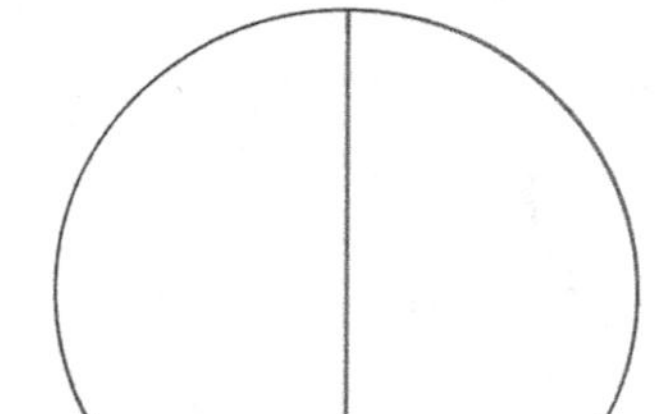

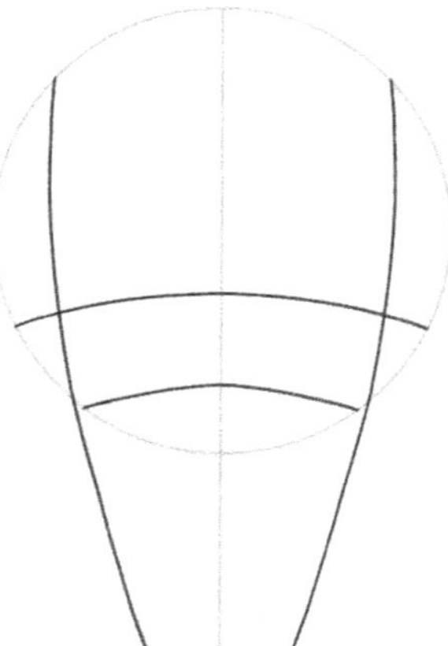

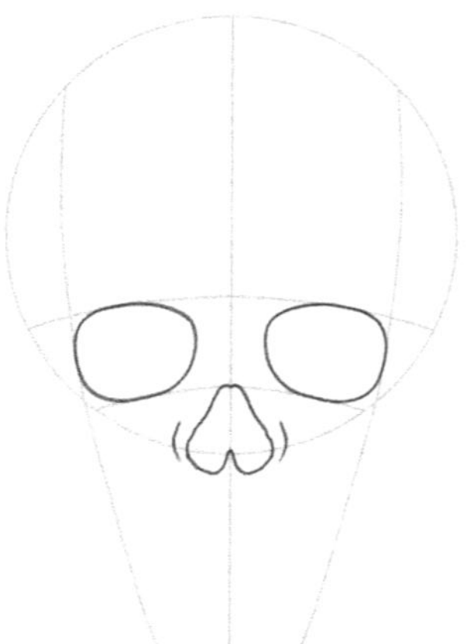

04

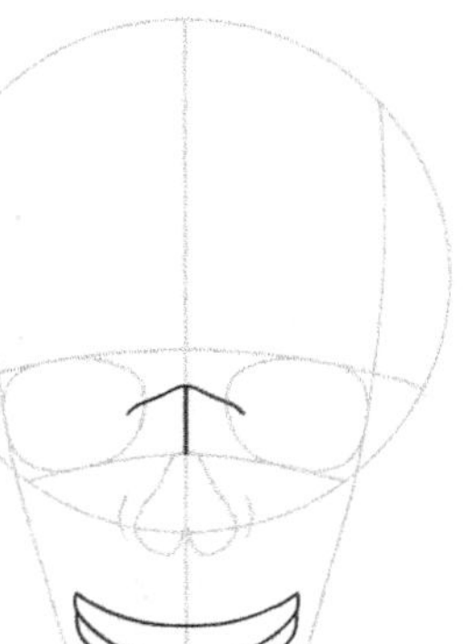

05

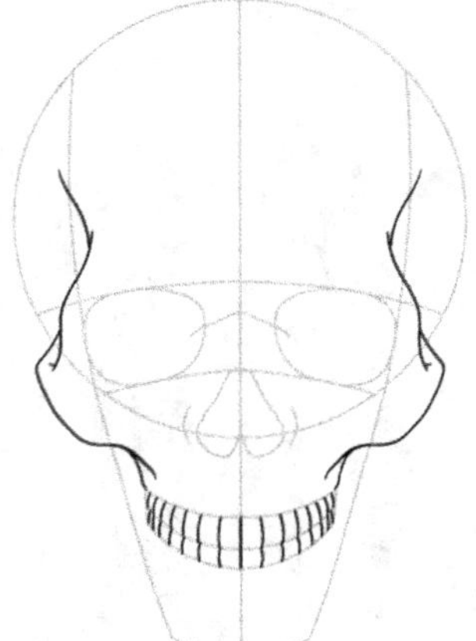

06

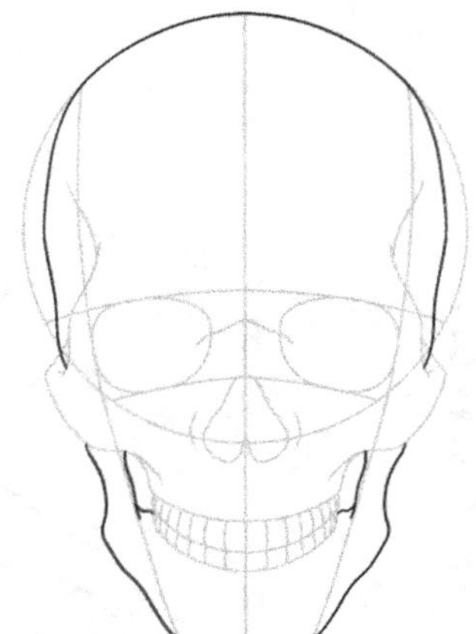

07

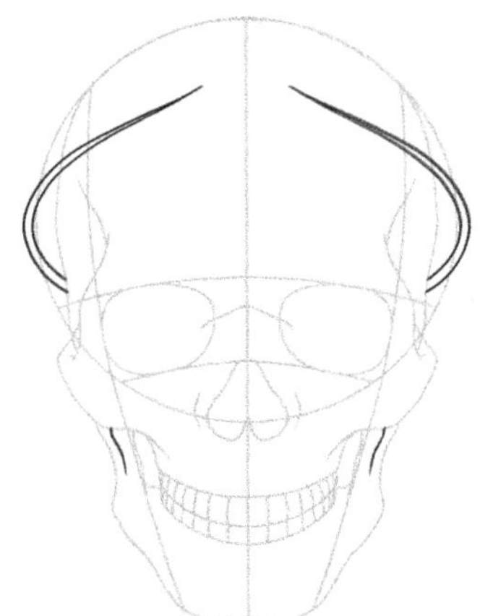

08

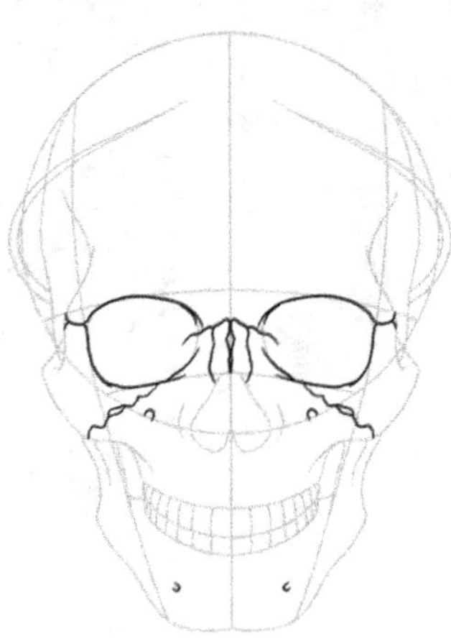

09

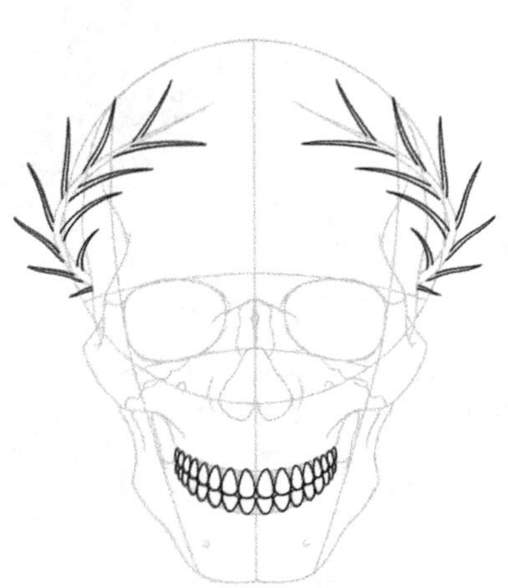

10

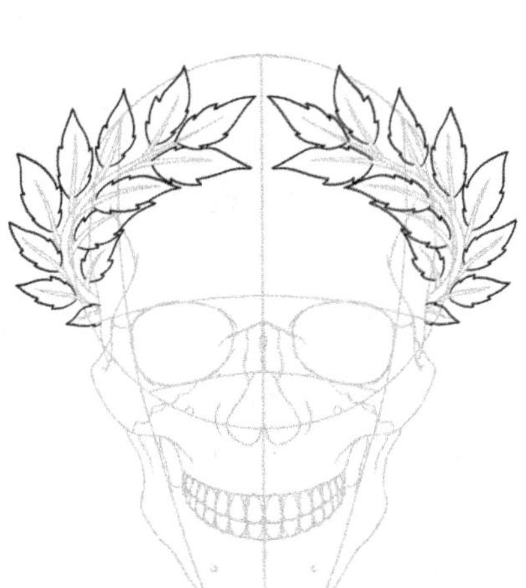

11

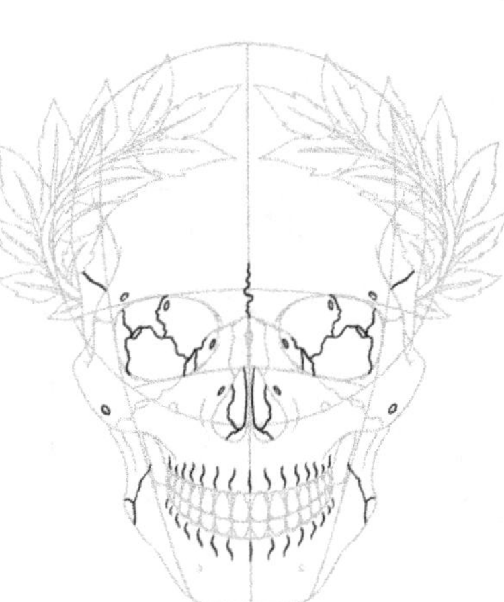

12

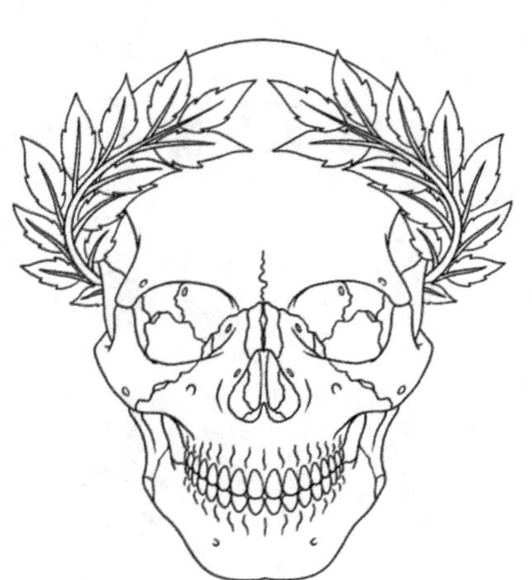

HOW TO DRAW SKULLS

SKULL & FUNGI

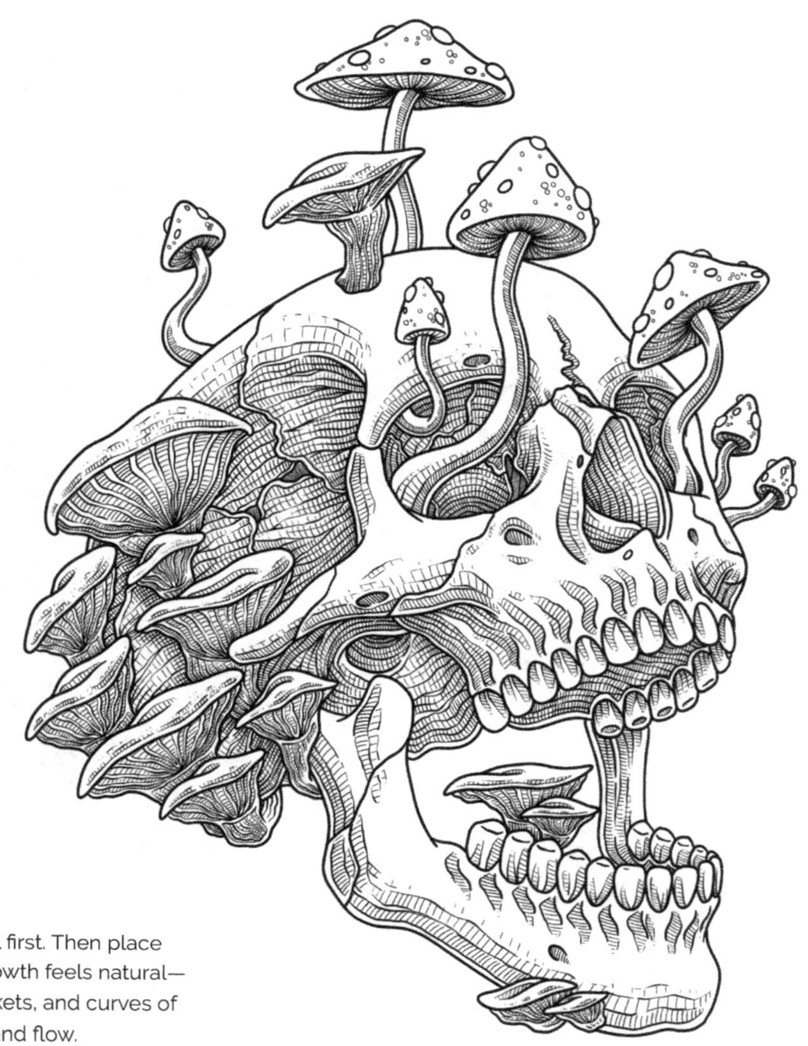

Pro Tip: Draw the skull first. Then place mushrooms where growth feels natural—along cracks, eye sockets, and curves of the bone for balance and flow.

01

02

03

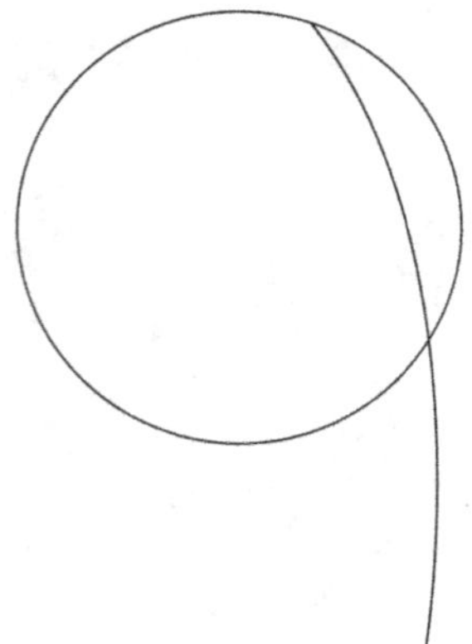

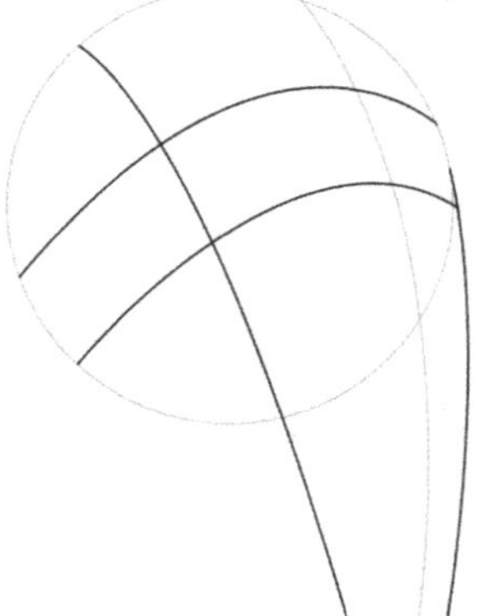

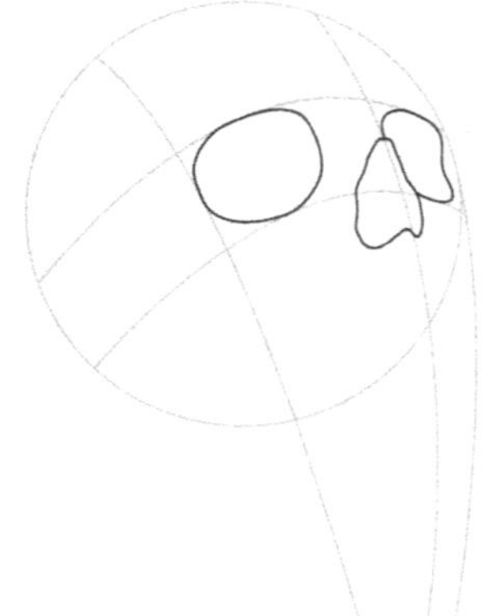

04

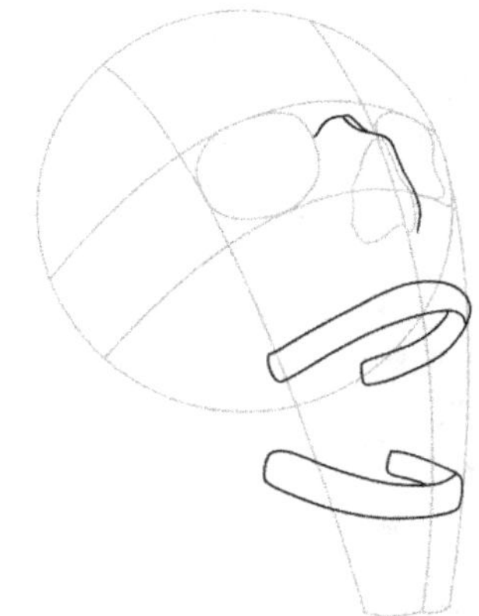

05

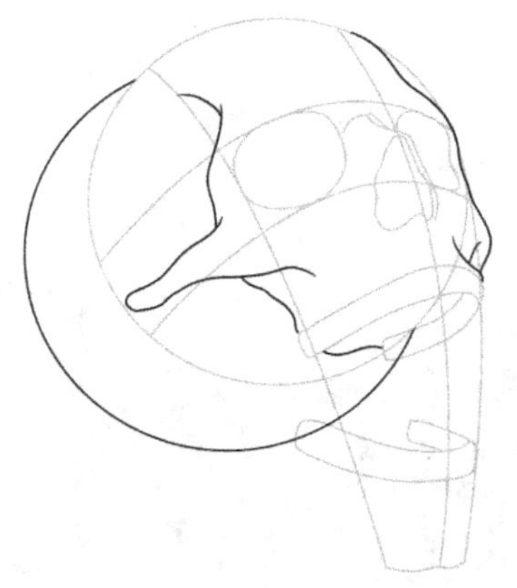

06

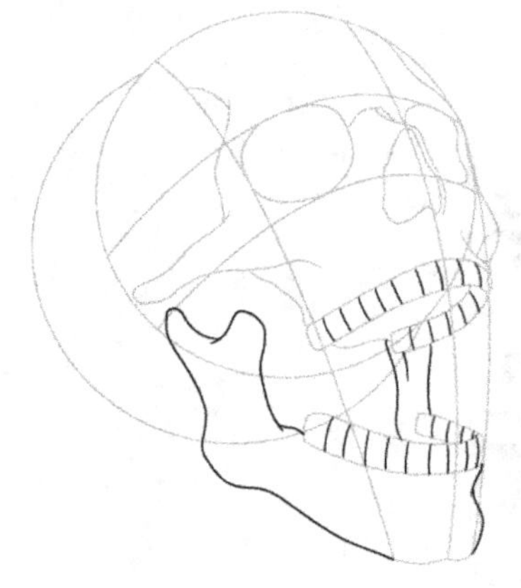

07

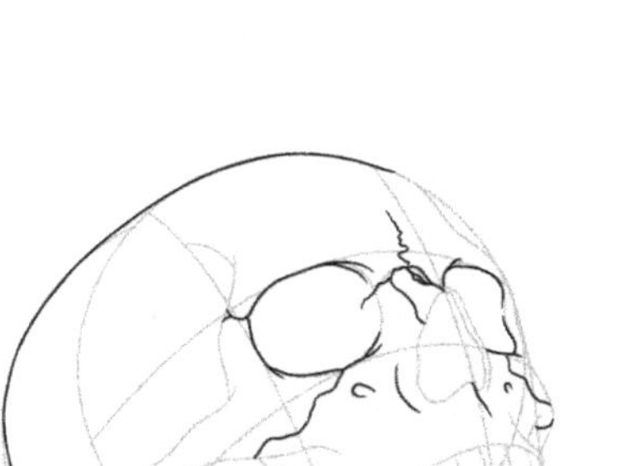

08

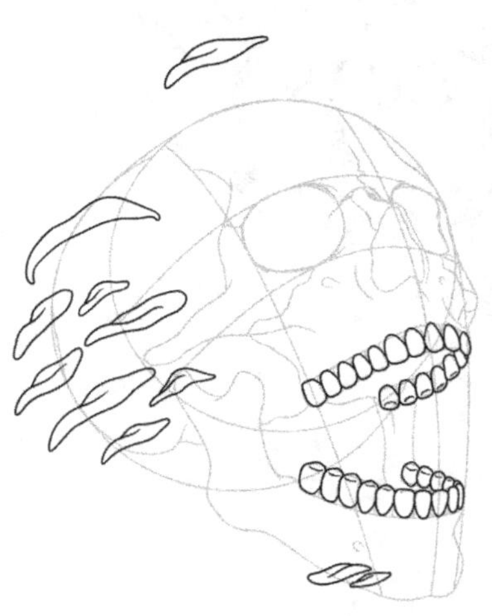

09

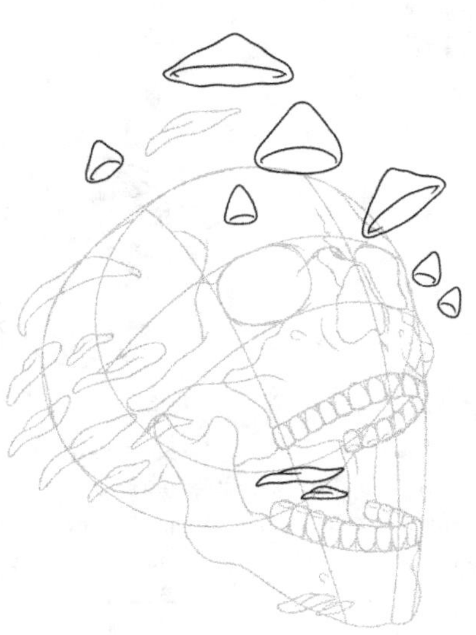

10

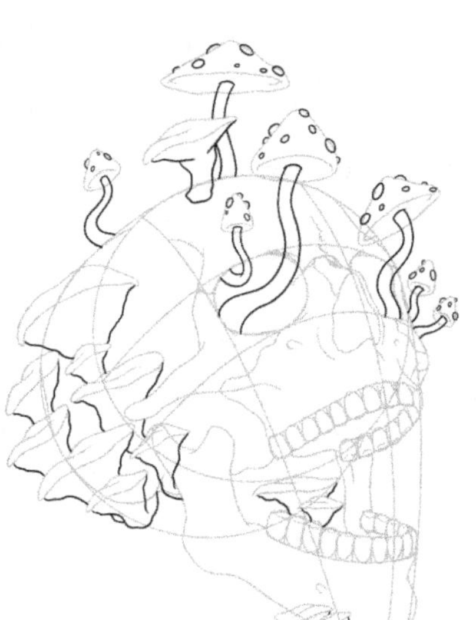

11

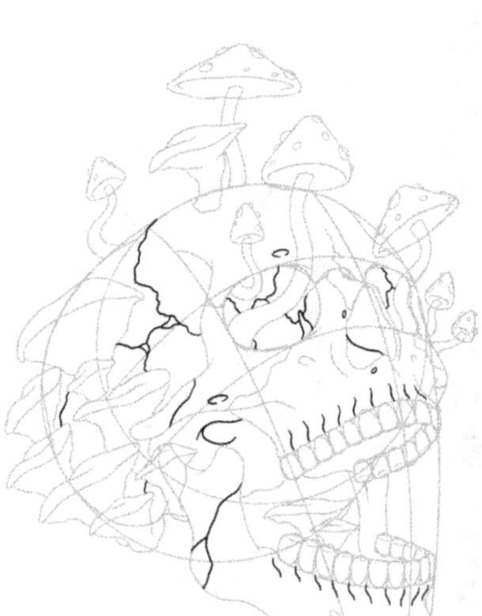

12

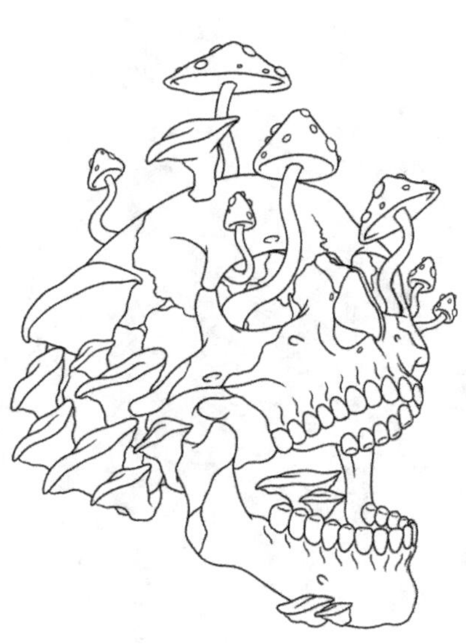

HOW TO DRAW SKULLS

SKULL WITH PIPE

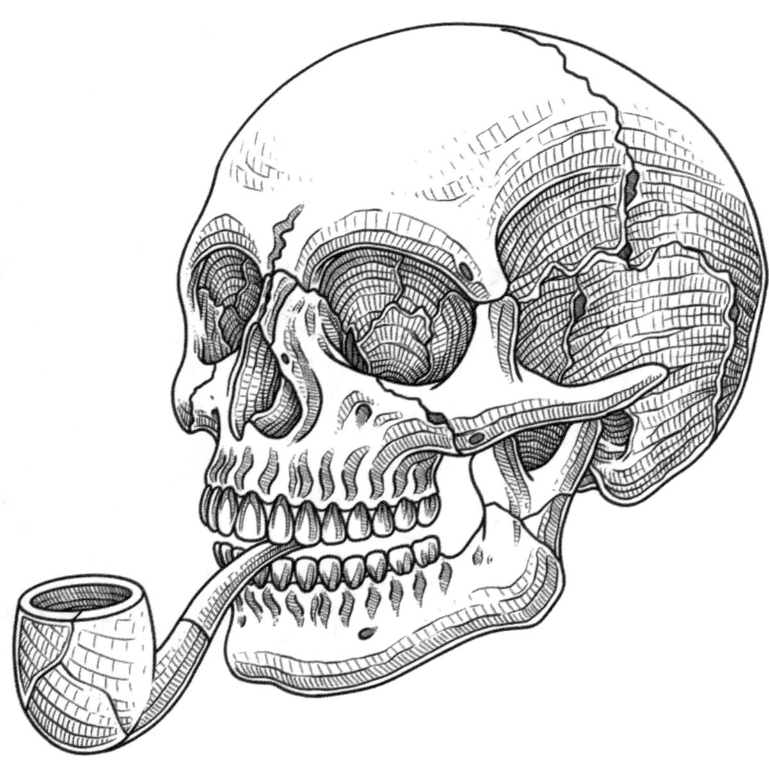

Pro Tip: Start with the skull's form. Then draw the pipe resting between the teeth, aligning the stem with the mouth's opening and adjusting the angle for a natural look and feel.

01

02

03

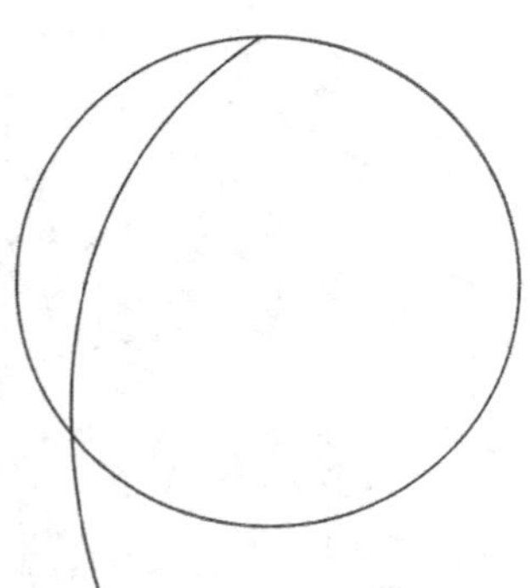

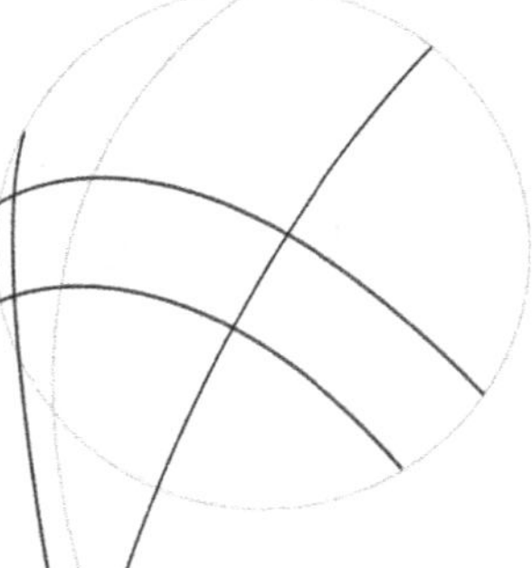

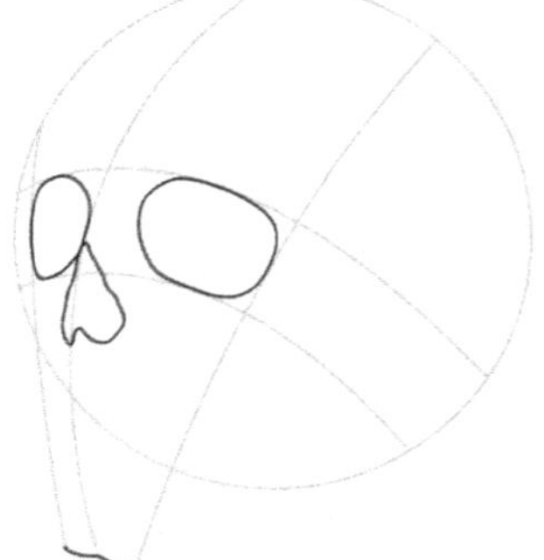

04

05

06

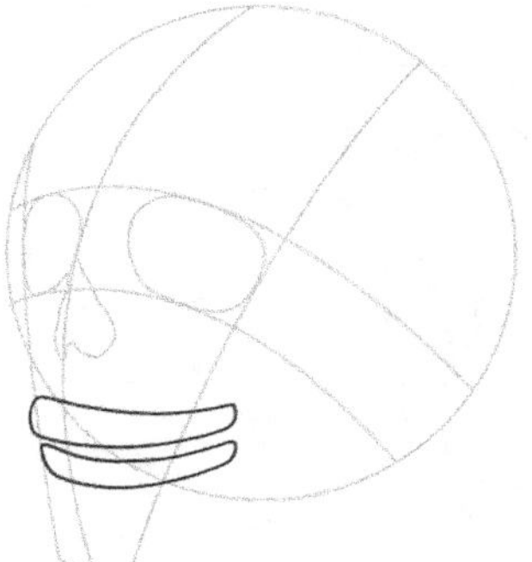
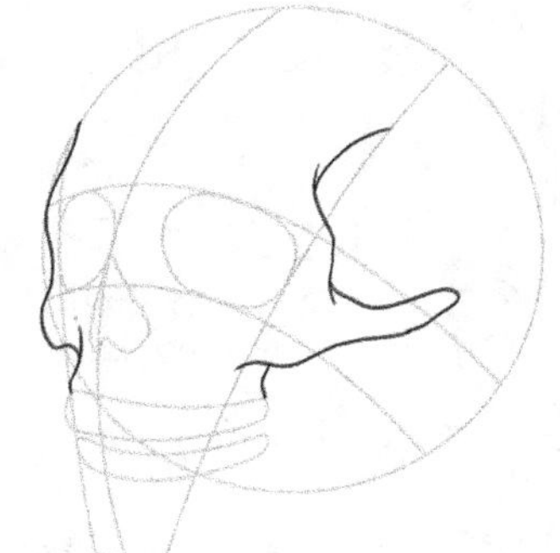
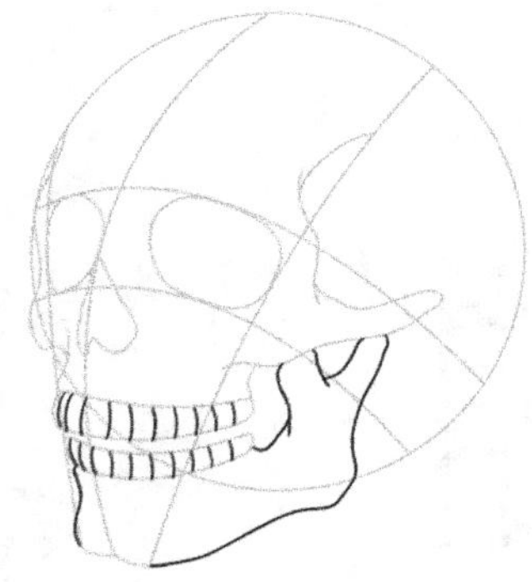

07

08

09

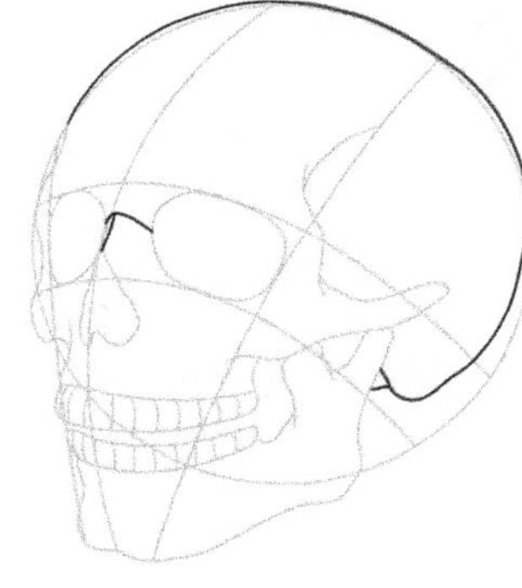
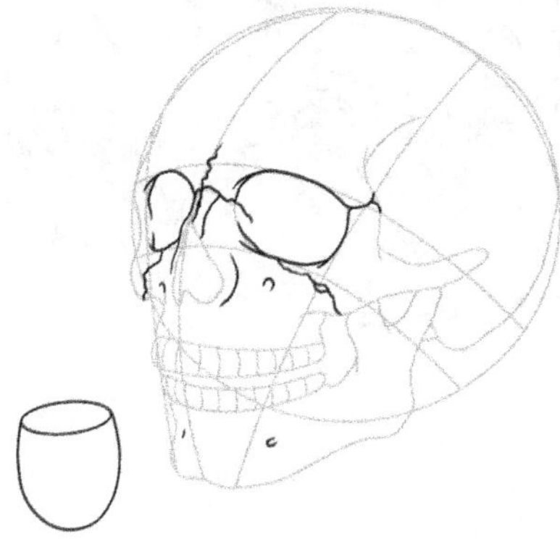
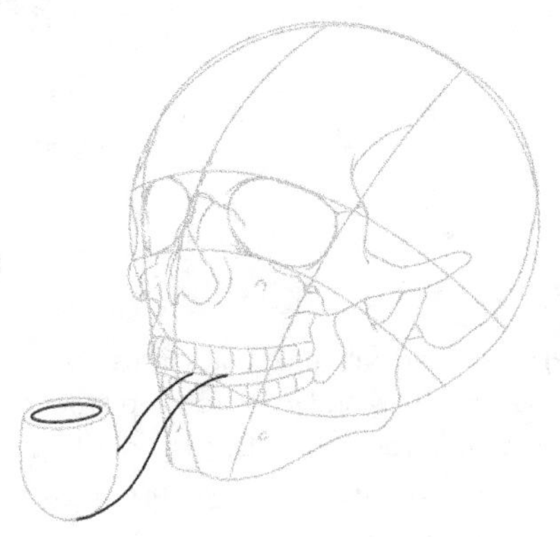

10

11

12

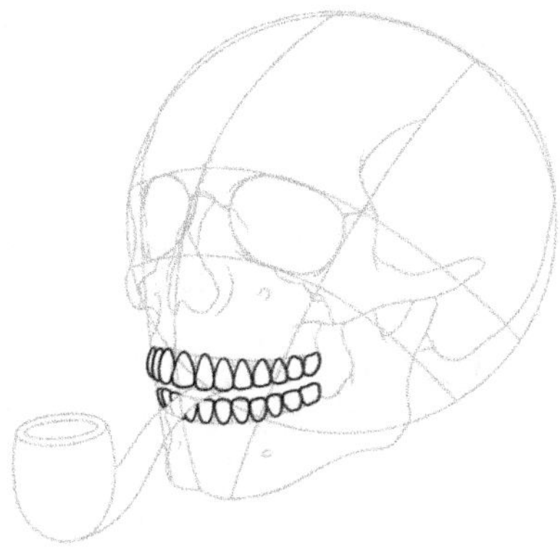
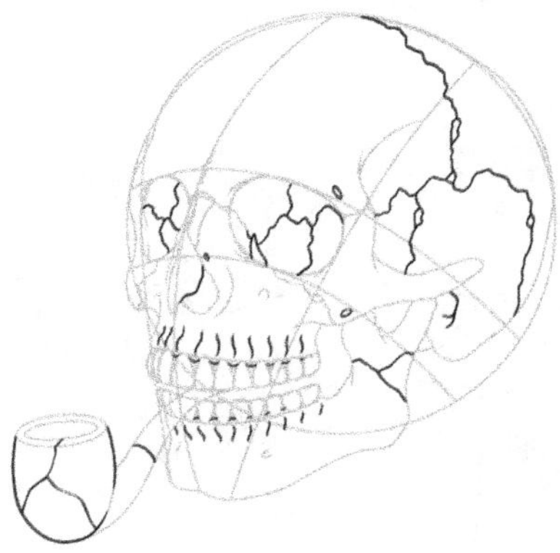
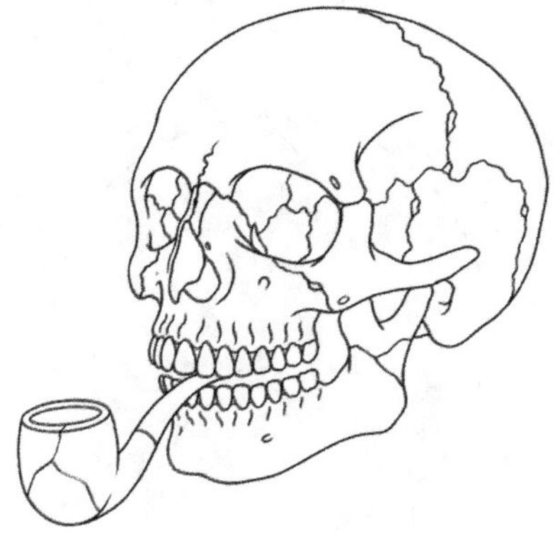

SKULL & ROSES

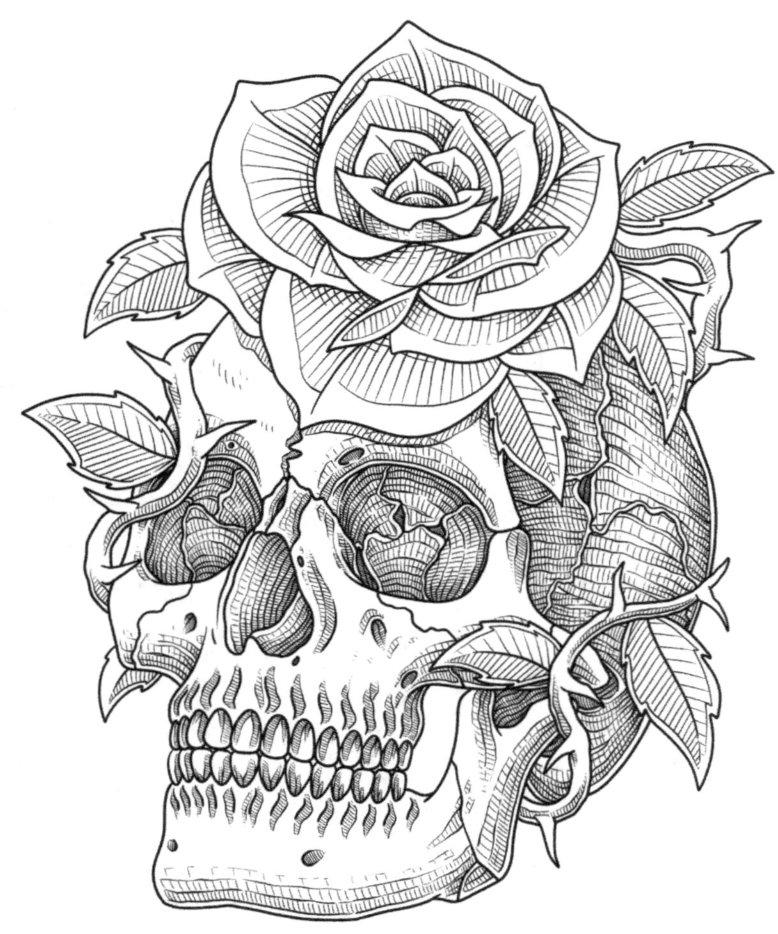

Pro Tip: Start with the skull's form. Then build the roses and vines to wrap around the cranium and cheekbones, adjusting placement for a balanced composition.

01

02

03

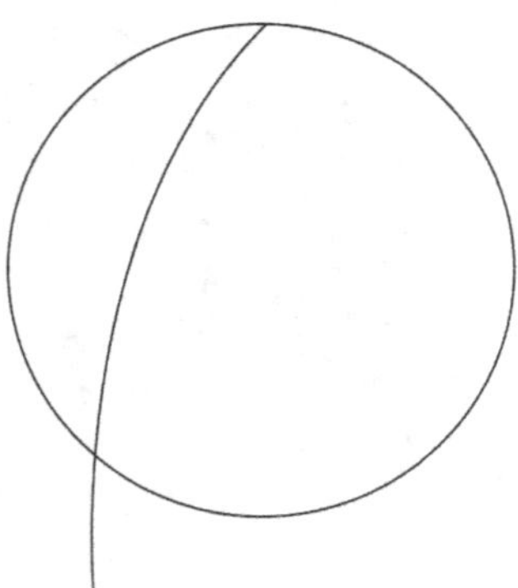

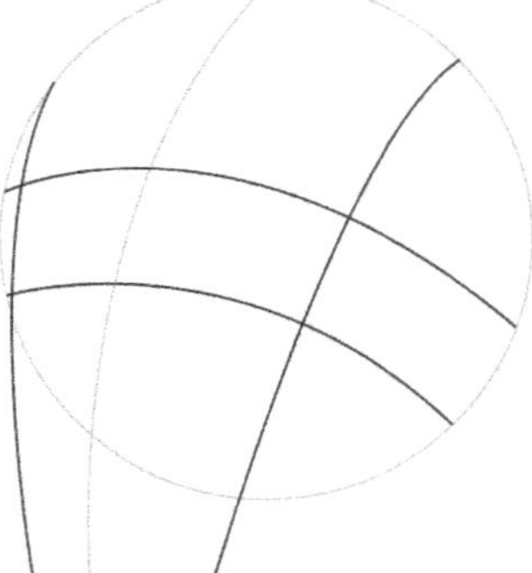

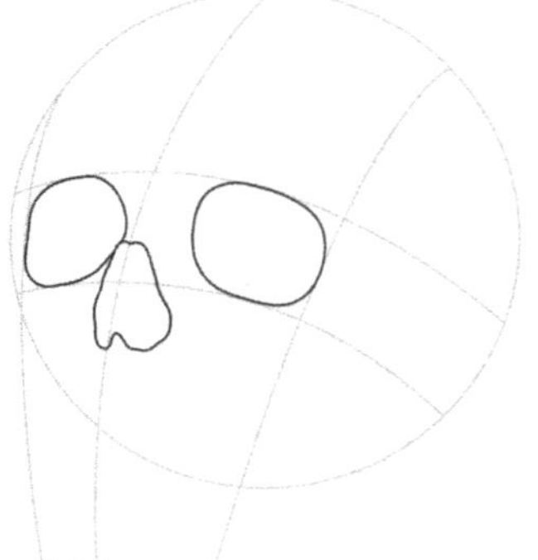

04

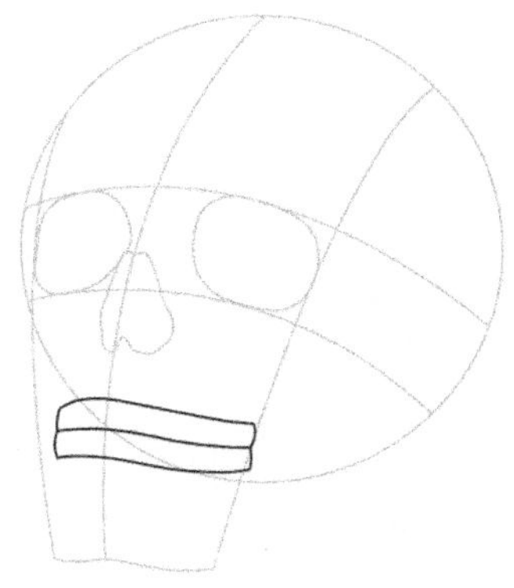

05

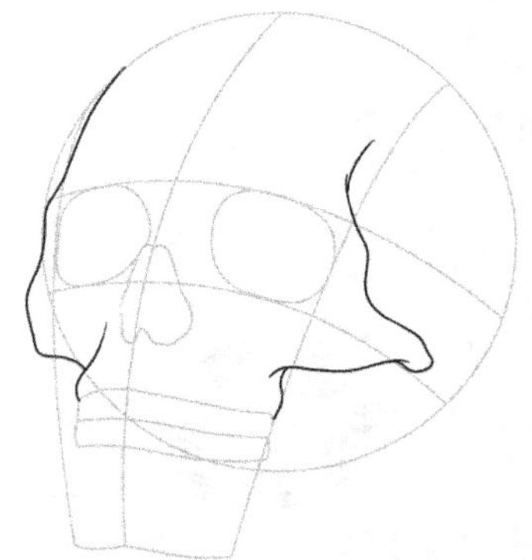

06

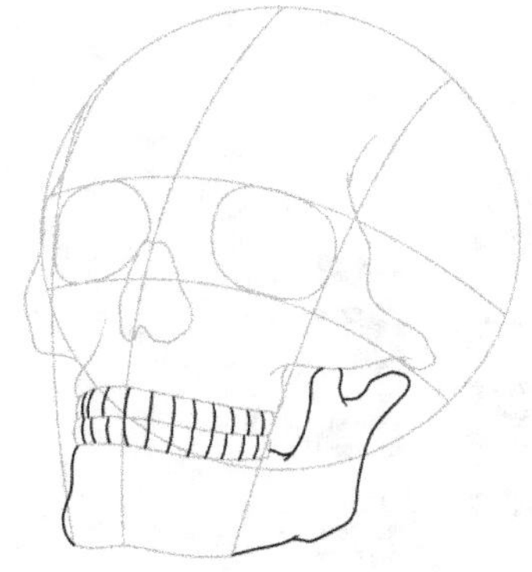

07

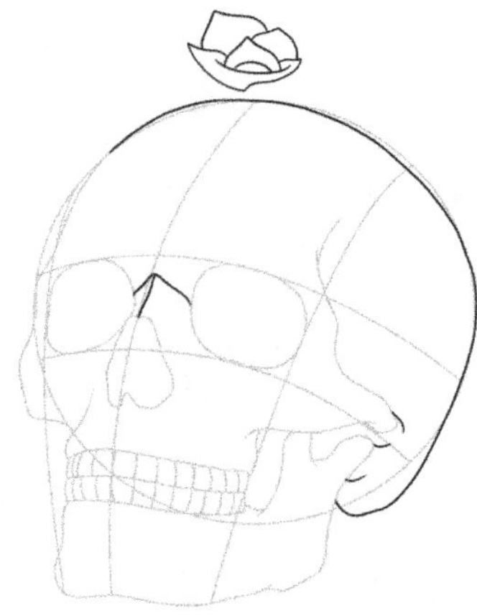

08

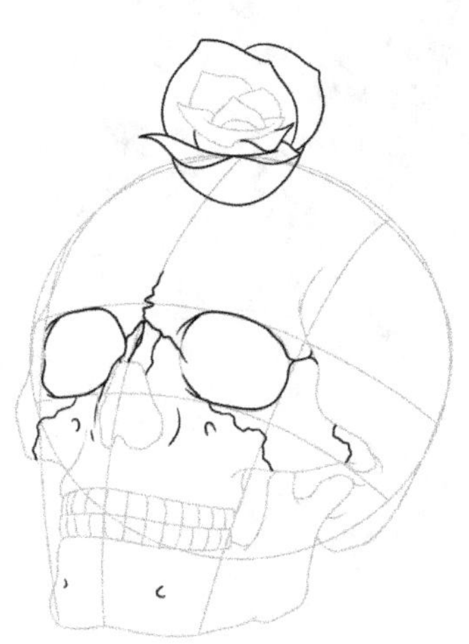

09

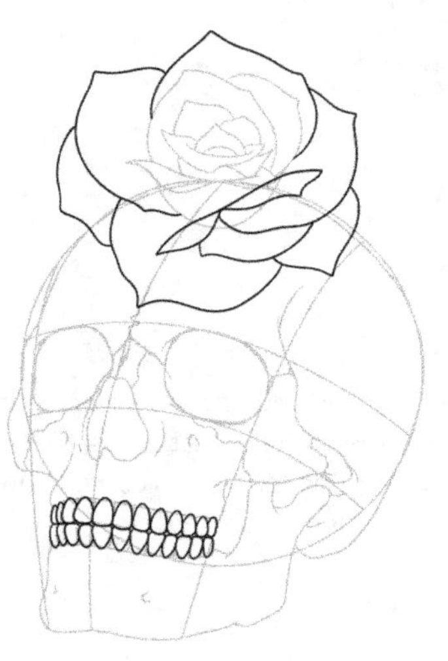

10

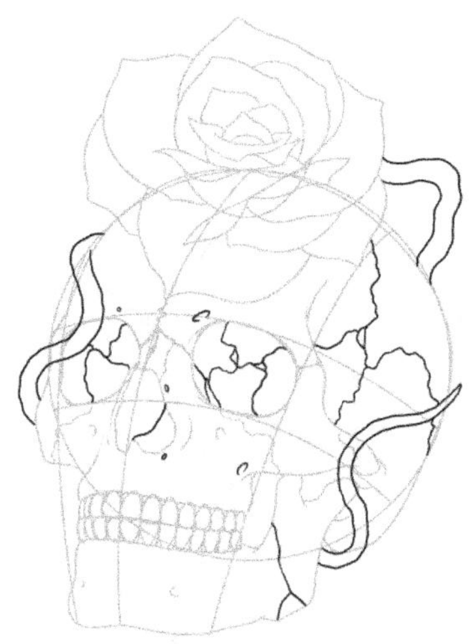

11

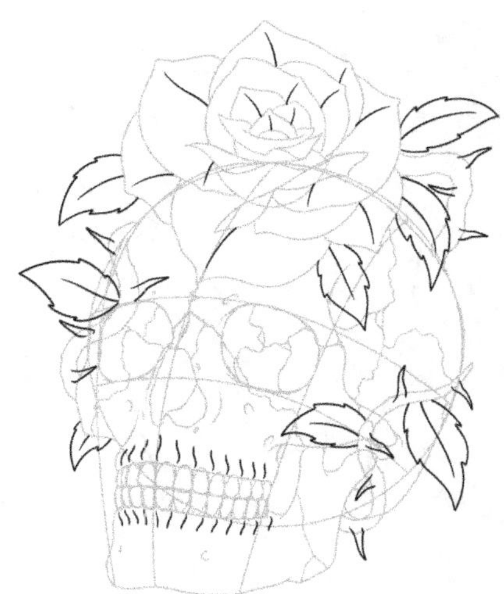

12

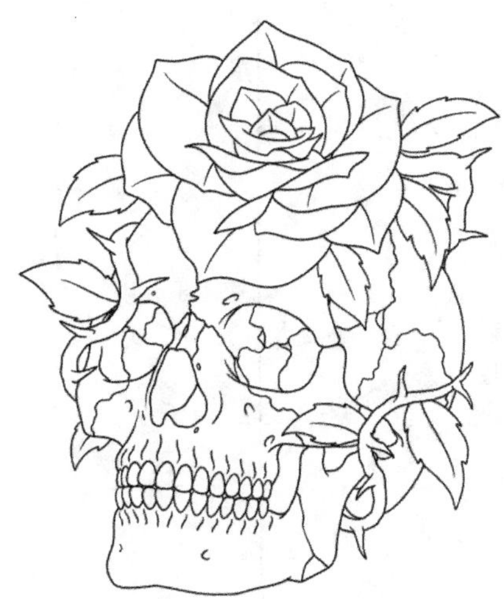

HOW TO DRAW SKULLS

MYSTIC SKULL WITH THIRD EYE

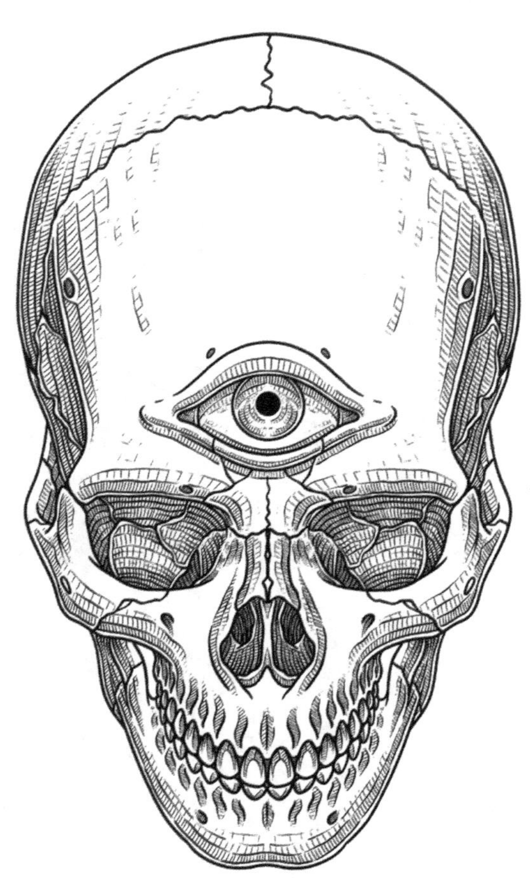

Pro Tip: Start with the skull's form. Then centre the third eye just above the brow line, using the forehead's curve to guide its shape and placement.

01   02   03

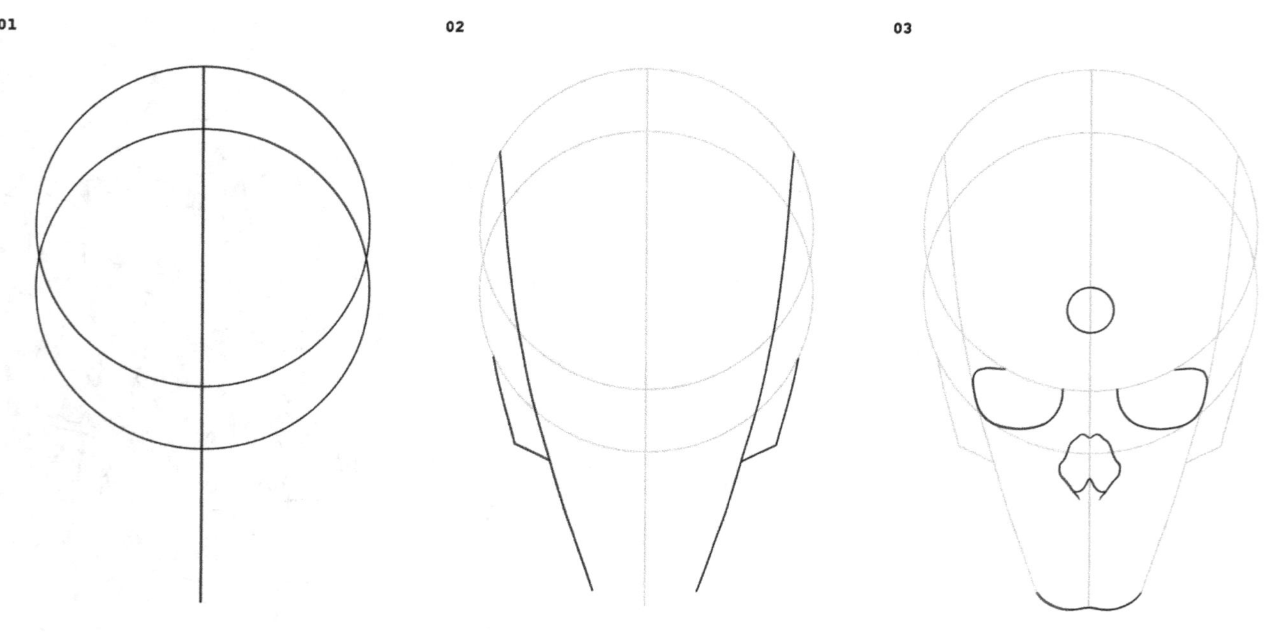

04

05

06

07

08

09

10

11

12

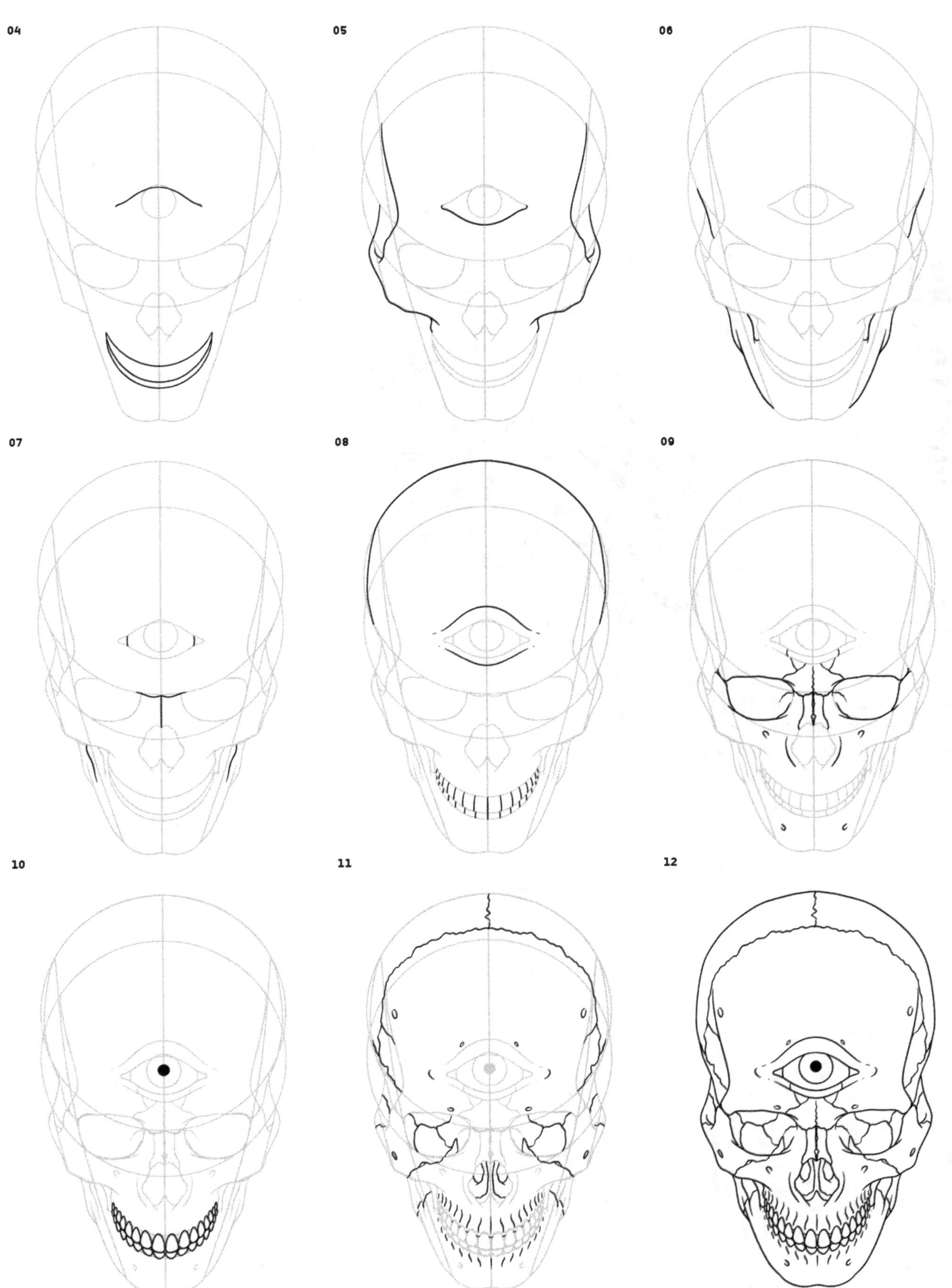

WINGED SKULL

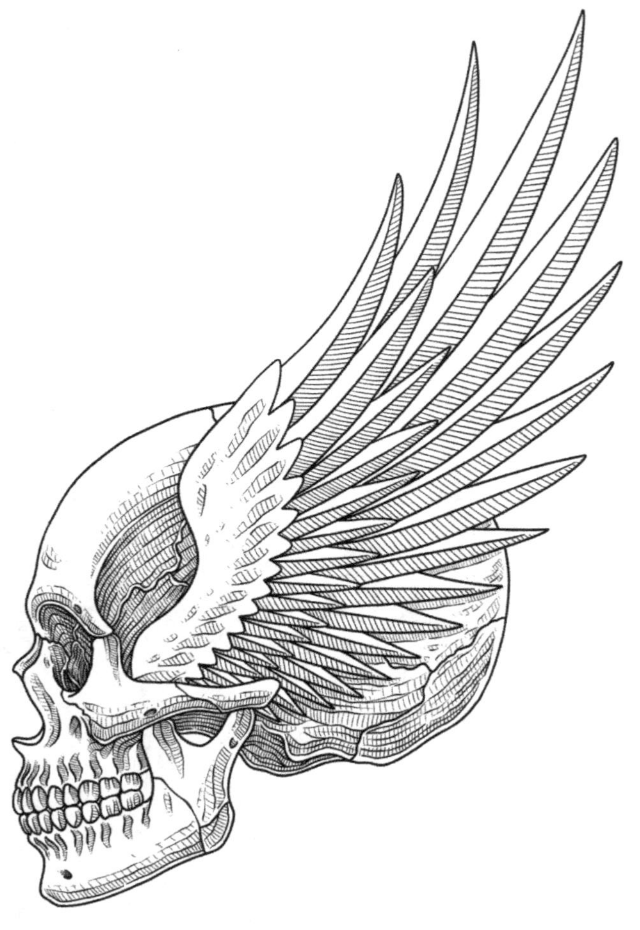

Pro Tip: Start with the skull's form. Then map the wing so it anchors behind the cheekbone, letting the feathers follow the curve of the cranium.

01

02

03

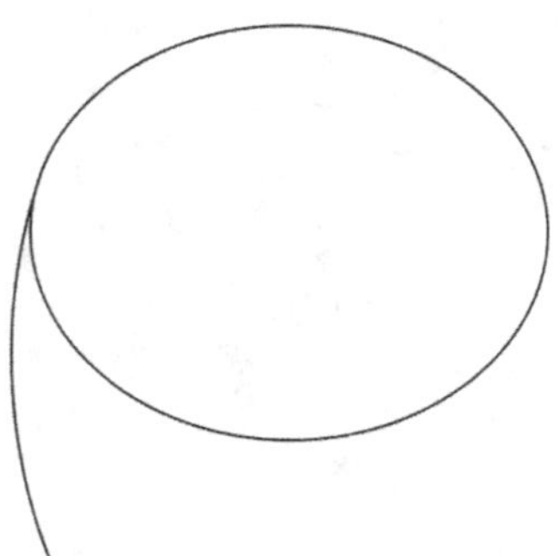

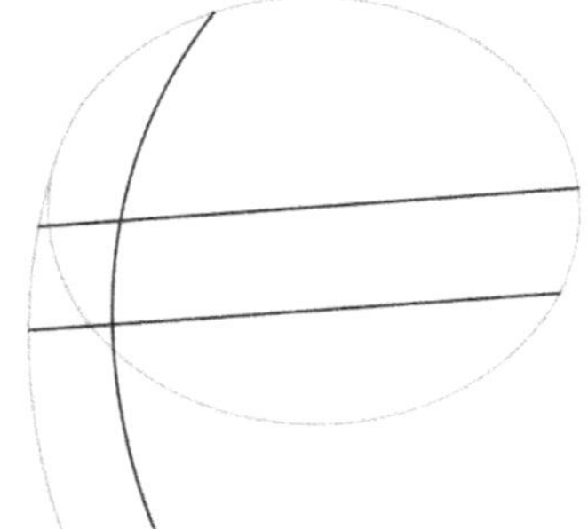

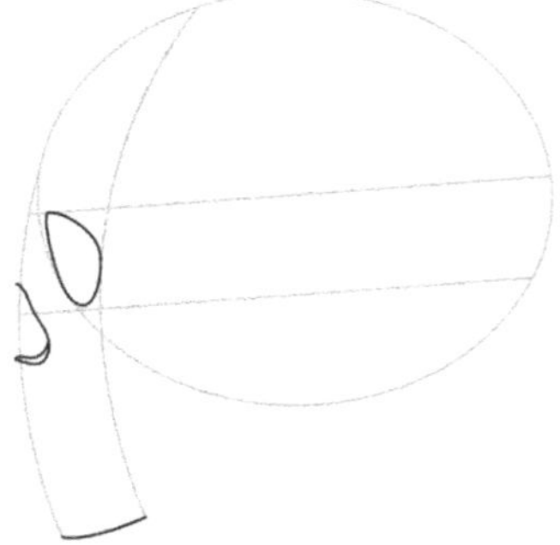

04   05   06

07   08   09

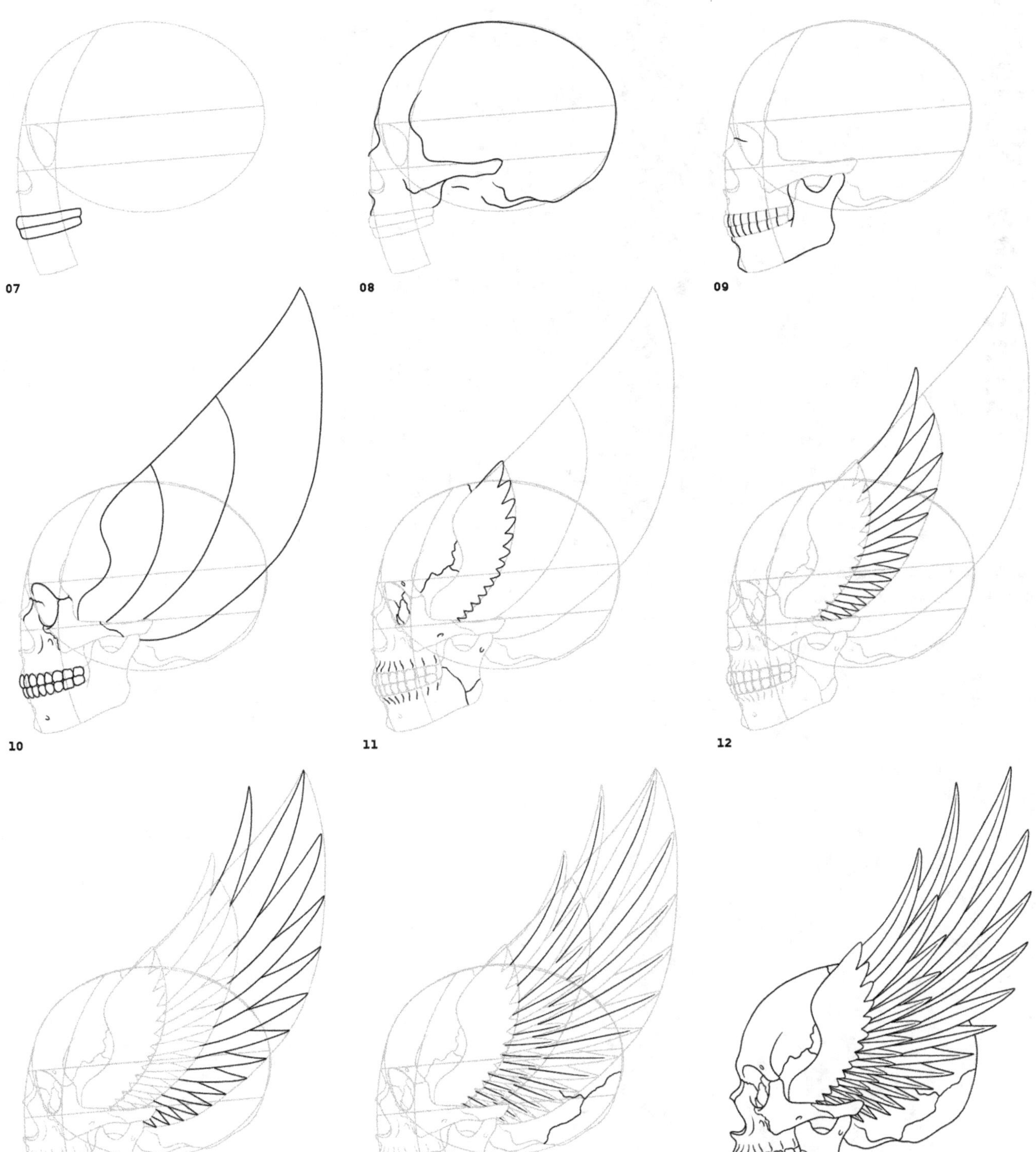

10   11   12

SKELETONS EMBRACING

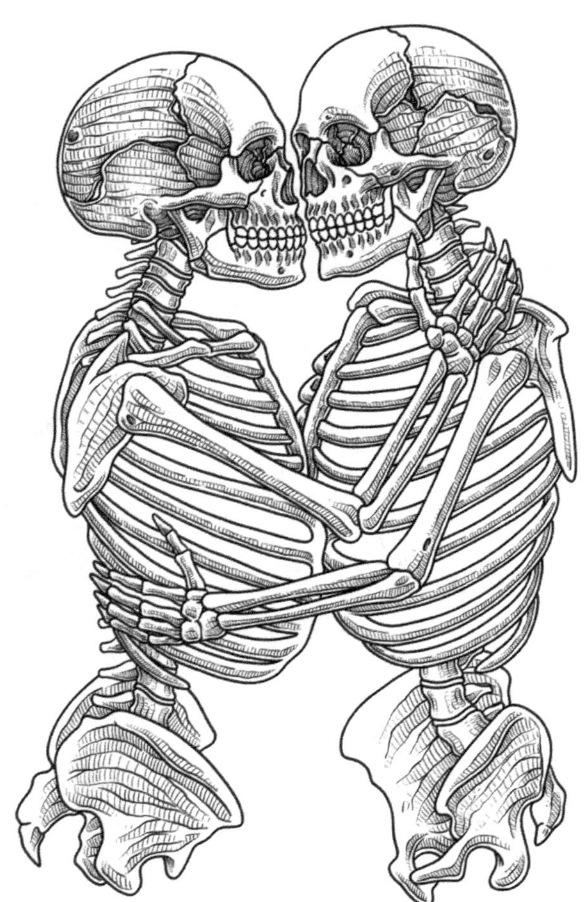

Pro Tip: Draw both skeletons together from the start, focusing on posture, proportion, and symmetry. Let the arms and hands interlock naturally to convey the embrace.

01

02

03

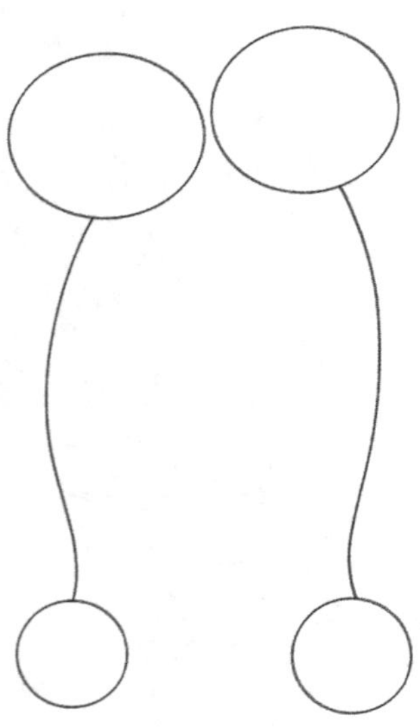

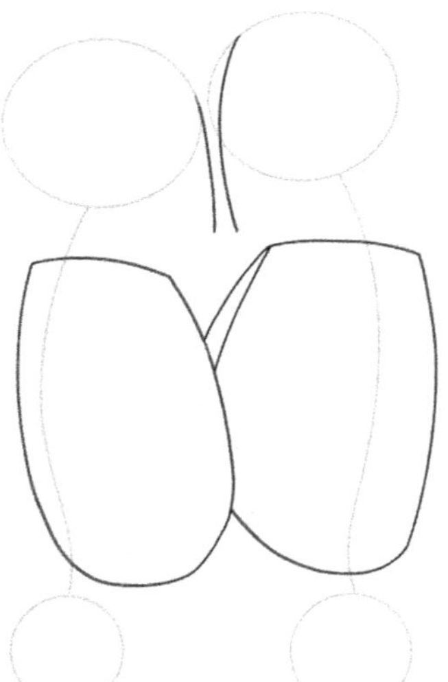

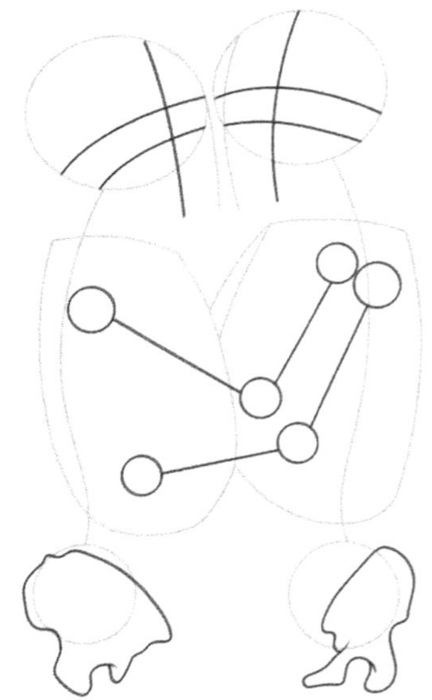

04

05

06

07

08

09

10

11

12

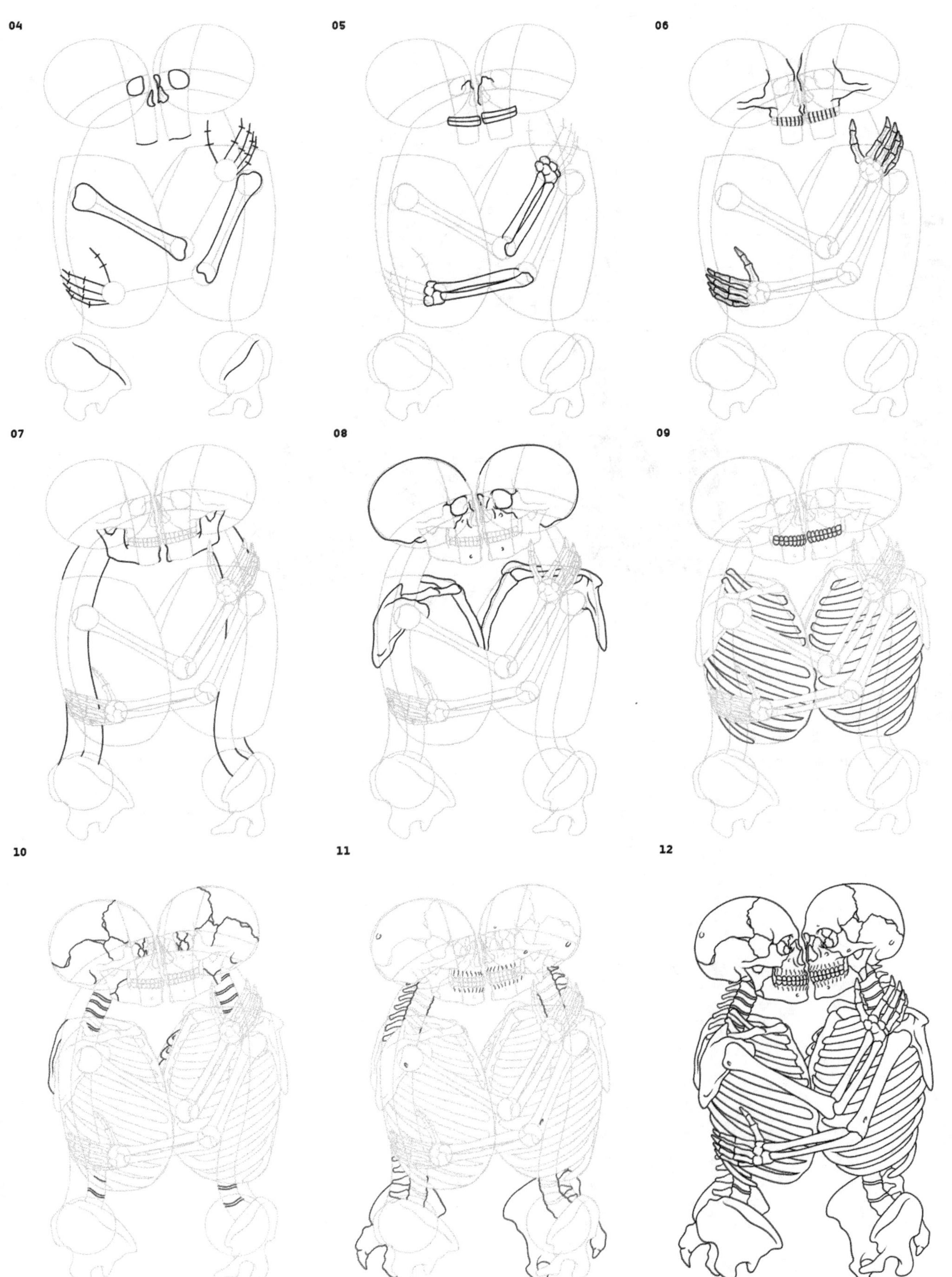

PILE OF SKULLS

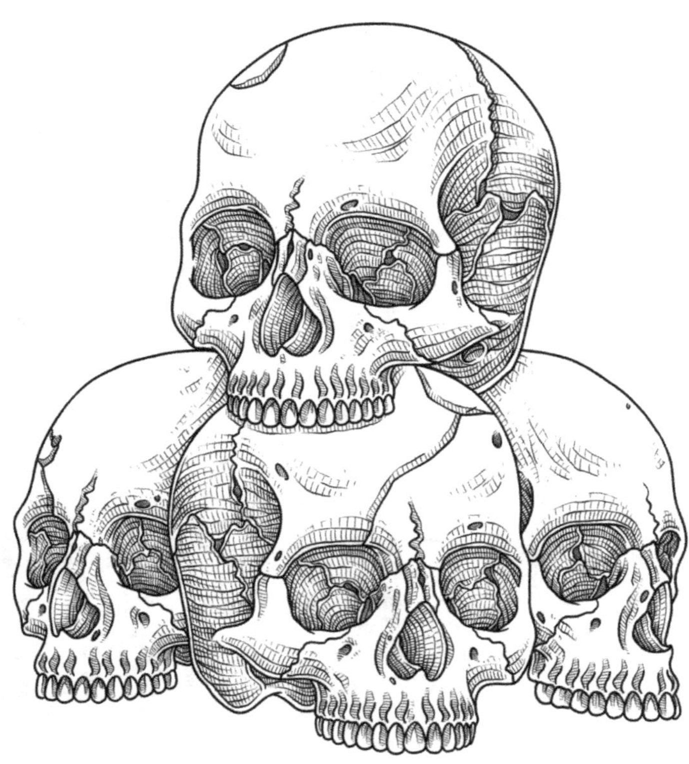

Pro Tip: Start with basic shapes to map the position, tilt, and overlap of each skull. Focus on varying the angles and layering to create depth before refining the forms.

01   02   03

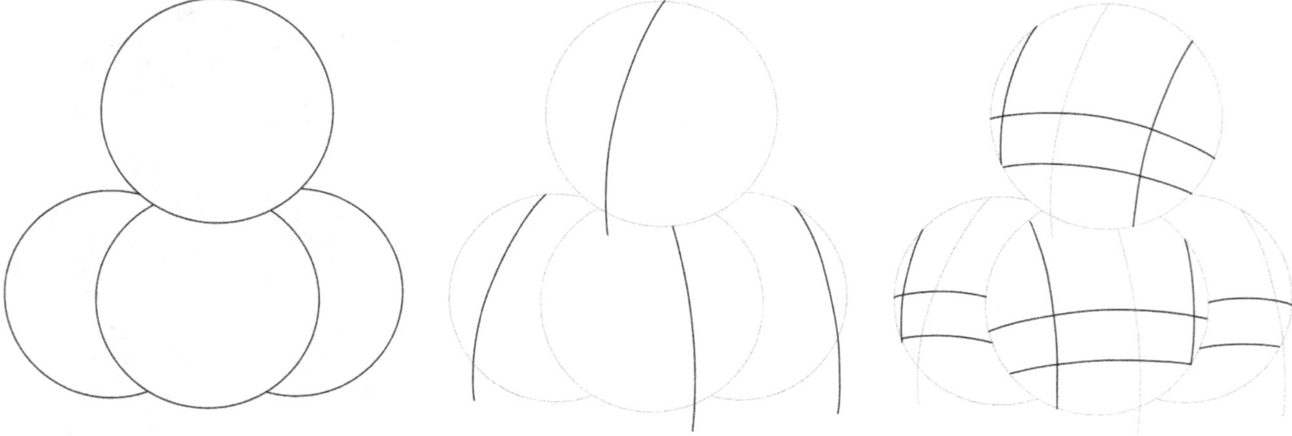

04

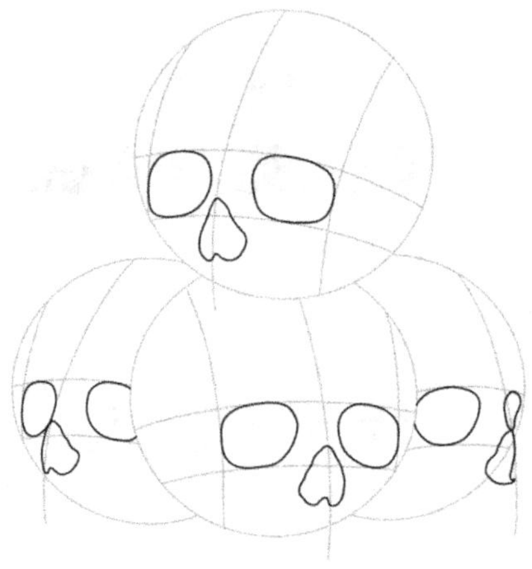

05

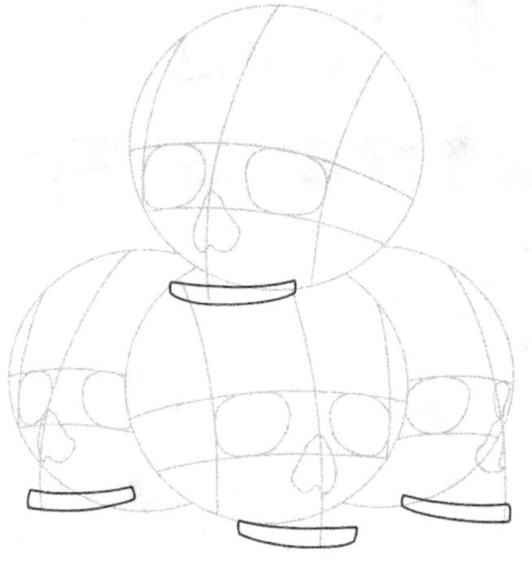

06

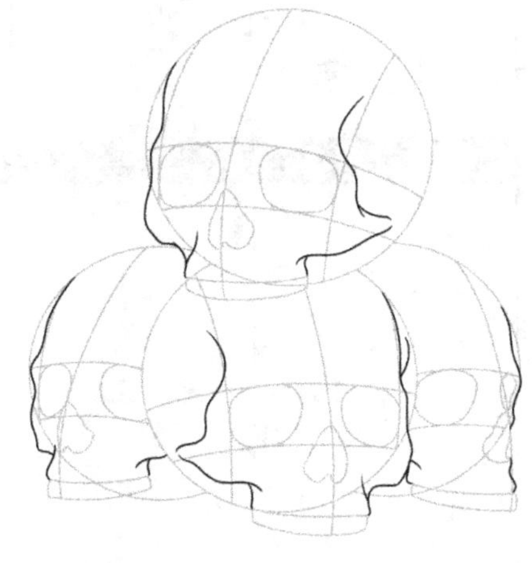

07

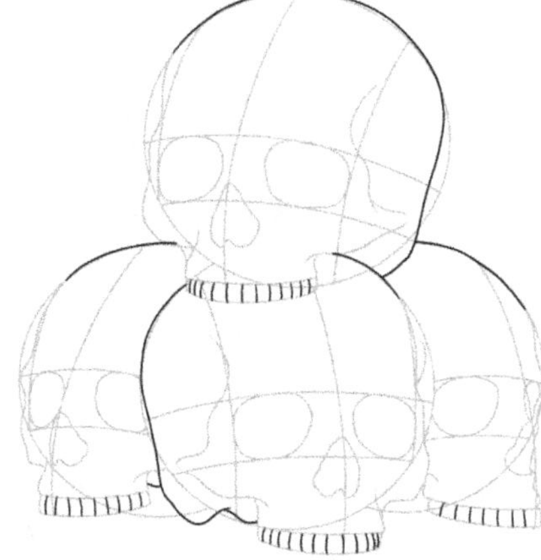

08

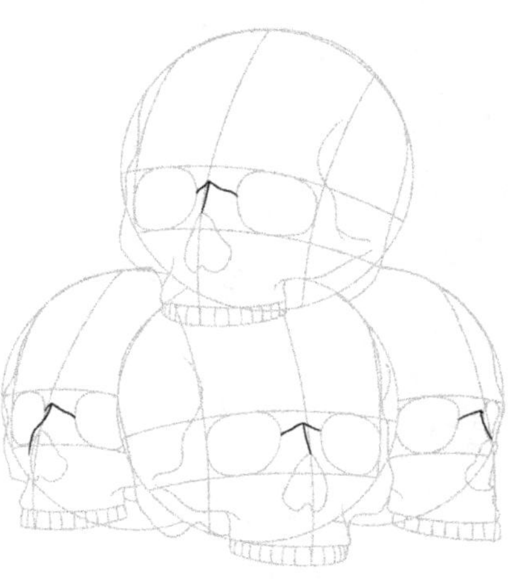

09

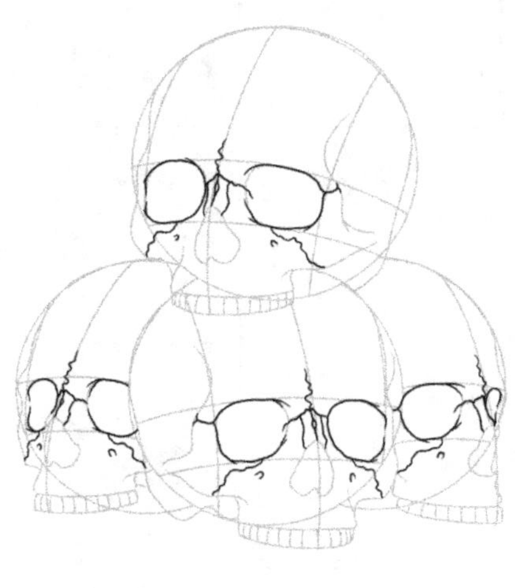

10

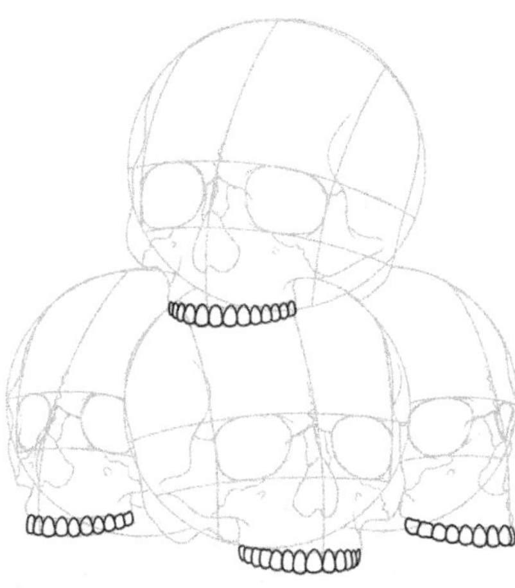

11

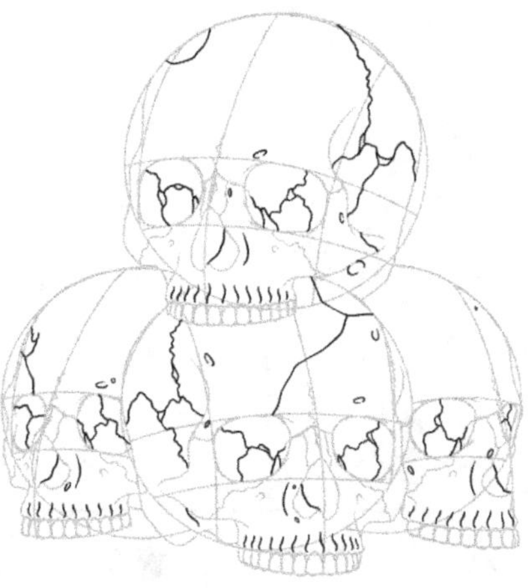

12

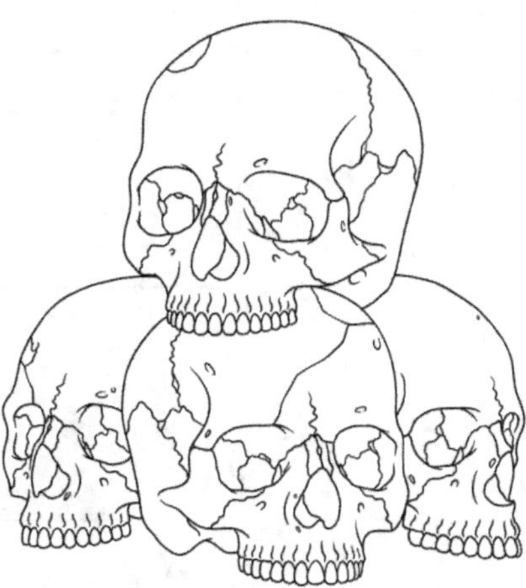

PRACTICE MAKES PERFECT
T R D   M R K

HOW TO DRAW
SKULLS

PRACTICE MAKES PERFECT
T R D   M R K

Vault Editions Ltd

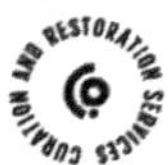

LEARN MORE

VAULTEDITIONS.COM

HOW TO DRAW SKULLS

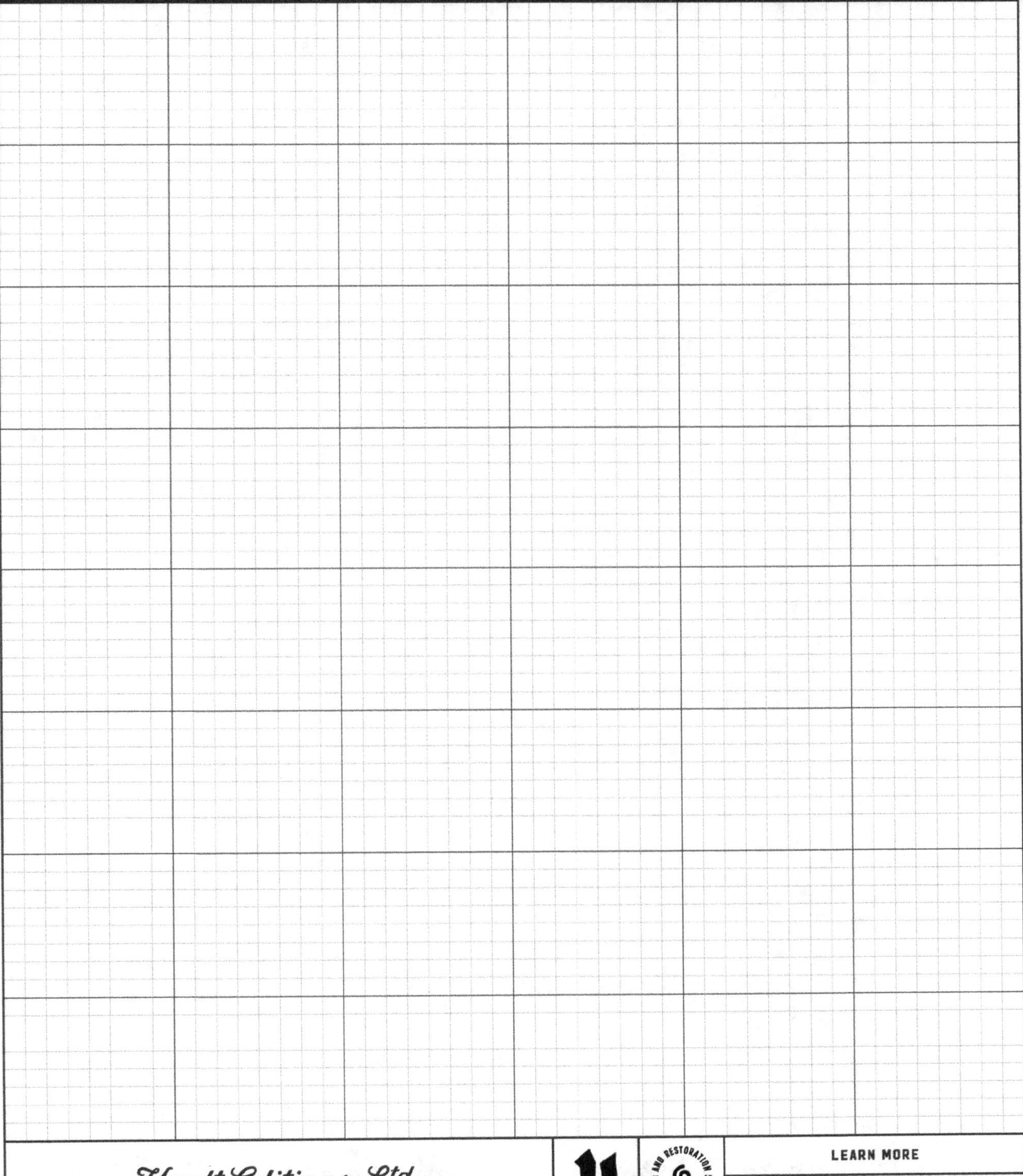

Vault Editions Ltd

LEARN MORE

VAULTEDITIONS.COM

HOW TO DRAW
SKULLS

HOW TO DRAW SKULLS

Vault Editions Ltd

LEARN MORE

VAULTEDITIONS.COM

HOW TO DRAW SKULLS

Vault Editions Ltd

LEARN MORE

VAULTEDITIONS.COM

PRACTICE MAKES PERFECT
T R D   M R K

HOW TO DRAW SKULLS

PRACTICE MAKES PERFECT
T R D   M R K

Vault Editions Ltd

CURATION AND RESTORATION SERVICES

LEARN MORE

VAULTEDITIONS.COM

PRACTICE MAKES PERFECT
T R D   M R K

HOW TO DRAW
SKULLS

PRACTICE MAKES PERFECT
T R D   M R K

Vault Editions Ltd

LEARN MORE

VAULTEDITIONS.COM

SERVICES CURATION AND RESTORATION

PRACTICE MAKES PERFECT
T R D   M R K

HOW TO DRAW
SKULLS

PRACTICE MAKES PERFECT
T R D   M R K

Vault Editions Ltd

CURATION AND RESTORATION SERVICES

LEARN MORE

VAULTEDITIONS.COM

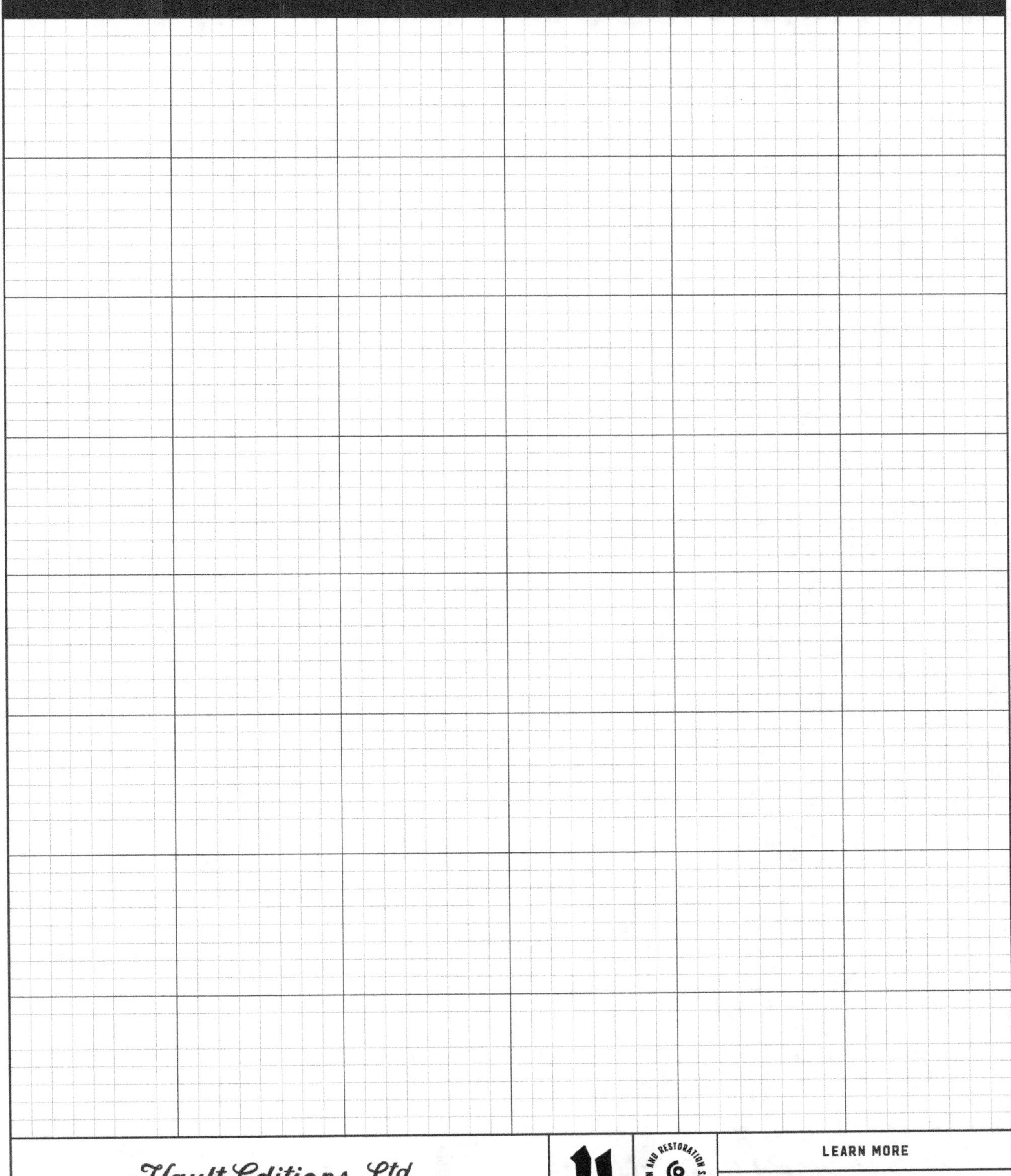

Vault Editions Ltd

LEARN MORE

VAULTEDITIONS.COM

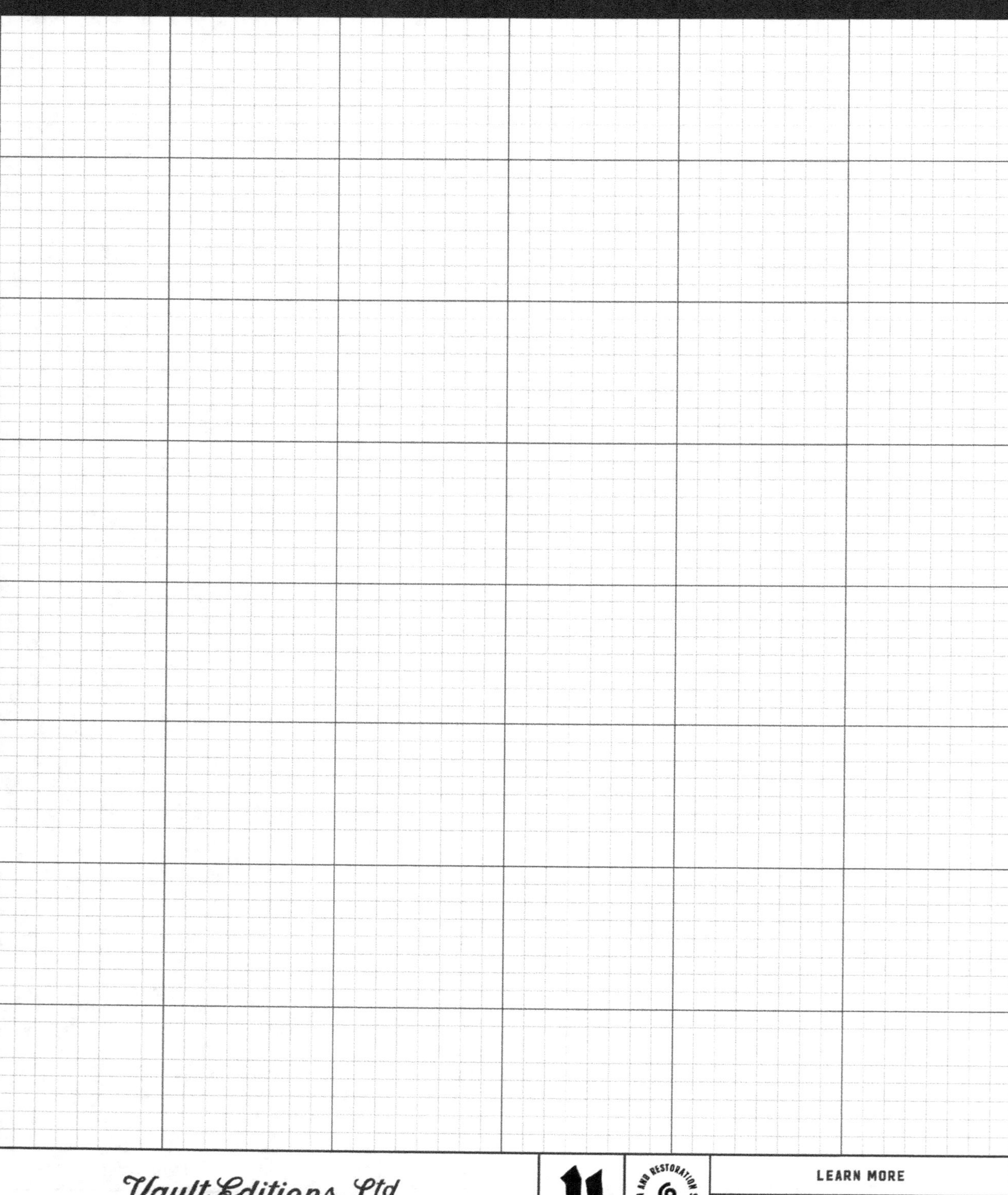
PRACTICE
MAKES
PERFECT
HOW TO DRAW
SKULLS
PRACTICE
MAKES
PERFECT
Vault Editions Ltd
LEARN MORE
VAULTEDITIONS.COM

HOW TO DRAW
SKULLS

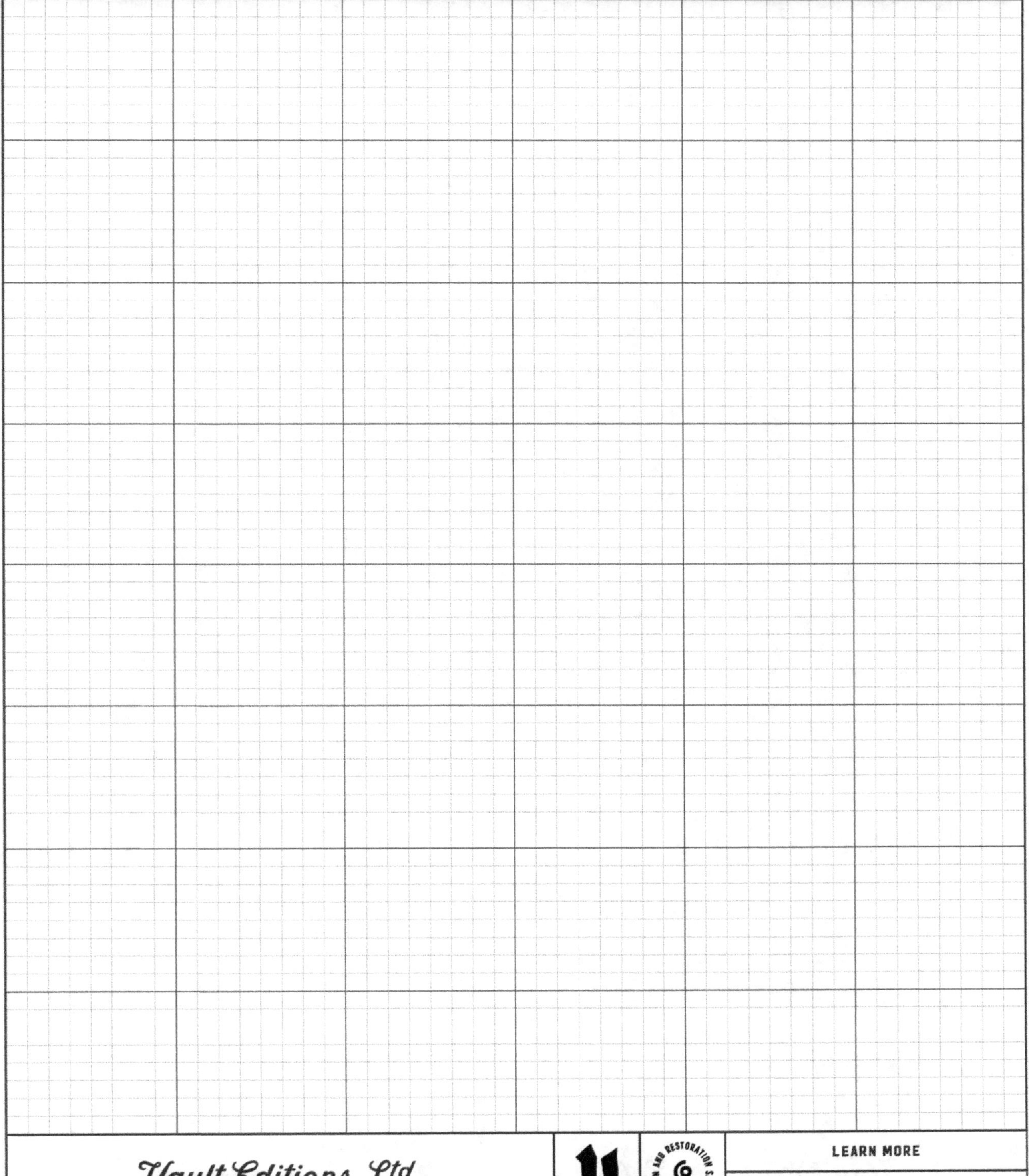

Vault Editions Ltd

CURATION AND RESTORATION SERVICES

LEARN MORE

VAULTEDITIONS.COM

HOW TO DRAW SKULLS

PRACTICE MAKES PERFECT
T R D · M R K

HOW TO DRAW
SKULLS

PRACTICE MAKES PERFECT
T R D · M R K

HOW TO DRAW SKULLS

Vault Editions Ltd

LEARN MORE

VAULTEDITIONS.COM

PRACTICE MAKES PERFECT
TRD MRK

HOW TO DRAW
SKULLS

PRACTICE MAKES PERFECT
TRD MRK

Vault Editions Ltd

CURATION AND RESTORATION SERVICES

LEARN MORE

VAULTEDITIONS.COM

HOW TO DRAW
SKULLS

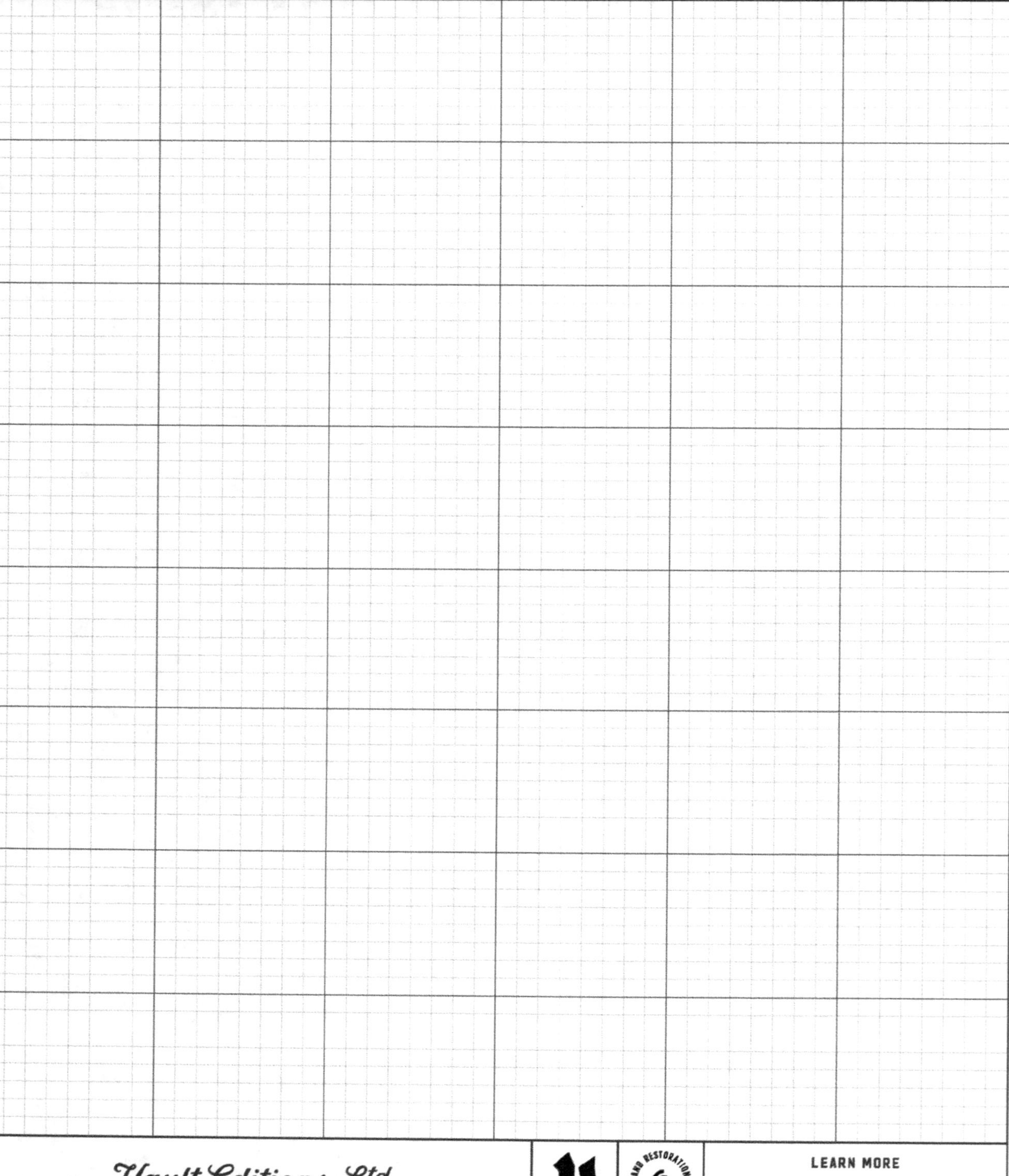

Vault Editions Ltd

ART AND RESTORATION
CURATION SERVICES

LEARN MORE

VAULTEDITIONS.COM

PRACTICE MAKES PERFECT
T R D
M R K

HOW TO DRAW
SKULLS

PRACTICE MAKES PERFECT
T R D
M R K

Vault Editions Ltd

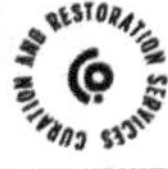

LEARN MORE

VAULTEDITIONS.COM

CONCLUSION

By working through the designs in this book, you've built a solid foundation for drawing skulls with confidence, accuracy, and style. You've learned how to construct the skull from multiple angles, how to balance complex compositions, and how to combine the skull with other classic motifs like flowers, snakes, wings, and fire.

The goal of this book was never for you to copy the artwork perfectly, but to give you the tools to develop your own approach, to understand structure, flow, and form well enough that you can bend, stylise, or exaggerate it however your work demands.

As with anything, repetition is key. Keep drawing skulls. Explore new angles, new variations, and new ideas. Use these designs as references, springboards, or foundations for your own compositions.

Skulls are a timeless symbol, whether they represent mortality, strength, rebellion, or transformation. Mastering them will only strengthen your creative toolkit as an artist, tattooer, or designer.

Thank you for joining us on this creative journey. May your study of skulls continue to sharpen your skills, fuel your curiosity, and deepen your understanding of this timeless symbol.

ABOUT THE ARTIST

Syadat Baihaqi, known as Blasphemy Ink, is an illustrator specialising in dark, intricate artwork that draws on themes of death, mythology, and the occult. His black-and-white compositions often feature skeletal figures, decayed forms, and surreal, otherworldly imagery inspired by gothic art, metal music, and symbolic ideologies.

Blasphemy Ink's work is defined by its fine linework, rich textures, and a strong sense of atmosphere. Each illustration invites the viewer into a world where the grotesque meets the beautiful, where decay is rendered with precision and reverence. His style balances classical drawing techniques with a contemporary edge, resulting in pieces that feel both timeless and raw.

Syadat's art has been used across various creative projects, including album covers, apparel, and personal commissions. His illustrations are visually bold, emotionally charged, and deeply rooted in storytelling—offering a distinctive voice in the world of dark art.

LEARN MORE

At Vault Editions, our mission is to provide the highest-quality reference materials for artists and designers, offering meticulously curated resources that inspire and empower creativity. If you've found value in this book, we invite you to explore more of our expertly crafted titles at vaulteditions.com, where you'll discover a world of visual inspiration and practical tools designed to elevate your creative work.

REVIEW THIS BOOK

As a family-owned and operated independent publisher, reviews are essential to the success of our business. Please leave an honest review of this book wherever you purchased it.

JOIN OUR COMMUNITY

Are you the creative and curious type? If so, you will love our community on Instagram. Every day, we share bizarre and beautiful artwork ranging from 17th and 18th-century natural history and scientific illustrations to mythical beasts, ornamental designs, anatomical drawings and more; join our community of 300K+ people today by searching @vault_editions on Instagram.

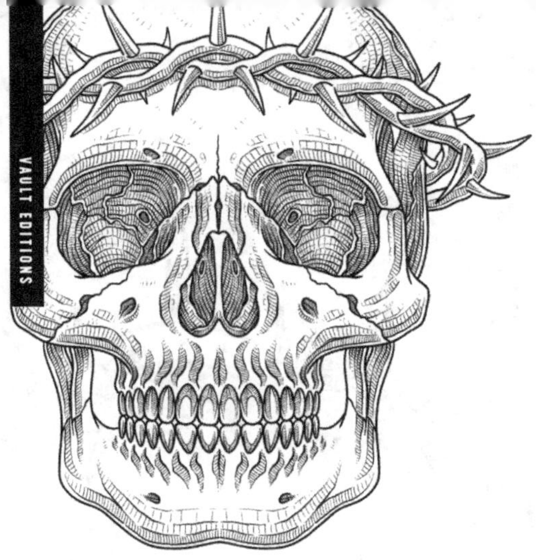

DOWNLOAD YOUR FILES

To enhance your creative journey, How to Draw Tattoo Flash comes with a digital PDF version of the book and a specially designed set of Procreate brushes. These resources are tailored to help you refine your skills and streamline your workflow, whether you're working traditionally or digitally.

The digital PDF provides easy access to the book's contents on any device, so you can reference the designs anytime, anywhere. It's perfect for artists on the go, allowing you to study and practice whenever inspiration strikes.

The custom Procreate brushes are designed to replicate the look and feel of traditional tattoo flash designs, from bold outlining to shading techniques. These brushes make it easier for digital artists to create authentic-looking designs in a digital medium, offering precision and flexibility as you sketch, refine, and finalise your artwork. Whether you're experimenting with new ideas or perfecting your final designs, these brushes allow you to bring your creations to life with the same iconic style that defines classic tattoo flash.

Download yours now and get creating!

STEP ONE

Enter the following web address on a desktop or laptop computer in your web browser.

vaulteditions.com/pages/hts

STEP TWO

Enter the following password to access the download page:

hts77636sxda

STEP THREE

Follow the prompts to access your high-resolution files.

CONTACT

For technical support, please email: info@vaulteditions.com

Copyright © 2025
Vault Editions Ltd

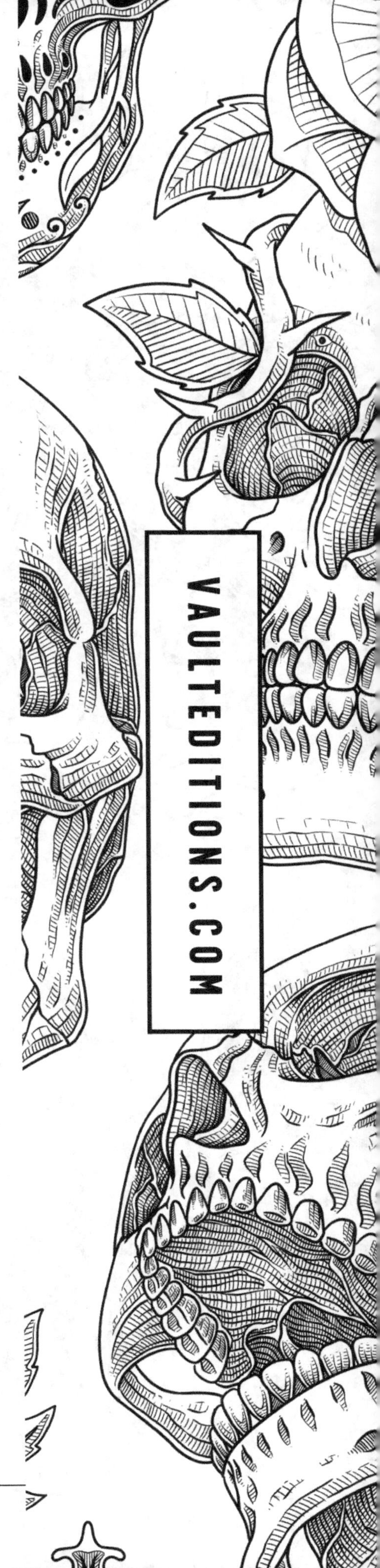

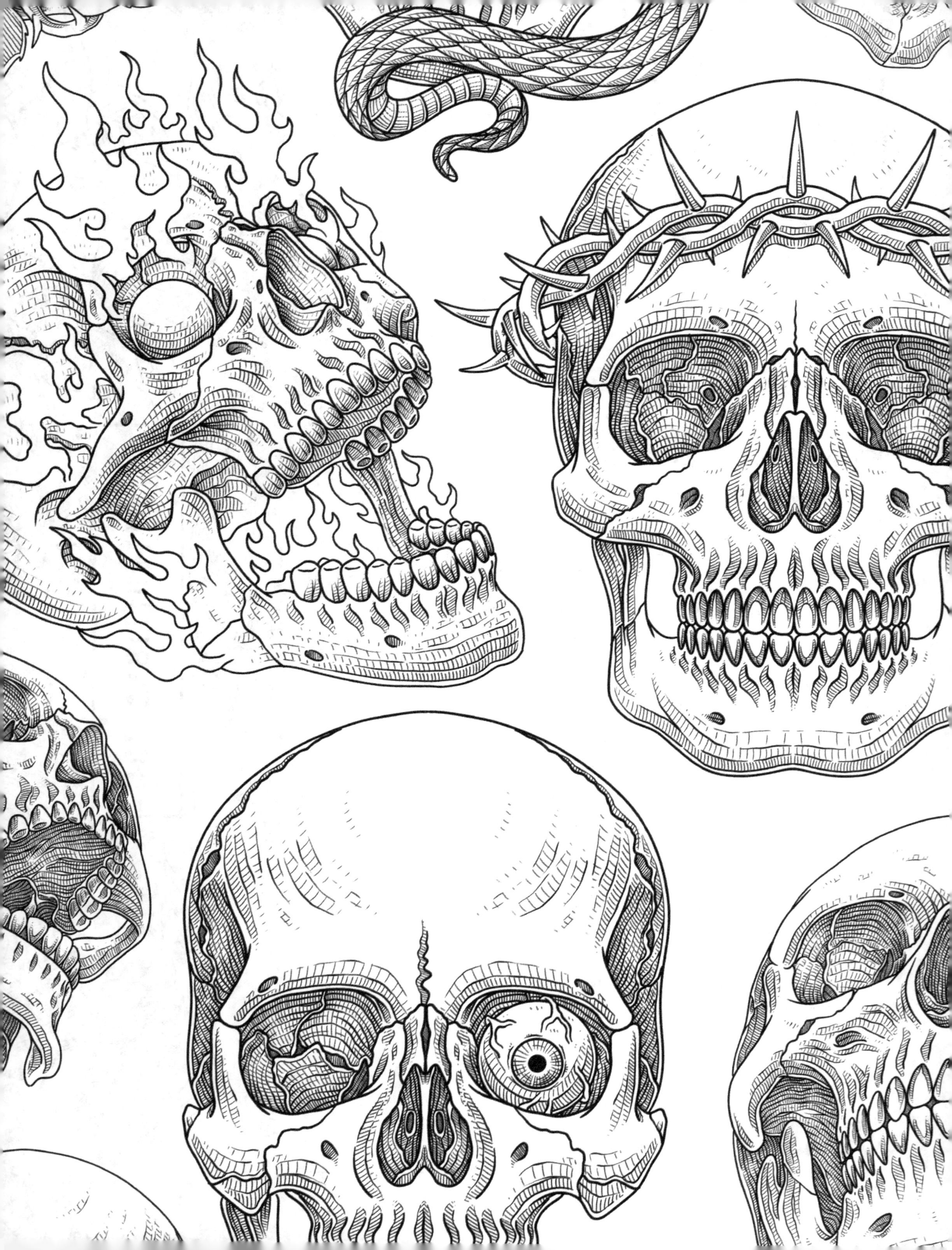